Geopolitics and Democracy

Advance Praise for *Geopolitics and Democracy*

"Timely and compelling, *Geopolitics and Democracy* argues that since the end of the Cold War, government leaders in the West broke the social contract underpinning the liberal international order they built. By focusing their efforts on market globalization and the pooling sovereignty at the international level, while reducing social protections at home, Western government leaders overstretched public support for their actions, paving the way for growing anti-globalization sentiment. The book is a model for how to bridge insights from international relations and domestic politics, and does an exceptional job of marshaling a wealth of available evidence to make nuanced arguments about the state and future of the Western-led liberal order. I strongly encourage everyone to read it."

—Catherine E. De Vries, Professor of Political Science,
Bocconi University

"In this tour de force, Trubowitz and Burgoon offer a new and compelling portrait of the shifting and fraught domestic foundations of Western democracy and its postwar leadership of the liberal world order. Beautifully written and deeply researched, *Geopolitics and Democracy* chronicles the decades-in-the-making erosion of support for liberal internationalism in Western societies—and points to ways in which liberal democracies might once again bring their ambitions and capacities back into line."

—G. John Ikenberry, Albert G. Milbank Professor of Politics and
International Affairs, Princeton University

"Trubowitz and Burgoon offer a highly readable and persuasive argument about the interaction between populism and the unraveling of the liberal international order. A notable contribution helping us understand our politics today."

—Kathleen R. McNamara, Professor of Government and
Foreign Service, Georgetown University

"This ambitious book synthesizes existing scholarship and also breaks new ground, theoretically and empirically. The authors argue convincingly that the embrace of 'globalism' by Western political elites has been accompanied by domestic reforms that have undermined public support for the liberal international order. A must-read for students of comparative welfare-state politics as well as international political economy and international relations."

—Jonas Pontusson, Professor of Comparative Politics,
Université de Genève

"*Geopolitics and Democracy* is essential reading for everyone who wants to grasp the root causes of the anti-globalist pressures in today's liberal democracies and the resulting crisis of the liberal international order. Based on a rigorous analysis of a wealth of data, Trubowitz and Burgoon challenge standard accounts of liberal internationalism's decline and show how trade liberalization and neoliberal governance have contributed to the widening gap between governments and voters in the West."

—Wolfgang Wagner, Professor of International Security,
Vrije Universiteit Amsterdam

"*Geopolitics and Democracy* is a thought-provoking book that studies the challenges to the liberal international order from a broad perspective. Drawing on insights from different subfields that are usually studied in isolation, paying attention to different levels of analysis, and presenting a vast array of empirical findings, this book provides a provocative new perspective on why the Western liberal world order has come under pressure and what could be done to change this."

—Stefanie Walter, Professor of International Relations and
Political Economy, University of Zurich

"A big, grand sweeping and important argument. *Geopolitics and Democracy* makes a powerful case that Western governments got well ahead of what their populations would support when they decided to deepen and broaden the liberal international order after 1990."

—William C. Wohlforth, Daniel Webster Professor of Government,
Dartmouth College

Geopolitics and Democracy

The Western Liberal Order from Foundation to Fracture

PETER TRUBOWITZ AND BRIAN BURGOON

OXFORD
UNIVERSITY PRESS

OXFORD
UNIVERSITY PRESS

Oxford University Press is a department of the University of Oxford. It furthers the University's objective of excellence in research, scholarship, and education by publishing worldwide. Oxford is a registered trade mark of Oxford University Press in the UK and certain other countries.

Published in the United States of America by Oxford University Press
198 Madison Avenue, New York, NY 10016, United States of America.

Library of Congress Cataloging-in-Publication Data
Names: Trubowitz, Peter, author. | Burgoon, Brian, 1965– author.
Title: Geopolitics and democracy : the Western liberal order from
foundation to fracture / Peter Trubowitz, Brian Burgoon.
Description: New York : Oxford University Press, 2023. |
Includes bibliographical references and index.
Identifiers: LCCN 2022035036 (print) | LCCN 2022035037 (ebook) |
ISBN 9780197535417 (paperback) | ISBN 9780197535400 (Hardcover) |
ISBN 9780197535431 (epub) | ISBN 9780197535448 |
Subjects: LCSH: Liberalism—Western countries. | Geopolitics—Western
countries. | Political planning—Western countries. | Western
countries—Social policy. | Western countries—Economic integration. |
World politics—1989–
Classification: LCC JC574 .T736 2023 (print) | LCC JC574 (ebook) |
DDC 320.5109182/1—dc23/eng/20221107
LC record available at https://lccn.loc.gov/2022035036
LC ebook record available at https://lccn.loc.gov/2022035037

DOI: 10.1093/oso/9780197535400.001.0001

To our families

Contents

Figures

Preface and Acknowledgments

War has given Western democracies a renewed sense of unity and purpose. In response to Vladimir Putin's invasion of Ukraine, Western governments have imposed tough economic sanctions on Moscow, sent weapons and aid to Kyiv, ratcheted up military spending, strengthened their security ties, and thrown open their doors to millions of Ukrainian refugees. The speed, breadth, and vigor of the West's response have raised hopes that Putin's brutal war marks a turning point for a liberal international order whose rules and norms have been badly battered and weakened by the forces of autocracy and nationalism. Whether the liberal order gains a new lease on life will depend on more than Western democracies' resolve in the current international crisis, however. The liberal order's future will be determined by the push and pull of domestic politics as well as by geopolitics.

Geopolitics and Democracy is about how international and domestic politics have shaped and reshaped the liberal world order from its postwar origins through the height of the Cold War to the present era. For decades, the liberal order's political foundations were sturdy and strong. Geopolitics and social democracy were self-reinforcing, the one buttressing and fortifying the other. Today, the liberal order's foundations are fractured, riven by anti-globalist and populist insurgencies and democratic backsliding. We explain how this happened and consider what might be done to restore domestic support for the liberal order. In telling this story, we draw on ideas and concepts that will be familiar to scholars of international relations, comparative politics, and political economy, combining and testing them in new ways.

What emerges is an account that traces today's disorder and discontent back to choices and missteps that Western leaders made at the height of liberal triumphalism after the Cold War. Chief among them was Western governments' failure to balance the pressures to rapidly globalize markets and pool national sovereignty at the supranational level against the demands for greater social protections and economic security at home. Western democracies succeeded in expanding the liberal order, but the resulting imbalance between foreign and domestic policy came at the cost of mounting public disillusionment and political division at home. In short, Western governments' efforts to globalize the liberal order exceeded what their domestic politics would allow.

Closing this gap will be critical if Western leaders hope to put the liberal order on solid domestic footing again in their nations. In one democracy after another, the turn to globalism has weakened the political center and fueled ideological extremism. As we show, this has proven costly internationally as well as domestically. As Western democracies have become more internally fragmented, the pace of globalization and international institution-building they have long set has slowed. Meanwhile, Western party democracy, once a source of Western attraction, has lost much of its international luster and appeal. If Western democracies hope to reverse these international trends, understanding how they got themselves into this political fix is an essential first step. In writing *Geopolitics and Democracy,* we have tried to keep this goal front and center.

We began this collaborative journey in 2015 as part of the Dahrendorf Forum on Europe's future, a joint initiative by the Hertie School in Berlin and the London School of Economics and Political Science, funded by Stiftung Mercator. After co-authoring a couple of articles on the erosion of domestic support for the liberal order in the US, European, and other Western democracies, we decided to deepen and expand the argument in a book. We began working on the project in earnest shortly before the COVID-19 pandemic struck, traveling back and forth between Amsterdam and London and then, like so many others, meeting over Zoom. For both of us, it was a labor of love as the book engages issues that touch core themes of our research interests. It was also an opportunity to rekindle and deepen an old friendship forged many years before when teaching and studying at UCSD in La Jolla, California.

At various stages of the project, we have benefited from the comments, suggestions, and insights of colleagues and friends at LSE and the University of Amsterdam, as well as from seminars and conferences at Columbia University, the Hertie School, Princeton University, Université de Genève, the University of Konstanz, and the University of Tokyo where we have presented parts of the argument and analysis. We are especially grateful to Catherine Boone, Alexander Trubowitz, Wolfgang Wagner, and three anonymous reviewers for extremely helpful suggestions on how to improve the book. At Oxford University Press, we wish to thank Dave McBride for his sound advice and encouragement. The book has also benefited from Alexcee Bechthold's attention to detail during the production process. We would also like to thank Stella Canessa and Beatriz Da Silva for their expert research assistance.

We have accumulated many debts in writing this book, but none is greater than the ones we owe to our respective families. They have been a source of inspiration and support, especially in the face of the many challenges that COVID-19 presented for work and family life while this book was being researched and drafted. Peter thanks Catherine, Joshua, and Alexander for their constant encouragement and many insights about this research and the immense challenges facing liberal democracies today. Brian thanks Nicole, Max, and David for their support and wisdom on the project (and on life outside the project). We dedicate this book to them.

1

The Solvency Gap

In a speech before the American Society of Newspaper Editors in April 1950, Secretary of State Dean Acheson observed, "There is no longer any difference between foreign questions and domestic questions. They are all part of the same question."[1] Acheson's view about the relationship between international and domestic politics was not a uniquely American perspective. Many of his Western contemporaries had reached the same judgment. After a decade of economic depression and war, international security and domestic stability were considered inseparable, each required to guarantee the success of the other. In the years and decades that followed, the imperatives of geopolitics and social democracy would reinforce and buttress this view in Western democracies. Political leaders had to guarantee their citizens "freedom from want" as well as "freedom from fear" if they hoped to sustain popular support for international openness and cooperation within the West, and to blunt the appeal of communism, socialism, and fascism at home. International and domestic politics were aligned.

Today, Western democracies are struggling to keep international and domestic politics in balance. Since the end of the Cold War, foreign and domestic policy have become disconnected, each operating in isolation and increasingly, at cross-purposes with the other. In the absence of a common foe, the West's international ambitions expanded globally. New international markets and supranational institutions were created; visions of a new global security architecture were promulgated. Western governments' commitment to social stability did not keep pace, however. Western investment in social protection and welfare slowed. Economic insecurity and inequality increased. Ideological extremism resurfaced. On issues ranging from international trade to global governance, domestic support for the liberal world order fragmented. A large and widening gap opened up between the West's international ambitions and its domestic political capacity to support them.

Much of the debate over the West's weakening commitment to the liberal international order has focused on recent developments: Donald Trump's turbulent presidency, Britain's surprising decision to leave the European

Geopolitics and Democracy. Peter Trubowitz and Brian Burgoon, Oxford University Press.
© Oxford University Press 2023. DOI: 10.1093/oso/9780197535400.003.0001

Union, and the spread of populist and nationalist sentiment in France, Germany, and other Western democracies. *Geopolitics and Democracy* shows that the decline in domestic support for what we call the "Western-led liberal order" is not as recent as these examples suggest. Drawing on an array of cross-national data on Western governments, parties, and voters, we show that anti-globalist pressures have been building in Western democracies for over three decades.[2] We trace these pressures back to decisions that Western governments made after the Cold War ended. The key decisions were to globalize markets and pool sovereignty at the supranational level, while at the same time relaxing the social protections and guarantees that domestic support for international engagement had long rested upon. As we show, this combination of policies succeeded in expanding the Western-led system, but at the cost of mounting domestic discontent and division.

Geopolitics and Democracy is about how and why Western governments overreached internationally, and what they can do to bring international ends and domestic means back into balance at a time when the problems of great power rivalry, spheres of influence, and reactionary nationalism have returned. The book focuses on three separate, yet interrelated, political processes: Western governments' backing away from the foreign policies and social bargains that defined and supported liberal internationalism through the long East-West struggle for primacy; the steady decline in public support for international openness and institutionalized cooperation in Western democracies since the Cold War ended; and the associated fragmentation of the liberal order's domestic foundations in Western party systems. Each is part of the larger story that *Geopolitics and Democracy* tells about the West's efforts to globalize the postwar liberal order in the wake of the Soviet Union and communism's collapse and the resulting problems of strategic overextension that plague Western democracies today.

International relations scholars use the term "overextension" to describe nations that make international commitments beyond their means. Often, those means are equated with military or economic capabilities.[3] However, a country's "political solvency" can be more critical than its material means. This is especially true for democracies that depend on the consent of the governed. In the pages that follow, we argue that Western democracies today are suffering from a democratic "solvency gap": the many foreign policy commitments that Western governments have made to promote greater economic integration and institutionalized cooperation since the end of the Cold War have come to exceed what their domestic publics are willing to bear.

A once virtuous cycle between party democracy and international openness, each strengthening and reinforcing the other, has been transformed into a vicious cycle. Populist and nationalist parties, marginalized and isolated during the Cold War, have steadily gained political ground by attacking core principles of liberal international order-building. Established mainstream political parties that were the backbone of the Western liberal order in national parliaments and electorates—Social Democratic, Christian Democratic, and Conservative and Liberal—have been forced onto the political defensive.

In developing this argument about the fracturing of the Western liberal order, we focus on two separate, yet interrelated, drivers: the end of the Cold War and of bipolar superpower rivalry, and the breakdown of the postwar compromise between free-market capitalism and social democracy associated with "embedded liberalism."[4] Briefly, we argue that the Cold War had a disciplining effect on party politics in Western democracies, at once strengthening mainstream parties' commitment to embedded liberalism while marginalizing parties espousing globalism, isolationism, or nationalism that voters deemed too weak, extreme, or belligerent to be entrusted with power. With the end of the Cold War, political space in Western democracies opened up, making it easier for once-marginalized parties to gain political traction by pushing anti-globalist and nationalist agendas. Western leaders inadvertently lent those parties a helping hand by more fully integrating and institutionalizing international markets while slowing the growth of, and in some cases, actively rolling back, social protections governments once guaranteed their citizens. As the costs to many ordinary citizens in terms of economic security and national autonomy became clear, Western voters grew increasingly receptive to anti-globalist parties' platforms.

In combination, these developments go far in explaining why Western electorates have grown increasingly dissatisfied over the past thirty years with efforts to integrate and institutionalize international markets, and dissatisfied with the political elites and parties advancing this foreign policy agenda. In general, we show that the level of domestic support for liberal internationalism in Western democracies has depended greatly on the level and intensity of international threat those democracies face *and* the extent to which their governments provide social protection from market forces for their own citizens. Broadly speaking, the less "geopolitical slack," or room for strategic error, Western democracies have internationally, and the more extensive their welfare and social safety net provisions are at home, the stronger domestic support for liberal internationalism is likely to be in Western polities.[5] Conversely, the lower the perceived threat and the thinner the social safety net, the less citizens will endorse expansive internationalist projects. We show that these two drivers are critical in understanding why domestic political support for the Western-led liberal international order was so abundant during the Cold War. This means that popular claims today that the "West is back" should be viewed with caution.

The future of the Western liberal order depends on the ability of leaders in America, Germany, France, and other advanced industrialized nations to nourish and support it. However, the more these democracies invest in economic integration and institutionalized cooperation, the more internally divided and polarized they risk becoming. This is the West's strategic conundrum, and the reemergence of great power politics alone will not solve it. A common threat can concentrate the West's collective mind, as Russia's invasion of Ukraine reminds. Yet as *Geopolitics and Democracy* shows, the liberal order did not rest on fear alone. Throughout the long Cold War, it depended critically on the economic security and welfare that Western governments guaranteed their citizens. In the absence of a renewed commitment to those social purposes, Western democracies will struggle to find a collective grand strategy that their domestic publics will support.

In making this argument it is important not to overstate the West's coherence and inclusiveness. The West is not a monolith and the liberal order was never as benign as some analysts and commentators would have it. The liberal order has excluded countries in the developing world (some also opted not to join "the club"), and penalized some of them. In Western democracies, the principle of social protection that was so central to the practice of embedded liberalism typically excluded peoples immigrating from their former colonies and other nations.[6] Liberal order-building has also involved the use of hard power to create "buffer zones," protect strategic "choke points," and "guarantee access" to strategic materials in the Middle East and elsewhere.[7] Nations at the receiving end of American and Western power projection have sometimes paid a steep price for nationalizing Western assets, attacking their neighbors, or harming their own citizens. Western democracies sometimes fall short domestically of the high standards they hold others to. During the Cold War, fears of communism and Soviet "fifth columns" led Western leaders to trample on individual rights in the name of national security, intervene in places like Vietnam, and suppress democracy in developing countries. This too is part of the Western-led liberal order's long trajectory stretching from the postwar era to the present.

We are also mindful that there is a long arc of writings about the West's woes. Like the greatly exaggerated reports of Mark Twain's demise, historians, political scientists, and commentators have been predicting the West's death since Oswald Spengler published *The Decline of the West* after World War I.[8] *Geopolitics and Democracy* is not another monograph about the West's inexorable decline. Our purpose is different. In the pages that follow, we argue that Western democracies' foreign policies have overrun their political foundations, but that it is within their power to bring international ends and domestic means back into balance. To do so, a necessary first step is to correctly diagnose how the West got itself into this fix. As we show, today's anti-globalist pressures in Western democracies owe more to the breakdown of their commitment to social democracy at home than the headlong pursuit of democracy promotion abroad, however checkered the history of the latter. It is here, in Western efforts to build an open, institutionalized order, that the gap between international ambition and domestic politics is greatest. If Western leaders hope to rebuild domestic support for international engagement, this is where they must concentrate their efforts, and their governments' resources.

In the rest of this introductory chapter, we sketch out the theoretical framework, research design, and methods we use to track Western democracies' foreign policies, and domestic support for them, over the past seventy-five years. We begin by developing a typology that distinguishes between four basic foreign policy strategies: globalism, liberal internationalism, isolationism, and nationalism. We then provide an overview of our argument about how Western governments' foreign policies changed in the 1990s, and why they overran their domestic foundations. We turn next to how we develop and test our argument empirically, and describe how our argument differs from other explanations for the rise of anti-globalism and the causes of Western overreach. Finally, we summarize the book's three empirical chapters, along with the book's concluding chapter on possible strategies for bringing international ends and domestic means back into balance. Our principal aim in this book is to explain the widening gap between Western governments and their publics over foreign policy. Yet our analysis of Western foreign policy does point to a number of "dos" and "don'ts" for those hoping to bridge the gap and make the liberal order more solvent.

VARIETIES OF STATECRAFT

Geopolitics and Democracy combines a novel theoretical framework and empirical strategy to systematically analyze the correlates of change in the foreign policies of Western democracies since the postwar era, as well as the long-run causes of the widening gap between governments and their voters on foreign policy. Our theoretical framework draws on the fields of international security, international political economy, comparative political economy, and comparative party politics. These four fields of inquiry are rarely combined, but there are theoretical and empirical payoffs in doing so.[9] Indeed, one of our objectives in writing this book is to show how our understanding of the evolution of the Western system over the past seventy-five years can be enhanced by taking into account the interaction between geopolitics, political economy, and party politics. As we show, the political solvency of the liberal world order has depended far more on party democracy, and especially on the electoral dominance of mainstream parties, than is generally appreciated by international relations scholars. The reverse is also true. Populism and nationalism's steady rise in Western democracies over the past three decades owes more to geopolitical developments than current models of comparative party politics allow.

Power and partnership

In making these and related arguments about the Western liberal system's evolution since World War II, we model Western statecraft along two separate foreign policy dimensions that we call "power" and "partnership." These are depicted in Figure 1.1. By power, we mean military power, one of statecraft's oldest tools and a key indicator of a foreign policy strategy's ambition and cost. International relations scholars and defense analysts measure military power in different ways, though most agree that the percentage of GDP a country invests in building up and maintaining its military power is a good barometer of how much weight or value its leaders and citizens attach to military might and defense preparedness as part of their nation's overall foreign policy strategy.[10] Nations that are located on the right end of the horizontal axis strongly favor investing in building up national militaries and national defense capabilities and maintaining military preparedness. Those located at the opposite end of the horizontal axis strongly oppose investing a large share of gross domestic product.

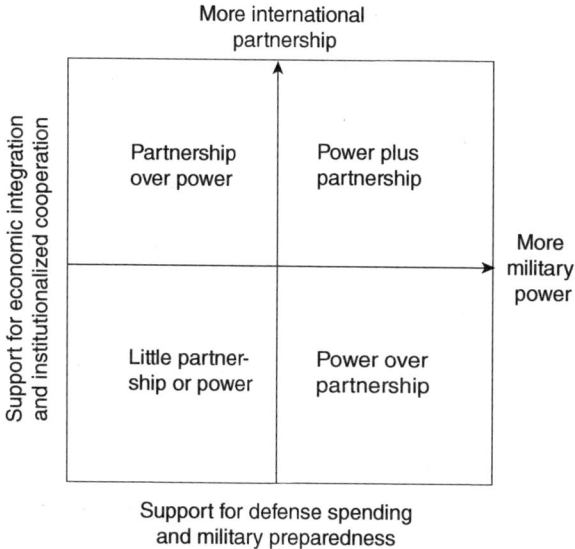

Figure 1.1 Power and partnership: dimensions of international statecraft

Where states lie on this continuum thus tells us something about the relative weight they attach to military strength, balance of power, and power projection in foreign policy. There is an extensive literature by international relations scholars on how, why, and when states come to occupy different points or positions on this power continuum. Motivations can vary from protecting national sovereignty, to checking the expansionist ambitions of other states in the international system, to establishing spheres of influence. Where states land on this continuum also depends on pressures *within* states, from economic interests (e.g., industrialists, merchants) seeking private gain from militarism and war-making, to peace movements that seek to reduce the impetus toward war through disarmament, collective security, or international federation.[11]

The position of each state on the power continuum also offers a rough sense of their international and domestic spending priorities.[12] This is because states' resources are limited. As the American strategist Bernard Brodie famously put it, "Strategy wears a dollar sign."[13] Political leaders must decide how much military power is enough to meet their foreign policy objectives, and whether to favor foreign policy strategies that make fewer demands on the government's resources and national wealth.[14] Political leaders must also consider whether and how those decisions might affect what they hope to achieve domestically. Political economists often describe this trade-off as a choice between guns and butter. Choices must be made on how much of the state's resources to invest in national defense (guns) versus how much to invest in domestically oriented policies and social programs (butter). While there is ample evidence that political leaders frame many foreign policy choices in guns-versus-butter terms, in practice the trade-off is rarely as harsh and unbending as modern economic texts portray it to be.[15] Countries can and often do invest in both guns and butter, relying on increased taxes or large budget deficits to reduce the severity of the trade-off.

As many historians, sociologists, and political scientists have shown, this compatibility between guns and butter exists especially when states face a common enemy or threat.[16] One reason for this is that leaders see domestic spending as a means to gain popular support and legitimacy for their foreign policy initiatives.[17] Another reason is to preempt, or at least neutralize, adversaries' efforts to sow internal division and factionalism.[18] In the 1880s, Otto von Bismarck introduced social insurance in Germany, partly in an effort to tame a growing internal socialist movement and to contain the spread of revolutionary ideas from other European states.[19] During the Cold War, Western leaders saw the welfare state as a means to blunt the appeal of communism at home and as a political weapon in the East-West struggle.[20] The German Social Democrat Ludwig Preller spoke for many elected officials when he claimed that welfare state "battalions" would play a decisive role in determining the outcome of the Cold War.[21]

In Western democracies, political parties play a critical intermediary role between governments and society by framing public debate, and by mobilizing popular support for and against specific military policies and programs in national parliaments and legislatures.[22] In the postwar era, these party debates have focused on Western "burden-sharing" (i.e., the percentage of GDP Western democracies spend on national defense) relative to one another, as well as more sharply defined questions concerning the strategic necessity and risks of military doctrines (e.g., NATO's nuclear "first use" doctrine) and weapon systems (e.g., the UK-US "Skybolt Crisis" in the 1960s; the "Euromissile" deployment in the 1980s). Debates over military preparedness, and arms control and disarmament (e.g., Britain's Campaign for Nuclear Disarmament in the late 1950s and early 1960s; the 1980s' Nuclear Freeze movement in the United States) have also frequently figured in party platforms and positioning over the domestic opportunity costs of military spending, as well as its benefits for local economies and regional development. Often these distributional struggles are played out as partisan debates over the strategic necessity of peacetime military spending ("peace through strength," "weakness invites aggression") and the domestic dangers of excessive militarism ("corruption," "atavism," "despotism," "militarism").

Partnership is international statecraft's second dimension. By partnership, we mean political support for international openness (e.g., trade liberalization; capital mobility), institutionalized cooperation, and multilateral governance. Here, too, governments face choices and trade-offs. Political leaders and policymakers must decide how much discretion over national policies to surrender in order to comply with standards set by international institutions, treaties, and agreements, and how much regulatory and adjudicatory power to transfer to international bodies like the European Union. There is also an extensive literature on when and why states elect to voluntarily pay these "sovereignty costs," and when they are most likely to oppose doing so.[23] Motivations for transferring national authority to the international level can vary from gaining access to larger markets and capital, to harmonizing tax, regulatory, and social standards, to neutralizing contentious domestic issues by going beyond national borders.[24]

The vertical dimension in Figure 1.1 tells us something about states' willingness to cooperate internationally to achieve their ends and, conversely, how much they worry about the loss of political sovereignty to international bodies beyond their control.[25] States that are located at the top end of the vertical axis strongly favor investing in international partnership; the advantages they see in economic integration and international cooperation outweighs whatever concerns they may have about the loss of national autonomy. Those located at the opposite end of the vertical axis can be expected to strongly oppose transferring domestic discretionary authority to international institutions of any type. They worry more about the intrusiveness and costs of these institutions: that is, how much they constrain national decision-making authority, impose limits on states' redistributive and regulatory capacity, and risk foreign entanglement and entrapment.

As in the case of military power, how intensively governments invest in international partnership cannot be divorced from the domestic interests that win or lose from greater international openness, institutionalized cooperation, and multilateral governance. There is a large literature on the uneven domestic effects of trade liberalization and economic integration, as well as their repercussions for mass politics.[26] There is also considerable evidence that voters are sensitive to the distributional benefits and costs, real and imagined, of international cooperation and multilateral governance.[27] Here, too, political parties play a key role in framing public debates over international trade and institutionalized cooperation and, as Britain's debate over withdrawing from the European Union reminds us, in mobilizing voters for and against international openness and sovereignty-pooling arrangements.[28]

Foreign policy strategies

We now have a way of describing variation in the types of foreign policy strategies that countries can choose. These strategies can be broadly classified in terms of their relative reliance on power and partnership. This yields four permutations: "partnership over power" (quadrant 1), "power plus partnership" (quadrant 2), "little partnership or power" (quadrant 3), and "power over partnership" (quadrant 4). These combinations are broadly consistent with four foreign policy strategies that are summarized in Figure 1.2. We have labeled them globalism (quadrant 1), liberal internationalism (quadrant 2), isolationism (quadrant 3), and nationalism (quadrant 4). This is not

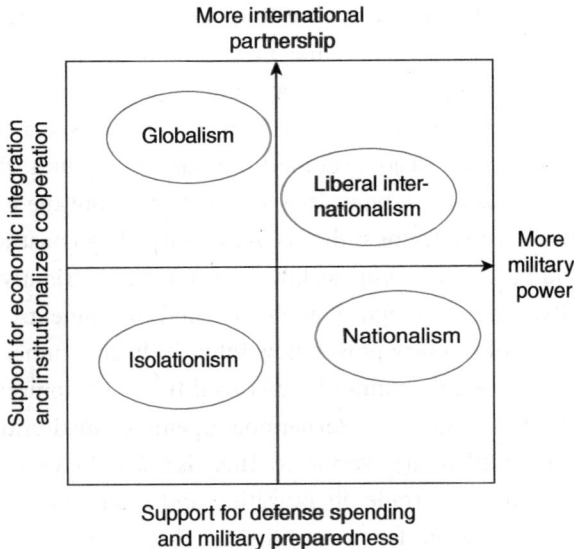

Figure 1.2 Foreign policy strategies by power and partnership

an exhaustive list of foreign policy approaches that fit into these quadrants, and the relative weight that different governments, parties, or voters attach to each of these dimensions—power and partnership—can also vary within quadrants.[29] We describe each of these four foreign policy approaches, beginning with globalism in quadrant 1.

Globalism

Globalism favors partnership over power. Globalists consider national sovereignty to be the root cause of international instability and war, and look to economic integration and institutionalized cooperation as remedies.[30] While viewing a common defense and foreign policy as indispensable for settling disputes and guaranteeing collective external security, they see political and economic union as essential prerequisites to overcoming the frictions caused by self-interested sovereign states. In the 1940s, this diagnosis of sovereignty's pernicious effects was shared by leading American, British, and European public intellectuals of varying political persuasions. They argued that international federation, of one form or another, offered the most promising path to removing the barriers of national economies, improving economic and social well-being, and reducing the risk of international conflict among self-interested sovereign states.[31] Today's supranational European Union, which pools sovereignty and guarantees the free movement of goods, capital, services, and people across borders, arguably stands as the fullest expression of this midcentury globalist vision, albeit on a regional scale.[32]

Globalists give pride of place to economic integration and institutionalized cooperation, but they are not opposed to investing in or using military power under all conditions.[33] In general, though, globalists favor investing relatively few resources in peacetime militaries and, importantly, see military power as a means for collective self-defense and enforcing international laws rather than as a tool for maintaining international order through balance of power. This view of when, how, and to what end military power should be used in international affairs is not wholly different from Woodrow Wilson's vision of a "community of power." For Wilson and other supporters of the League of Nations, the purpose was not only to guarantee peace through the threat of collective action against aggressors, but also importantly, to gradually transcend traditional *raison d'état* and balance of power politics by transforming "how states and peoples thought about rights and obligations and the imperatives to uphold them."[34]

Liberal internationalism

If globalists favor partnership over power, liberal internationalists (quadrant 2) see both as essential and complementary.[35] Liberal internationalists also see international openness, institutionalized cooperation, and multilateralism as means to foster a more peaceful and prosperous world. However, they worry more about the sovereignty costs of institutionalized cooperation than do globalists. They also think that international order and peace depend on balance of power politics and the willingness to use military power to uphold it. In a world of sovereign states, liberal internationalists do not think the Hobbesian problem of anarchy can be solved through international institutions and laws, but they think those challenges can be managed and lessened if partnership is buttressed by a heavy investment in military power. This very intuition lies at the core of the liberal international order that Western democracies built after World War II, and in the thinking of its chief architect, Franklin Delano Roosevelt.[36]

Liberal internationalism and globalism are often conflated. It is easy to see why. Like globalism, liberal internationalism entails a commitment to economic integration and institutionalized cooperation. Yet the liberal internationalism championed by Roosevelt and his successors in the United States and elsewhere differs from globalism in two important ways. First, unlike globalists, who view international federation as a substitute and remedy for domestic interventionism, liberal internationalists see government intervention as a means to correct for international market failures and to respond to domestic demands for social justice. In schematic terms, liberal internationalists are thus located lower on the vertical axis in Figure 1.2 than are globalists, even if both liberal internationalists and globalists are more favorably disposed to international openness and multilateralism than isolationists and nationalists (see below). Second, unlike globalists who look to international law and institutions to restrain the dogs of war, liberal internationalists also rely on power politics to guarantee security, even as they try to devise institutional arrangements to manage great power rivalries, armament races, and destabilizing technologies. Where globalists focus on the promise of a world free of balance of power, spheres of influence, and militarism, liberal internationalists see wisdom in realist adages of "peace through strength" and "weakness invites aggression."

Isolationism

In contrast to globalism and liberal internationalism, isolationism (quadrant 3) attaches comparatively little weight to international institutions, preferring self-sufficiency to multilateral cooperation.[37] In general, political leaders and parties that favor isolationism oppose institutionalized cooperation, focusing less on potential benefits (e.g., larger markets; burden-sharing) and more on the potential risks (e.g., unstable international markets, economic exploitation by foreigners, foreign entanglement). Isolationists also take a dim view of heavy investment in military power, seeing high costs in terms of butter (or higher taxes) and unnecessary risk, be it centralized power, or imperial ambition, or military overexpansion. In principle, proponents of isolationism oppose or are deeply skeptical of both power and partnership. However, in the real world, this "ideal point" is nearly impossible to achieve. As a practical matter, they often find themselves playing defense, arguing for "restraint" to minimize the risk of strategic overextension and, in the case of smaller powers, for neutrality, to minimize the dangers of foreign influence and economic harm.

A strategy of isolationism does not mean diplomatic inactivity, let alone closure to the outside world. Nor does it necessarily preclude the movement of goods, services, and people across national borders, provided it does not involve surrendering national control and autonomy to international institutions. In the nineteenth century, isolationist America combined tariffs on foreign manufactures with exports of agricultural goods. Isolationism also does not imply nativism, even if this, too, has been a strain in isolationism's long history. Often associated with libertarianism today, isolationism, like globalism, has progressive as well as conservative variants, and not only in the United States where progressives such as Senator William Borah and socialist Eugene Victor Debs, among many others, championed it in the first quarter of the twentieth century.[38] As we will see, many parties on the far left in Europe's multiparty democracies have also populated this quadrant in Figure 1.2. Radical-left parties were staunch opponents of Atlanticism and early efforts at European integration in the postwar era, and also actively campaigned for unilateral nuclear disarmament and neutrality in the East-West conflict.[39]

Nationalism

Nationalists (quadrant 4) share isolationists' strong aversion to trade liberalization, international institutions, and multilateral governance. At best, they see international institutions as a temporary expedient to leverage power advantages or export their nation's socioeconomic model; at worst, they consider institutionalized cooperation, especially security cooperation, to be a source of moral hazard and strategic entrapment. However, unlike isolationists who worry as much about the dangers of militarism for civil liberties and democracy as about the risks of pooling sovereignty in international institutions, nationalists strongly support building and maintaining large militaries. In this respect, nationalists are similar to liberal internationalists who consider military power essential for guaranteeing *national* security and welfare. Where nationalists part company with liberal internationalists on military power is over the latter's willingness to also rely on multilateral arrangements to check foreign threats and advance vital national security interests (e.g., access to raw materials).

Nationalists come in many guises.[40] Certainly, nineteenth-century mercantilists, and their twentieth-century neo-mercantilist heirs, belong in this quadrant.[41] They favored targeted trade restrictions and other forms of government economic activism to make strategic domestic industries more competitive in world markets. Geopolitical rivalry and economic competition were considered two sides of the same coin. Today's economic nationalists bear a strong family resemblance. In her run for the French presidency in 2017, French populist Marine Le Pen vowed to invest more of France's GDP in national defense while liberating French firms and workers from the "tyrannies" of globalization and the European Union.[42] Donald Trump, whose foreign policy evoked comparisons to the country's first populist president, Andrew Jackson, arguably belongs here, too. Trump attached comparatively little weight to multilateral cooperation, but he did not hesitate to invest in military power or use it for narrowly defined national purposes.[43] As we will see, many of today's nationalists populate this quadrant.

OVERVIEW OF THE ANALYSIS

We now have the pieces in place to distinguish between different foreign policy strategies, and to measure variations across and within each approach. In the chapters that follow, we use this conceptual framework to identify and map out Western democracies' foreign policy preferences along each of these key dimensions of statecraft and how they have changed over time. In doing so, we focus the analysis on three political actors: governments, parties, and voters. *Governments'* foreign policies make up the strategies we examine in these pages. *Parties* and their leaders occupy positions of power within governments and influence foreign policymaking by framing policy choices and mobilizing voters on behalf of their preferred foreign policy strategies (combinations of partnership and power). *Voters* select political parties to represent their collective interests and preferences in the corridors of power at the national level. We track the foreign policy preferences of all three to identify where and when they overlap and, just as importantly, where and when they diverge.

Party democracy and liberal order

For roughly half a century after World War II, liberal internationalism was the West's lodestar. A strategy of international order-building that was at once liberal and realist, postwar liberal internationalism relied on international partnership and military power. Forged in the shadow of the Cold War, the West's liberal internationalist strategy was organized around two great regional axes, with the United States at the center. One was an Atlantic axis binding North America and Western Europe; the other, a Pacific axis tying Japan and other non-communist Asian nations to the United States. Together, they defined the geographic core of the Western system and the dense networks of military, economic, and diplomatic ties that made the whole greater than the sum of its parts. Sometimes described as *Pax Americana*, the Western system was dominated by the United States. However, it was not a distinctively American system, or unilaterally imposed by Washington. European and Asian democracies also saw benefits in foreign policies that offered protection from Soviet geopolitical ambitions and delivered high rates of economic growth.

To be sure, the Western system fell short of the universal liberal world order that Franklin Delano Roosevelt and other Western leaders envisioned as World War II was coming to a close. Even within the West, the level of support for liberal internationalism varied, as did the precise mix of power and partnership that member states favored. And economic nationalists in the emerging postwar "Third World" were often penalized or undercut. Nevertheless, the system achieved a level of international openness, economic interdependence, and political integration that exceeded what postwar planners thought possible, and that set the West apart from the rest—something the empirical analysis in Chapter 2 lays bare. Trade, foreign investment, and monetary cooperation grew rapidly along the system's Atlantic and Pacific axes. Western democracies' commitment to the common defense deepened. So, too, did the West's commitment to party democracy. In sharp contrast to the interwar years, when ideological extremism ruled in much of Europe and Asia, the postwar era was one of domestic consensus and coalition-building across party lines. Socialists and conservatives, Christian Democrats, and secular liberals found common ground in liberal internationalism.

During the Cold War, the Western liberal international order benefited from what political scientist Robert Dahl called a "surplus of consensus."[44] Mainstream parties dominated the electoral landscape and controlled the machinery of national government. Their dominance did not guarantee domestic consensus over foreign policy across the board. Public support for partnership often sagged during economic downturns. When fears of nuclear Armageddon dwarfed concerns about Soviet ambition, public support for military spending softened too. Yet for most of the Cold War, Western governments' foreign policies enjoyed broad and consistent domestic support. At the same time, Western governments' commitment to liberal internationalism provided grounds for consensus within Western democracies. Western leaders could advance liberal internationalist policies, confident that those policies would garner the support of a broad cross section of political parties representing the majority of voters in their countries. What was good for liberal internationalism was good for mainstream parties, and vice versa.

This virtuous cycle between foreign policy and party democracy in Western democracies did not last. The first cracks in liberal internationalism's domestic foundations appeared in the 1970s, but it was not until the Cold War ended that the virtuous cycle between foreign policy and party democracy broke down. In the 1990s, Western governments shifted from a strategy of liberal internationalism that combined power with partnership to a strategy of globalism that relied increasingly on partnership, and a particular market-oriented variant thereof. Military spending declined. International markets and institutionalized cooperation expanded. Trade and investment boomed. New international bodies were formed and older ones were enlarged, many promoting the expansion of global markets. Countries that once languished on the edges of the liberal world order, or that the Cold War had effectively locked out, were suddenly in play as destinations for Western investment. In the 1990s, the Western system was globalized.

Domestic support did not keep stride, however. We show that, even before the 1990s were out, popular support for liberalized trade, institutionalized cooperation, and multilateral governance was declining in Western democracies. The erosion of domestic support was starkest in the European democracies, but similar patterns emerged in America, Japan, and in most OECD countries. Across the West, a large and widening gap opened up between governments and voters over international partnership. While Western governments' support for international partnership continued to rise each year, support among Western voters for international partnership, and the mainstream parties championing it, declined steadily. The pace of trade liberalization and institutionalized cooperation slowed in the 2000s, but the gap between Western governments' global ambitions and what voters were willing to support continued to widen. Mainstream parties paid a hefty price for the growing disjuncture between governments' foreign policies and voters' policy preferences. Anti-globalist parties on the far left and especially, the far right, successfully exploited these gaps. Mainstream parties advocating international partnership lost significant electoral ground to these once marginal parties.

The pace and extent of these shifts in public support for partnership and power have varied across the West, and by party families within countries. Yet we show that this downward spiral in voter support for the liberal order has posed challenges for Western leaders everywhere. The more Western leaders invested in trade liberalization, institutionalized cooperation, and multilateral governance, the more vulnerable their parties became to anti-globalist parties and the more fragmented Western party systems became. Ultra-left parties, such as Greece's Syriza and Spain's Podemos, capitalized on growing Euroskepticism and anti-internationalist sentiment, which was fueled by the 2008 financial crash and the ensuing eurozone crisis. On the far right, France's *Front National* (FN), Austria's Freedom Party (FPÖ), and the Danish People's Party (DPP), among others, found that anti-globalism could be wielded as a "wedge issue" to exploit cracks within mainstream parties' electoral coalitions.[45] They used this to peel off voters no longer convinced that economic integration and supranational institutions were in their self-interest, or their country's best interest. By the time Britain voted for Brexit and Donald Trump was elected president, the once virtuous cycle between foreign policy and party democracy had become a vicious one.

Explaining Western insolvency

How did Western foreign policy ends become so disconnected from domestic political means? What explains this widening gap between Western governments and their publics? In the chapters that follow, we argue that popular support for the Western-led liberal order was contingent on a particular configuration of geopolitical pressures and domestic bargains. Geopolitically, the Soviet challenge was a defining reality for Western leaders and voters. For over half a century, worries about communist expansion on the Eurasian landmass and the associated danger of nuclear war pushed Western leaders toward liberal internationalist foreign policies. Soviet power and the nuclear arms race made most Western voters skeptical of foreign policies that were too trusting or too belligerent. For the "median voter," a liberal internationalist strategy that balanced liberalism with realism was far preferable to globalism, nationalism, or isolationism, especially if waging Cold War did not require sacrificing butter for guns.

Cold War constraints gave Western leaders and voters strong incentives to support liberal internationalism. So did the practical realities of domestic coalition-building in what Peter Mair calls the "age of party democracy."[46] For most of the second half of the twentieth century, political parties had to build cross-class coalitions to win power. This led Western leaders to pursue mixed-economy growth strategies at home, combining state intervention and free-market policies. In foreign policy, this meant striking a balance between international openness and social protection, and between institutionalized cooperation and national sovereignty. International openness and multilateral institutions were needed to promote and sustain growth; national autonomy and social protection were needed to correct for international market forces and ensure working-class voters' support. This was the compromise of embedded liberalism that balanced international openness with domestic policy objectives—full employment, economic equity, unemployment insurance, and social welfare, at least for labor market insiders.

For thirty remarkable years—*les trente glorieuses*—Western democracies' commitment to the liberal world order deepened. It was not until the 1970s and 1980s that the first cracks in liberal internationalism's domestic foundation appeared. This is when Western leaders, led by Ronald Reagan and Margaret Thatcher, began "liberalizing" the Western system by shifting the balance between international openness and social protection in favor of markets. The West's turn toward neoliberalism set in motion forces that would ultimately come back to haunt mainstream parties by weakening public support for the liberal order and opening the door to political parties advancing anti-globalist platforms. However, it was not until the Cold War ended, and Western governments fully embraced an agenda of international market expansion and welfare state "reform," that a clear gap emerged between political leaders and their domestic publics.

In the 1990s, globalization became the West's new elixir. Those who argued that too much economic integration would trigger a political backlash were dismissed as Cassandras. At the height of Western triumphalism over "winning" the Cold War, political leaders doubled down on international partnership, driving economic integration and international rule to new heights. The new supranational European Union and World Trade Organization pooled sovereignty far more extensively than their forerunners—the European Community and the General Agreement on Tariffs and Trade (GATT). With the lifting of the Iron Curtain, West European industries moved production to low-cost East European countries and, soon, opened their doors to workers from Eastern Europe. American and Western investment in China accelerated. At the same time, Western leaders, including center-left politicians like Bill Clinton, Tony Blair, and Gerhard Schröder, continued to liberalize domestic economies and loosen social protections. In the early 2000s, Japan's Koizumi Junichiro followed suit.

For Western leaders, globalization's promise of greater national wealth and security served as a substitute for Cold War imperatives—a new way to sustain the Western system in the absence of a common threat. However, domestic support for foreign policies to promote greater international openness and multilateral cooperation had never depended on geopolitics alone. This support also rested on social guarantees to Western workers, especially those who formed much of the backbone of the mainstream parties. And therein lay the problem. After a decade of market liberalization and privatization at home, Western leaders had less and less domestic political room to maneuver in foreign policy. Public opinion was shifting against the new orthodoxy. We show that, by expanding the global liberal order through the European Union, the WTO, and other global initiatives in the 1990s, but doing so without also expanding social protection at home, Western leaders set in motion the anti-global political dynamics we see today. While foreign policies that resulted in greater access to low-wage markets in Asia and Eastern Europe appealed to many middle-class voters who benefited from cheaper goods and low-cost immigrant labor, those same policies fueled working-class discontent and anti-globalist politics.

In the chapters that follow, we document how the end of the Cold War and the growing reliance on globalism combined to make liberal international order-building less attractive to Western electorates. While the electoral strategizing of parties on the far left is part of the story, we show that it is the parties on the radical right that have been particularly adept at converting anti-globalist policies and platforms into electoral support. Once champions of traditional values and laissez-faire economic orthodoxy, far-right parties adopted nationalist and nativist foreign policies while moving their domestic economic policy agendas to the left. This made radical-right parties more appealing to the swelling ranks of disaffected working-class voters. It also put mainstream parties on the center-right on the political defensive. Western governments' failure to uphold the postwar social bargains they had struck with their citizens does not fully explain the hollowing out of the liberal order's domestic foundation, but we show that it has contributed significantly to the fragmentation of Western party systems and to the political divisions over the purposes of foreign policy that we see today.

RESEARCH DESIGN AND METHOD

Geopolitics and Democracy relies on historical, aggregate, and inferential analysis to develop and test these descriptive and causal claims about the shift from liberal internationalism to globalism, the international and domestic sources of Western overreach, and the concurrent fragmentation of Western party systems. The analysis spans twenty-four Western democracies, over four hundred political parties, and nearly seventy years. We combine large-N quantitative analysis of government policies, party platforms, and voter behavior with more fine-grained historical analysis of foreign policy and party dynamics in the West's major players—the United States, Japan, and the European states that would come to comprise the European Union. In developing the quantitative and historical analysis throughout the book, we draw on the work of scholars in the fields of international security, international political economy, comparative political economy, and comparative party politics that shed light on the origins and evolution of the liberal order, the changing relationship between party democracy and foreign policy, and the rise and spread of anti-globalist sentiment in Western democracies.

We develop and test the argument at the country, party, and voter levels of analysis.[47] We also use this multi-level approach to compare and contrast actual government foreign policies with party and voter support for those policies. The inferential analysis of the country, party, and voter dynamics draws on a variety of cross-national and cross-party time series data. For the country-level analysis of governments' foreign policies, we leverage widely used Stockholm International Peace Research Institute (SIPRI) indicators measuring the share of national wealth invested in military power and KOF Swiss Institute indices measuring the degree to which our 24 OECD countries' foreign policies promote international partnership through economic openness, membership in international organizations, and multilateral diplomacy. Because these measures vary over large time spans, we are able to compare the foreign policies of the West to those of "the rest" over time. At the country level, we also rely on a battery of cross-national indicators that vary over time to gauge states' international security environment (their relative vulnerability to geopolitical rivals and international threats) and their commitment to social protection and overall social welfare.[48]

At the party level, we rely principally on data from the Manifesto Project Database (MPD), a widely used database that summarizes political parties' policy positions through systematic content analysis of their electoral manifestos (platforms) by country and election year.[49] The database includes all twenty-four OECD countries and over 455 political parties between 1950 and 2018. We use the Manifesto data to identify, summarize, and compare, cross-sectionally and longitudinally, political parties' foreign policy preferences on our two foreign policy dimensions: international *partnership* and military *power*.[50] We do not assume that parties always implement their platform pledges when they are in power. In fact, we show that party platforms and government policies frequently diverge. We also do not assume that voters read party manifestos. Party manifestos can, however, tell us something important about what policy positions parties think will help them win national elections.

At the voter level, we also use the Manifesto database to indirectly measure Western voters' support for international partnership and military power. Our strategy is different from relying on available direct measures of public support for partnership and power. The problem with such a direct approach is that public opinion survey data on foreign policy issues is very patchy and inconsistent over time and cross-nationally, leaving too many gaps to adequately address the issues and questions we are raising.[51] The Manifesto database provides a useful and more empirically complete way to manage this issue. It provides a proxy for voter attitudes, with coverage and focus matching our party and policy measures, where we can weight each party's manifesto score for partnership and power by the electoral vote share the party won, based partly on their manifesto positions on these key foreign policy positions.[52] The resulting scores can be interpreted as behavioral indicators of voters' support for partnership and power, or what economists call "revealed preferences."[53] They do not tell us directly what voters think, but they capture voters' policy preferences based on voting behavior (e.g., whether they favor parties for or against trade liberalization).[54]

Our multi-tiered approach to analyzing the liberal order has several advantages. First, it enables us to assess the validity of our arguments descriptively and inferentially at multiple levels of analysis, using different data sources. Second, it allows us to evaluate some common arguments about the liberal order that are pitched at different levels of analysis and, sometimes, at multiple levels at once. For example, some international relations scholars argue that there never really was a "golden age" of liberal order-building—that there was little consensus *between* or *within* Western democracies in favor of liberal internationalism.[55] This argument does not hold up to empirical scrutiny. We show that there was a domestic consensus in favor of liberal internationalism in Western party systems and that it was remarkably robust for decades. Moreover, using different measures of support for partnership and power, we see the same pattern at the level of Western governments. Showing that our arguments about the liberal order hold up at different levels of analysis, using different data sources, increases confidence in the findings.

SIGNIFICANCE OF THE ARGUMENT

Most international relations scholars and foreign policy analysts agree that the liberal world order has fallen on hard times.[56] Yet there is considerable disagreement about how and why liberal internationalism lost its way, and debate over what steps Western democracies should take to rebuild international and domestic support for the liberal order. Our analysis starts from the assumption that there is much to be gained by viewing the current anti-globalist backlash against a larger historical canvas—that is, by tracking the ebb and flow of domestic support for liberal international order-building across many Western democracies, different issue areas, and over many decades. Adopting such a comparative, historical approach reveals many things about the liberal international order's trajectory, but perhaps the most essential is that the anti-globalist backlash we see across the West today has deep roots. As we show, anti-globalist domestic pressures have been steadily building in Western democracies, large and small, old and new, for over three decades.

Establishing when the West's retreat from liberal internationalism began is important for several reasons. For one thing, it helps us understand why early, highly influential prognostications about the post–Cold War world were so far off the mark. In the 1990s, Western commentators were proclaiming the "end of history" and the arrival of the "unipolar moment."[57] The end of the Cold War, they argued, represented the permanent victory of liberal democracy and capitalism over the forces of illiberalism and nationalism. America's unparalleled power put it in a position to ensure liberal democracy's triumph by consolidating, protecting, and extending the liberal international order. As we show, these arguments sorely underestimated the risks of Western overreach because they rested on mistaken assumptions about the sources of popular support for liberal internationalism during the Cold War. They assumed that Western leaders' success in winning cross-partisan support for their foreign policy was due to voters' commitment to liberalizing the world order, and thus that it would continue after the Cold War. In fact, Western leaders' success was contingent on geopolitical imperatives and social guarantees that would soon disappear and weaken.

If many observers underestimated the risk that Western ambition would outstrip its domestic supports, others have misread how ends and means became so misaligned in the ensuing years. The most popular explanation for Western overreach attributes it to political leaders' overreliance on military power and democracy promotion in the Middle East and elsewhere.[58] That the West's misguided pursuit of overly expansive liberal goals like democracy promotion in the Middle East contributed to voter disillusionment seems clear. Yet, as we show in *Geopolitics and Democracy*, domestic disenchantment with the liberal order set in well before Western efforts to spread democracy to the Middle East, the former republics of the Soviet Union, and elsewhere. The evidence in this book makes clear that it was Western governments' unbridled pursuit of trade liberalization, institutionalized cooperation, and multilateral governance after the Cold War, rather than their failed military ventures (e.g., the Iraq War) or their strategic gambits (e.g., the effort to expand democracy to Ukraine on Russia's doorstep), that put these governments at odds with their publics over foreign policy.

Explanations that attribute the anti-globalist backlash to globalization itself are closer to the mark. Many cross-national and country-specific studies indicate that anti-globalist parties have gained national vote share by hammering Western leaders for outsourcing jobs to low-wage countries like China, and for putting too much power in the hands of unelected bureaucrats in supranational institutions like the European Commission and the WTO.[59] Our analysis supports these findings. Yet it also indicates that anti-globalists' arguments about the costs of economic integration and multilateral governance succeeded in no small part because Western leaders no longer felt compelled by geopolitical necessity to uphold the social protections that had buoyed their foreign policies during the Cold War. Instead of taking steps to shore up domestic support for liberal international order-building, Western leaders' domestic reforms made it easier for populist and nationalist politicians to use nativism, Euroscepticism, and calls for protectionism to play on voters' concerns about the sovereignty costs of globalization and, as we show, increase their parties' share of the national vote.

Geopolitics looms large in our account of the West's retreat from the strategy of liberal internationalism that guided it for over half a century. This story is not only about how the presence, and absence, of Cold War imperatives have impacted Western solidarity—the province of international relations scholars. It is also about how international politics have shaped and influenced Western leaders, *domestic* policy choices and electoral strategies, matters central to the study of comparative politics. In showing how the Cold War superpower bipolar competition reinforced mainstream parties' electoral clout and commitment to social protection and, conversely, how the end of the Cold War weakened mainstream parties' hold on their electorates and fueled the fragmentation of Western party systems, *Geopolitics and Democracy* reminds us that the connection between geopolitics and domestic politics runs deep.[60]

ORGANIZATION OF THE BOOK

In the chapters that follow, we explore how and why Western democracies overreached, and what their political leaders can do to set things right. We begin in Chapter 2 by focusing on the widening gap between Western governments and their voting publics over foreign policy. Using the two-dimensional model described above, we show that, starting in the 1990s, Western governments began turning away from the Cold War strategy combining partnership and power (liberal internationalism) to one that relied increasingly on partnership as opposed to power (globalism). We show that this was true of Western democracies in general, but it was also true of the West's preeminent power: the United States. America's commitment to international partnership also increased, albeit less conspicuously and less fully than did Europe's, Japan's, and other OECD nations. The West's commitment to globalism also deepened in the 2000s, through the war on terrorism and the 2008 financial crisis. Western voters did not keep pace with their governments, however. We show that, as Western governments shifted from liberal internationalism to globalism, their foreign policies grew increasingly out of step with what their electorates were willing to support. Anti-globalist sentiment spread.

Chapter 3 picks up where Chapter 2 leaves off by focusing on the sources of Western overreach and the anti-globalist backlash. We argue that Western governments' turn toward globalism led to a domestic backlash because it was shorn of many of the social guarantees and protections that liberal internationalism originally entailed and that Cold War strategic exigencies reinforced. We show how sensitive Western domestic support for international partnership and military power is to the level of international threat facing Western democracies and to their governments' commitment to economic security for their citizens. In the absence of a "clear and present danger" to Western interests and softening government support for social protection, efforts to expand international markets and supernationalism were all but guaranteed to provoke a backlash. We conclude this chapter by considering why, in the face of these anti-globalist pressures, Western leaders did not alter course, by trimming their internationalist sails or providing greater social compensation.

Chapter 4 considers the consequences of the anti-globalist backlash for Western democracies and the liberal order. We show that, while mainstream party support for liberal internationalism has not collapsed, it has weakened in the face of declining voter support for trade liberalization and multilateral institutions. It has also contributed to the process of political fragmentation that has been unfolding in Western democracies for the past three decades. In contrast to the Cold War, when liberal internationalism strengthened the mainstream parties' hold on national electorates, Western governments' turn toward globalism cost parties on the center-left and the center-right at the polls. We show that, since the 1990s, the more mainstream parties promoted economic integration and multilateral governance the more fragmented Western party systems became. Parties running on anti-globalist platforms, especially on the far right, steadily increased their share of the national vote in Western democracies. The splintering of political authority in Western democracies has made them less effective and credible as models of good governance. One consequence we show is that international efforts to deepen the liberal order through institutionalized cooperation have slowed significantly.

In the book's concluding chapter, we consider the implications of our analysis for Western solvency and the liberal world order. We begin by summarizing our findings about the sources of Western overreach, the causes of anti-globalist backlash we see today, and the hollowing out of the liberal order's domestic foundations in the advanced industrialized nations. We compare and contrast our analysis to other explanations of Western overreach, anti-globalism, and political fragmentation. In the last section, we take up the coming debate over the liberal order's future. We focus on three strategies that are likely to dominate foreign policy deliberations in Western capitals: one that urges Western democracies to retrench by scaling back internationally; another that seeks to rekindle Western solidarity and support for liberal internationalism through confrontation with China and Russia; and a third strategy that attacks the ends-means problem from the domestic side through policies of economic renewal. We assess each of these strategies in light of our analysis of Western party democracy and the liberal order.

2

A Widening Gyre

Writing two decades ago, Robert Kagan famously challenged the idea that
the countries of the West still shared a common approach to international
order-building. "On major strategic and international questions today,"
Kagan wrote about the post–Cold War world, "Americans are from Mars and
Europeans are from Venus: They agree on little and understand one another
less and less. . . . When it comes to setting national priorities, determining
threats, defining challenges, and fashioning and implementing foreign and
defense policies, the United States and Europe have parted ways."[1] Since the
Cold War, Americans, Kagan argued, had been more apt to rely on power
and coercion to promote international order and stability. By contrast,
Europeans preferred diplomacy, negotiation, and partnership to manage international conflict and strengthen the international order. Ever since, international relations scholars and foreign policy analysts have debated how best
to characterize these differences over foreign policy—as a clash of ideas, or
interests, or, as Kagan suggested, values.[2] But they did not contest the core as-
sertion itself. The idea that Western democracies' foreign policy differences
were more significant than their similarities became an article of faith in academic and policy circles.

   In this chapter, we show that Western democracies' approaches to foreign policy today are far more similar than such accounts assume. Indeed,
one reason that so many Western democracies today are experiencing anti-
globalist backlashes is that their governments made essentially the same foreign policy bet a quarter of a century ago. In the 1990s, Western governments
turned from the Cold War strategy of liberal internationalism that had balanced international openness and social protection to a strategy of globalism
that put greater emphasis on market-driven economic integration and institutionalized cooperation. This shift in strategy proved costly for Western
governments: as we show, it set in motion political forces that have weakened the liberal order's domestic supports. In this chapter, we take the first
step in explaining how and why Western domestic support for the liberal
order has declined by tracking Western government and voter support for

international partnership and military power cross-nationally from the postwar era to the present.

Briefly, we show that during the Cold War, the United States, Europe's democracies, and most of the rest of the OECD invested heavily in *both* power and partnership—they coalesced around a liberal internationalist foreign policy strategy. With few exceptions, the twenty-four Western governments in our sample favored foreign policies that relied on military power to check and contain the Soviet Union and on *managed* trade and international co-operation to promote growth, stability, and solidarity within the West. This commitment to liberal internationalism lasted until the end of the Cold War when Western democracies' foreign policy (and domestic) priorities shifted. In the 1990s, Western governments began investing fewer resources in power while relying more heavily on partnership. Western governments' reliance on trade liberalization, institutionalized cooperation, and multilateral governance increased while military spending as a percentage of GDP declined in most OECD nations. This pattern continued into the 2000s, when it began to stabilize, albeit at levels that dwarfed those achieved by Western governments at the height of the Cold War.

Western governments' enthusiasm for globalism was never matched by their publics, however. We show that, in contrast to the Cold War years, when the voting public backed Western governments' efforts to expand trade and institutionalize cooperation, voters' support for integration and multilateralism declined steadily after the Cold War. As Western governments invested in ever greater international openness and pooled more and more authority in multilateral institutions, a widening gap opened up between governments and their citizens over how heavily to rely on international partnership. The reverse is true of military power. While Western investment in military power as a share of GDP predictably fell during the 1990s, the voting public's support for military spending and preparedness did not; it increased. Cold War worries that Western governments were fueling the arms race by overinvesting in military power were soon replaced by concerns that national defenses were atrophying. Those concerns intensified in the ensuing years and, as we show in Chapter 4, contributed to populist parties' success at the ballot box.

The chapter is organized into three main sections. In the first section, we describe the origins, consolidation, and development of the Western-led liberal order from the early postwar years through the end of the Cold War. We show how the commitment to both international partnership and military power distinguished Western democracies and liberal internationalism from other nations' foreign policies. In Section Two, we show that the Western-led system was transformed in the 1990s as Western governments moved from a *managed* approach to liberal order-building to one that was increasingly market-led. We show that the turn toward what we call globalism was as true of the United States as it was of the European Union, and that to the extent that there is a gap between America's and Europe's vision of international order-building, it has narrowed, not widened, since the Cold War. In the chapter's final section, we show that, as Western governments came to rely increasingly on international partnership, voter support for their foreign policies declined. We show that this trend, which first appeared in the early 1990s and accelerated in the aftermath of the 2008 global financial crisis, is a Western-wide phenomenon.

THE WESTERN LIBERAL ORDER

For roughly half a century after World War II, the West embraced a strategy of liberal internationalism. After a decade of global depression and war, Western democracies converged on a strategy that relied on international partnership and military power to guarantee security and prosperity. The resulting Western-led liberal order fell far short of the "one world" liberal internationalist vision that Franklin Delano Roosevelt and others were advancing as World War II came to a close.[3] Global institutions like the United Nations (1945) and Bretton Woods (1944) championed by Roosevelt remained, but the exigencies of the Cold War led Western leaders to adopt a system that was less universal in ambition. Regional initiatives and programs such as the Marshall Plan (1947), the North Atlantic Treaty Organization (1949), and the European Economic Community (1957), backed up by a substantial American military presence and nuclear security guarantees, assumed a much larger role in promoting economic recovery and guaranteeing security than postwar planners had originally envisioned.

Cold War liberal internationalism

The United States was the dominant power in the Western liberal order, but it was not a solely American system. European and Japanese leaders saw benefits in the emerging order and American leaders found it necessary, for geopolitical as well as practical political reasons, to make concessions to their European and Japanese counterparts on matters ranging from tariffs, to monetary convertibility, to military burden-sharing.[4] In Europe, US officials, who initially opposed the idea of a European economic bloc, reversed course. They came to see the Schuman Plan (1950) to regulate European production in heavy industries and, then, the more ambitious European Economic Community, as essential steps to creating a barrier to communist expansion on the continent and a larger, more efficient market for European as well as American goods.[5] Americans' early hopes of avoiding a costly long-term military commitment to Europe were also set aside. Between 1950 and 1963, the United States forward deployed some 343,000 troops in Europe on average each year, a number that did not drop significantly until after the Soviet Union collapsed in 1991.[6]

Early postwar American plans in Asia were also revised to accommodate the region's rapidly changing geopolitical landscape. Initially, US officials planned to break up and decentralize Japanese industry to limit Tokyo's freedom of action internationally.[7] In a region where there was no obvious strategic counterweight to Japan, breaking up the Zaibatsu, Japan's industrial and financial conglomerates, made geopolitical sense. However, as Mao Tse-tung and the Chinese Communist Party gained ground in their decades-long struggle for control of China against Chiang Kai-shek's nationalist Kuomintang, and Japanese communists and socialists grew stronger domestically, the tide of opinion in Washington turned. Support mounted for reindustrializing Japan and turning it into a strategic bulwark against the spread of communism in Asia. The "fall of China" to the communists in 1949 and the outbreak of war on the Korean peninsula the following year made Japan indispensable to Washington. Tokyo became the lynchpin of the Western-led system in Asia that included Australia, New Zealand, South Korea, and Taiwan, among others.

The emerging Western liberal order was thus organized around two regional axes: an Atlantic axis linking North America and Western Europe, and a Pacific axis tying Japan and other non-communist nations in Asia to the United States. Similar economic, political, and military means were used to develop and expand both axes of this international order, albeit in different combinations and at different rates. US efforts to promote Asian economic growth, for example, focused more on production for export. Its approach in Europe focused as much on creating a continental market as it did on increasing European nations' share of the world market.[8] Meanwhile, America's NATO security ties with its European partners were more multilateral and symmetric than the bilateral "hub and spokes" partnerships with its Asian allies: Australia, Japan, the Philippines, South Korea, and Thailand.[9] The United States also enjoyed greater success in getting its European allies, especially Britain, France, and West Germany, to contribute to collective defense. Still, defense spending by US allies in both regions was considerable, averaging roughly 3.2 percent of GDP in the 1960s.[10]

Of course, security considerations were not the only reason Western democracies favored liberal internationalism. As John Ruggie and others have argued, Western support for liberal internationalism also rested on a crucial domestic bargain—the compromise of "embedded liberalism."[11] In the 1930s, Western democracies' commitment to full employment, social insurance, and the welfare state expanded. At Bretton Woods, Western policymakers looking to rebuild the postwar world economy agreed to preserve those domestic commitments, and the peace between capital and labor they bought. Policymakers struck a balance between international openness and national autonomy. New rules and mechanisms were devised to make currencies convertible and enable governments to manage exchange-rate imbalances while facilitating growth-oriented means of adjustment. Globalization was to be kept within manageable bounds. Unions and workers agreed to Bretton Wood's new international rules and mechanisms; business agreed to preserve and expand the existing system of social protection.[12]

The West versus the rest

The West's commitment to liberal internationalism deepened during the early decades of the Cold War. Foreign aid, international trade, overseas investment, and monetary cooperation grew rapidly along the North Atlantic axis. The institutional linkages tying the United States and Europe together soon eclipsed levels achieved during the era of laissez-faire internationalism in the late nineteenth and early twentieth centuries.[13] Within Europe itself, the European Economic Community was enlarged to include Britain, Denmark, and Ireland (1973), making it roughly equal in population to both the United States and the USSR and, in terms of international trade, comparable in importance to the United States. America's political and military ties with its Asian partners never reached comparable levels of institutionalization due to lingering resentment toward Japan after the war. Nevertheless, trade and investment ties in the Pacific region also expanded, especially after Washington concluded that boosting Japanese exports would do more to consolidate the Cold War alliance than demanding that Tokyo bear a greater share of the defense burden.[14]

The West's economic performance during this period was impressive. Annual GDP growth for OECD members averaged 4.3 percent between 1950 and 1975.[15] For America, Britain, France, West Germany, and Japan the average was about the same, at 4 percent. Per capita income in the West also grew by leaps and bounds, doubling for the OECD as a whole and tripling for the big five countries. Much of this growth was due to the huge expansion in trade spurred by postwar recovery and successive rounds of the General Agreement on Tariffs and Trade (GATT).[16] Between 1950 and 1975, OECD countries' imports and exports as a percentage of GDP rose from an average of less than 49 to more than 58 percent. Nation after nation experienced dramatic export growth. America, Britain, France, West Germany, and Japan alone grew 25 percent, on average, over the period. The overwhelming share of their trade was with each other and other members of the OECD. Trade ties were reinforced by the increasing interpenetration of foreign investment within the West. Most of this was in the form of foreign direct investment by multinational corporations, the bulk of them American.[17]

By the 1970s, the West had achieved a level of economic and political integration and coherence that set it apart from the rest. This is captured in Figure 2.1, which summarizes Western governments' support for partnership and power from 1970 through 1975.[18] We use total national defense expenditure (share of GDP) to measure a country's relative defense burden.[19] Countries that shoulder a greater relative defense burden are further to the right in the space; countries investing comparatively little in defense are further to the left. For partnership, we rely on KOF Swiss Economic Institute indices measuring government policies to promote and regulate economic and political globalization.[20] KOF's economic globalization policy index monitors variations in tariff rates, trade regulations and taxes, capital account openness, and foreign investment agreements—policy tools that Bretton Woods allowed governments to use to stimulate, restrict, and otherwise manage cross-border flows of goods, capital, and services.[21] KOF's political globalization policy index measures country membership in international organizations and the number and "diversity" of its international treaties and agreements.[22] Together, these measures capture the extent to which a government supports policies of economic integration and an international rules-based system.[23]

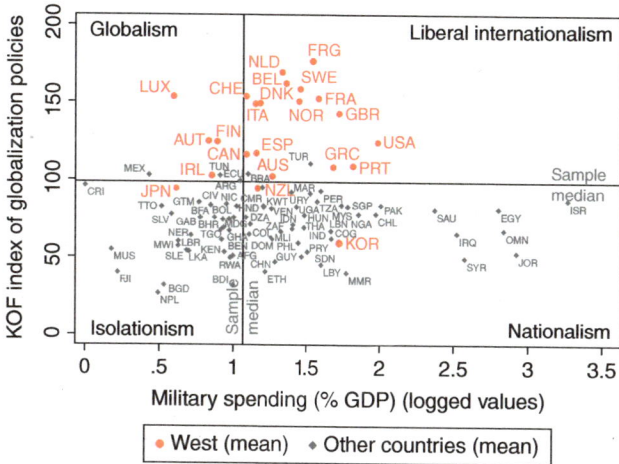

Figure 2.1 Government support for international partnership and military power by country, 1970–1975

As Figure 2.1 indicates, the West's commitment to partnership and power distinguished it from the rest of the world.[24] While countries from all regions of the world invested in military power during the Cold War, comparatively few countries invested in foreign policies promoting international partnership, and *only* Western governments invested in both. To be sure, there were exceptions within the West. For constitutional and political reasons, Iceland, Japan, and Luxembourg did not contribute their "fair share" to Western security during the Cold War. This is reflected in their location on the left side of Figure 2.1. South Korea, which did not join the Western liberal trading system until the early 1970s (and did not become a member of the OECD until 1996), is also an "outlier" in Figure 2.1. It is positioned below the horizontal line. However, America, Britain, France, West Germany, and most other Western democracies line up squarely in the liberal internationalist quadrant.[25] Most other countries supported more nationalist foreign policies (quadrant 4).[26] In short, liberal internationalism was a Western strategy.

THE CRISIS OF THE 1970s

In the 1970s, the Western liberal order's capitalist foundations were shaken. Growth in the advanced Western democracies suddenly slowed, dropping in the 1970s to half its postwar rate.[27] Unemployment doubled, and then tripled. Inflation surged. The price of oil fueling Western economies soared from three to thirty dollars a barrel as a result of crises in the Middle East. Currencies fluctuated wildly, following the collapse of the Bretton Woods regime and the end of capital controls. Political consensus in Western democracies over the proper mix of internationalism and nationalism buckled under the weight of mounting, conflicting demands for fiscal solvency, social redress, and global financial liberalization. Surveying the political landscape, one highly influential analysis of the period concluded that Western democracies were suffering from a "governability crisis."[28] Western governments, it argued, were struggling to cope with the escalating demands for public goods and services being placed on them. Something had to give.

Cracks in the order

For many, the deepening crisis in the West evoked disquieting comparisons to the onset of the Great Depression and the sudden breakdown of that era's international order. The causes of the laissez-faire international order's collapse in the interwar years were different, of course. The interwar international system had put too much faith in markets and business.[29] The question now was whether the reverse was true—whether Western democracies had come to rely too heavily on the state as a provider of goods and services for the public. Many political elites, business leaders, and academic scholars thought so.[30] They argued that Western governments' commitment to full employment and social protection had "overloaded" Western governments and stymied the full development of global markets. Labor unions, workers, and their elected representatives strongly disagreed. They urged Western officials to maintain distributive and redistributive policies and strengthen national control and regulation of their economies. At the time, the implications of all this for Western democracies' foreign policies were not immediately clear. One reason is that the crisis of the Western economic order coincided and intersected with unanticipated developments in the geopolitical realm.

In the late 1960s, cracks opened up on both sides of the Cold War divide. In the East, a growing rift between Moscow and Beijing led to military encounters in 1969 along the border separating the two communist powers. Compounding matters, Eastern Europe had grown increasingly restive under Soviet control. In 1968, the Soviet economic and political model was challenged in Czechoslovakia. Moscow crushed the Czechs' experiment in liberalization (the "Prague Spring"), but the movement was a harbinger of things to come elsewhere in the East. Meanwhile, on the Western side of the divide, America's war in Vietnam put enormous strain on transatlantic relations. Young Europeans, like many young Americans, took to the streets to protest the war. America's European partners were also less willing to follow its lead on security matters. Mistrust between Washington and Paris led the French to pull out of NATO's integrated military command in the mid-1960s. A few years later, West Germany's Willy Brandt, who had long favored German reunification, moved to improve relations with the Soviet Union and other Eastern bloc countries. Under Brandt's *Ostpolitik* policy, West Germany signed a nonaggression pact with Moscow in 1970. Later that year, Brandt also agreed to Polish territorial demands dating from 1945 that came at Germany's expense. Two years later, West Germany offered diplomatic recognition to its East German neighbor.

In principle, East-West détente meant that Western governments could invest less in guns and more in butter. The rationale for doing so was clear. Sluggish growth had resulted in a widening gap between welfare states' declining tax revenues and soaring social expenditures.[31] At the same time, a world less polarized along East-West lines could unlock new markets and investment opportunities in China, Eastern Europe, and in much of the Global South for Western businesses suffering from falling profits. This is the direction most Western governments moved. Between 1976 and 1991, defense spending as a share of GDP dropped 12 percent on average within the West; this happened despite the sharp but short-lived revival of US-Soviet tensions in the early 1980s.[32] The United States continued to outpace its Western allies, spending between 4.6 (in 1991) and 6.6 (in 1982) percent of GDP on defense in the period 1976 to 1991 (compared to the average for the rest of the West that ranged from 2.7 to 3.2 percent of GDP during this period). But America's defense burden was also now well below its average of 8.4 percent during the 1950s and 1960s.

Less investment in military power did not mean less reliance on international markets or international institutions. As the West's defense burden lessened, its commitment to economic integration and institutionalized cooperation intensified. America and Britain were the West's first-movers.[33] Under Ronald Reagan and Margaret Thatcher, the United States and the United Kingdom took steps to reduce government intervention in the economy, liberalize financial markets, and weaken organized labor. Internationally, the Reagan administration was also the driving force behind the 1986 Uruguay Round of multilateral trade negotiations that would lead to lower global tariffs and, in 1995, the creation of the World Trade Organization. Unlike the GATT, the WTO was designed to move from managed trade to freer trade and give international authorities more autonomy to settle trade disputes.[34] The idea was to make international trade less vulnerable to domestic political pressures by setting economic rule-making above the authority of the sovereign member states.[35] Meanwhile, Western governments tightened IMF and World Bank "structural adjustment" demands for assisting developing countries while negotiating new agreements to better protect the rights of Western investors.[36] These were the first glimmers of a post–Bretton Woods international order that would come to prioritize the rights of property over the rights of states.[37]

As part of this global liberalizing movement, Western governments also deepened their commitment to regional integration. Traditionally, regional markets were considered anathema to trade liberalization. It was not only geopolitical imperatives and the need for larger markets that led the West to turn to them in Europe in the 1950s. By the 1980s, Western thinking had undergone a sea change. As political economist Jeffrey Frieden puts it, regionalism was now considered the "antechamber of broader liberalization."[38] In an era where market liberalization was rapidly becoming the leitmotif for policymakers at both the national and global levels, Western government saw regional integration as a stepping stone to strengthening existing regional markets and creating new ones. In Europe, the European Community was expanded to include Greece in 1981 and Portugal and Spain in 1986; Austria, Finland, and Sweden followed in the 1990s. The "Single European Act" in 1986 created a single market in goods and services and transformed the European Commission into a powerful agent for market liberalization. In North America, the 1983 Caribbean Basin Initiative gave countries in and around the Caribbean greater access to the American market. It was followed in 1988 by the Canada–United States Free Trade Agreement that reduced trade restrictions between the two countries. In Asia, an Asia-Pacific Economic Cooperation (APEC) forum was created to promote freer trade in the region.

In the 1980s, Western democracies began to recalibrate. The state-based approach that had guided Western international engagement since the postwar era lost ground to a decidedly more market-based approach.[39] As Figure 2.2 indicates, between 1976 and 1991, Western governments relied more heavily on international partnership than they did during the earlier

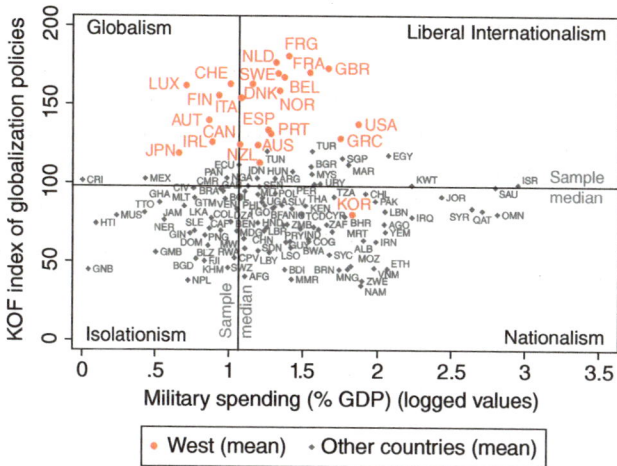

Figure 2.2 Government support for international partnership and military power by country, 1976–1991

period. Most Western democracies moved northward on the vertical (partnership) axis. Australia, Austria, Canada, Finland, France, Ireland, Japan, New Zealand, and the United Kingdom all invested more heavily in partnership. Newly democratic Greece, Portugal, and Spain also moved toward greater partnership. Less dramatic was the shift leftward along the horizontal (power) axis. Overall, Western defense budgets as a share of GDP declined during this period. However, compared to the global median, most Western governments remained firmly in the liberal internationalist quadrant. Even though Western democracies' relative reliance on international partnership increased, their comparative investment in military power held steady.

AGE OF GLOBALISM

In the 1990s, the West's approach to liberal order-building changed. Western governments shifted from a strategy of liberal internationalism that combined power with partnership to a strategy of globalism that prioritized partnership over power. International relations scholars have characterized this shift in different ways: "global neoliberalism," "liberal internationalism 3.0," and "postnational liberalism" to distinguish it from Wilsonian liberal internationalism after World War I and the liberal internationalism of the Cold War era.[40] What these labels have in common is a recognition that, in the

1990s, the West's approach to liberal international order-building began to rely more heavily on international markets and global institutions. The managed approach to globalization that held sway during the Cold War, favoring domestic policy objectives (e.g., full employment, social insurance) over economic integration and international institutions, was transformed into a new type of globalization that prioritized international trade, global finance, and supranational institutions as means to expand the liberal order and put it beyond the reach of domestic politics. The age of globalism had begun.

The turn to globalism

The surge in globalism that started in the 1990s is often equated with the rapid global expansion of economic activity of the late nineteenth and early twentieth centuries. There are similarities, to be sure. However, the globalism of the 1990s and 2000s owed far more to Western governments' efforts to actively promote the cross-border flow of goods, capital, and services and to shield that activity from vicissitudes of domestic politics by encasing them in supranational institutions.[41] During the 1990s, Washington, Paris, Berlin, and other Western capitals launched new institutional projects to deepen their economic ties as well as their reliance on international institutions. In Europe, the Maastricht treaty of 1993 formally established the European Union, including a new European Central Bank and a new common currency, the euro.[42] In North America, the Canada-US Free Trade Agreement was expanded to include Mexico, resulting in the 1994 North American Free Trade Agreement (NAFTA). In Asia, APEC expanded its goals, calling for free and open trade in the Asia-Pacific by 2010 for the region's more advanced economies and 2020 for its developing economies.

As the Western-led liberal order became more integrated internally, it also expanded outwardly into new markets. In the 1990s, countries that were on the periphery of the liberal order, by Western fiat or by choice, were suddenly in play as destinations for Western investment. Already, many countries in Asia, Latin America, and Africa had started reducing government involvement in their domestic markets and opening up their economies to cross-border flows of capital as well as expanded trade.[43] In the 1990s, the former Warsaw Pact countries and Soviet republics of Central and Eastern Europe followed suit. This gave them access to Western markets and capital. However, in most cases access came at a price: a commitment to the very market-oriented adjustments that Western democracies themselves had undertaken a decade earlier.

During the 1990s, the market-based movement of the 1980s gathered strength in the West, and in much of the rest. As Beth Simmons and her coauthors observe, the turn to privatization that Thatcher and Reagan had set in motion in the 1980s had become "a major element of economic policy in both the developed and developing world over the course of twenty years."[44] The so-called Washington Consensus that prescribed fiscal discipline, tax reform, privatization, deregulation, and trade liberalization became the new orthodoxy at the IMF, World Bank, and other financial institutions lending to those countries integrated as subordinate players into, or now joining, the Western liberal order. Yet the turn toward globalism was not only about markets and growth. In the 1990s, a bevy of new issues—from human rights to climate change—were thrust onto the international agenda by progressive voices in the developed and developing worlds. The result was a rapid expansion in the scope of institutionalized cooperation. Between the mid-1980s and late 2000s, the number of international government organizations more than doubled globally, from 3,546 in 1985 to 7,459 in 2008.[45]

In Central and Eastern Europe, publics that raced to join the West would later express resentment about the hardships, corruption, and inequities that so often accompanied market-induced liberalization.[46] However, in the 1990s, gaining access to Western foreign investment, the EU's market, and NATO's security umbrella were among many governments' highest priorities.[47] Political elites leading the transition from the Soviet centrally planned economies to the West's liberal economic system viewed access to Western capital and markets as essential to their countries' success, and to their own political fortunes. Western political and economic elites were no less enthusiastic about the advantages of gaining access to the low-cost, high-skilled labor that the former Warsaw Pact nations and Soviet republics had to offer their more developed economies. Over the course of the 1990s, Western capital flowed into Central and Eastern Europe. Hungary attracted over $20 billion in foreign direct investment; Poland, some $30 billion; the Czech Republic, $15 billion.[48]

Even more striking was China's rapid transition from the periphery of the world economy to its core. During the second half of the Cold War, Beijing and Washington's "tacit alliance" against Moscow had opened the door to China's economic liberalization and closer economic ties with the West.[49] Over the next two decades, Chinese exports grew from $20 billion to over

$170 billion, while United States, Japanese, and other foreign investors poured billions into China each year.[50] However, it was not until the late 1990s that Washington led a concerted effort to institutionalize China's integration into the world economy by normalizing trade relations with Beijing, paving the way for China's entry into the WTO. The idea was to encourage China to become a "strategic partner," as the Clinton administration put it.[51] The United States, and the West more generally, would benefit from China's integration into the rapidly globalizing world economy. China would benefit too, the thinking went. As its people began to reap the rewards of trade and economic growth, onlookers believed that there would be domestic pressure for social liberalization and bottom-up political change.[52]

In the 1990s, Western leaders also began reshaping and updating the Western liberal order's security architecture in Europe and Asia.[53] In Europe, this involved the unification of Germany and the integration of the former Warsaw Pact states and Soviet Baltic republics into NATO, along with their incorporation into the European Union. Poland, Hungary, and the Czech Republic joined the sixteen-member military and political alliance in 1999. Three years later, at NATO's Prague Summit, Bulgaria, Estonia, Latvia, Lithuania, Romania, Slovakia, and Slovenia were invited to join the security pact. In Asia, Washington and Tokyo reaffirmed their alliance commitments. Worries about Beijing's ambitions in East Asia following the 1996 Taiwan Strait missile crisis and North Korea's ballistic missile tests over Japan led Washington to commit to keeping 100,000 troops in East Asia. Tokyo signaled greater resolve, too, by broadening the role of its Self Defense Forces (SDF) from its traditional mission of territorial defense to regional and global multilateral operations and peacekeeping.[54]

As Western democracies' conception of security broadened, so did the range of missions they were prepared to support.[55] Democratic enlargement, democracy promotion, humanitarian intervention, and the Responsibility to Protect increasingly vied with more traditional conceptions of national interest and international security such as balance of power, collective security, and extended deterrence. Western governments worked to strengthen international laws to hold governments and their leaders more accountable for how they treated their populations, and began funding nongovernmental organizations with the hope of building civil society within states transitioning to democracy.[56] In the wake of the international community's failure to respond to the Rwandan genocide and Srebrenica massacre in Bosnia, Western governments also displayed a greater willingness to use coercion and force to achieve these goals. This was perhaps clearest in the case of the Balkans in 1999, when NATO pressured Yugoslav President Slobodan Milosevic to accept Kosovo's de facto independence.

On security as well as economic issues, the West relied increasingly on institutionalized cooperation. The West also continued to invest in military power. However, in the absence of a Cold War–style geopolitical rival, large outlays for defense were harder for governments to justify and sell to publics after a half-century of vigilance and, for many families, sacrifice.[57] Talk of a "peace dividend" was rife. In the 1990s, military expenditures as percentage of GDP fell in every NATO nation, including the United States.[58] In the wake of the September 11 attacks and with the onset of the war in Afghanistan, the United States, the United Kingdom, and France increased the share of GDP they invested in defense, but they were the exceptions. As Figure 2.3 makes clear, between 1992 and 2017, the center of gravity in the West shifted from liberal internationalism toward globalism. Every Western democracy moved left along the horizontal axis (power) and, notably, upward on the vertical axis (partnership).[59] The West was not alone. Now the vast majority of non-Western countries also clustered above the horizontal axis, signifying increased support for trade liberalization, institutionalized cooperation, and multilateral governance. In the age of globalism, the West and the rest were converging.

Of Mars and Venus

The ensuing years were not trouble-free years for the West, of course. The US-led war in Iraq in 2003 triggered the most significant rift in transatlantic relations since the Vietnam War. The debate over the war exposed European reservations about American power and the George W. Bush administration's willingness to flout liberal norms of sovereignty, multilateralism, and international law to overturn Saddam Hussein's Iraqi regime. Many Americans were put off by Europe's hand-wringing and second-guessing. It fueled suspicions that European capitals were no longer reliable allies or willing to make the tough choices thought to be necessary to keep citizens safe in the post-9/11 world. Speculation about the "end of the West" was widespread.[60] However, as Figure 2.3 makes clear, the war did not drive the West apart. The political storms over the Atlantic soon calmed. Western governments, most under new leadership, moved on. Despite their differences over Iraq, the United States and Europe remained committed to globalism.

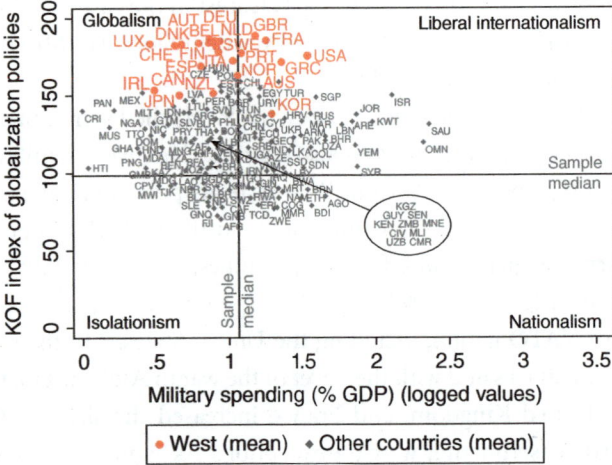

Figure 2.3 Government support for international partnership and military power by country, 1992–2017

In the 2000s, the event that arguably posed the greatest test of Western solidarity and the liberal order's durability was the 2008 global financial crisis. The scale and timing of the crisis, and the recession that followed, varied from country to country, but the crisis sent shockwaves across the OECD and beyond. Indeed, none of the 104 countries tracked by the WTO were spared its effects.[61] As the crisis cascaded across the globe, international trade plummeted. Unemployment spiked. International banks and financial institutions' asset values dropped sharply. In desperation, banks turned to their home countries' governments to be bailed out. By April 2009, the IMF concluded that the recession was the deepest economic downturn on record since the Great Depression.[62] After years of being told that markets free of domestic regulations are more efficient, national taxpayers, particularly in the United States, were now being asked to intervene to stabilize their economies, rescue the banks, and put an end to a crisis that sprang from their governments' increased reliance on market liberalization.

Much has been written about the effect of the 2008 economic crisis on Western support for international openness and global governance. On the surface, this key dimension of the liberal order appeared to be under threat during the first year of the crisis. Western and other governments initially responded by imposing "micro-protectionist" measures (e.g., local content requirements, export taxes and quotas, public procurement discrimination against foreign firms), often skirting the letter of WTO rules.[63] Even so, the beggar-thy-neighbor downward spiral in international trade many feared did not materialize. After the immediate shock, the surge in protectionism receded and cross-border capital flows rebounded, even if they remained below the 2007 highs for some time.[64] The initial drop in industrial output was steep, of course. Yet here, too, the rebound exceeded what many analysts had predicted in the early stages of the financial crisis.[65] Within four years of the recession's onset, global industrial output was 10 percent higher than before its start, partly because capital flows did not dry up.[66]

In the aftermath of the 2008 crisis, global trade, investment, and output resumed sooner and more forcefully than they had in the wake of the Great Depression of 1929. As a number of scholars have pointed out, one important reason for this is that the existing international institutional architecture proved to be more robust than one might have expected, given the severity of the crisis.[67] Existing global institutions such as the IMF and World Bank were arguably strengthened, not weakened. As the crisis deepened, the Group of 20 (G20) was transformed into a major forum for policy deliberation and coordination between the advanced industrialized countries of the West and the developing economies of the Global South.[68] In the area of international trade, the WTO was able to prevent or at least limit many forms of trade policy backsliding.[69] In short, the supranational architecture that Western democracies had invested in so heavily over the preceding decades helped them weather 2008's strong economic headwinds.

If globalism promoted the diffusion of the financial crisis, it also gave Western governments strong incentives to stick with the system rather than decouple from it.[70] It also arguably brought Western governments closer together. Evidence for this can be seen in Figures 2.4 and 2.5. Figure 2.4 tracks government support in the EU-15, Japan, and the United States for partnership and power from 1970 through 2018.[71] We see that, over the entire time period, there is very little distance between the EU-15 and the United States over international partnership (vertical dimension) and that, as EU support for international openness and cooperation increases, so does US support. By contrast, the distance between the EU-15 and the United States on the horizontal dimension (military power) narrows over time. Overall, though, the EU and the United States follow the same general pattern. In the 1990s, Western governments move away from liberal internationalism toward globalism, and this process continues through the 2000s and into the 2010s. While the United States never fully embraces globalism, it does follow a path

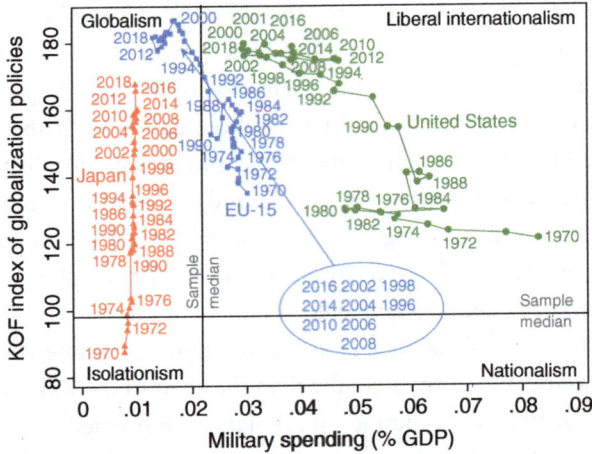

Figure 2.4 Government support for international partnership and military power by EU, Japan, and United States, 1970–2018

that is strikingly similar to the EU's. Indeed, if there is an outlier in Figure 2.4, it is Japan.

Japan's path toward globalism is clearly different from America's and Europe's. Not surprisingly, Japanese investment in power is low by Western standards. Japanese defense spending averaged 0.94 percent of GDP during the 1990s through 2000s. This is not significantly different from Japan's defense burden during the 1970s and 1980s, when it averaged 0.90 percent of GDP.[72] Yet like the EU-15 and the United States, Japan's investment in international partnership increased over time, and substantially so during the 1990s and especially, 2000s. This was a very active period of Japanese diplomacy. In the 2000s, Japan signed free trade agreements with Singapore (2002) and Mexico (2004). Similar trade negotiations were launched with the Philippines, Thailand, and Malaysia, among other countries in the region.[73] Tokyo also expanded its level of participation in multilateral peacekeeping and non-lethal international security missions.[74] In short, as Japan invested more heavily in international partnership, its foreign policy priorities more closely aligned with America's and Europe's.

The convergence of the United States, EU, and Japan in Figure 2.4 raises questions about the West, more generally. Did Western governments' foreign policy preferences also become more similar over time? The short answer is, yes. Figure 2.5 tracks Western government support for partnership and power from 1970 through 2018.[75] The dark-shaded areas in the figure

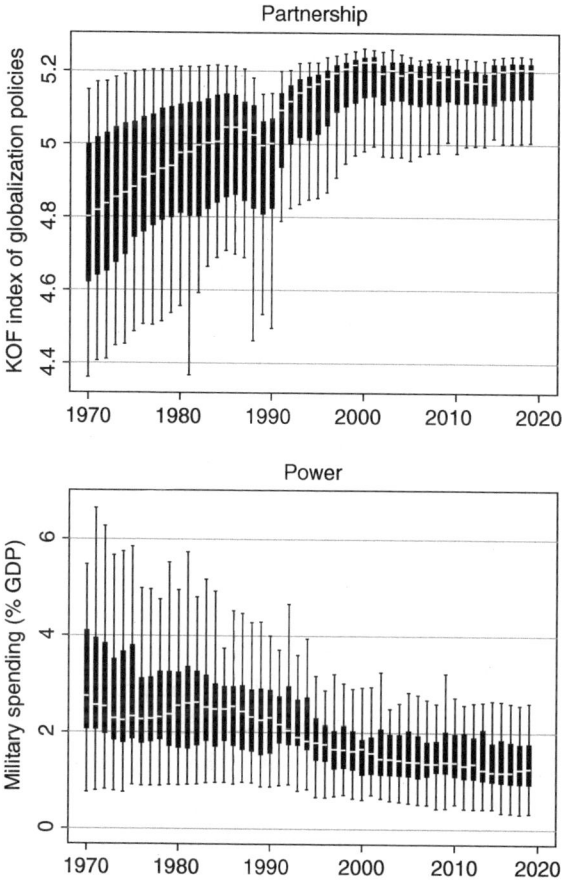

Figure 2.5 Cross-national variation in government support for international partnership and military power in Western democracies, 1970–2018

represent the bottom twenty-fifth and top seventy-fifth percentile of the interquartile distribution. The median value for the twenty-four OECD countries in our sample is denoted by white horizontal lines in the shaded areas. The "whiskers" in the plots represent the maximum and minimum value among Western countries in any given year. We see Figure 2.5a that policy differences among Western governments over trade liberalization and institutionalized cooperation have narrowed considerably over time. We see a similar trend in the case of defense spending and military preparedness in the bottom panel. Here, the relative defense burden shouldered by Western governments narrows considerably between 1970 and 2000. It expands slightly after 2001 due to the spike in US defense spending for the wars in Afghanistan and Iraq, before narrowing again. In short, the post–Cold War decades were a time of increasing policy convergence, not divergence, among Western governments. The same could not be said about Western governments and their publics, however.

GLOBALISM'S DISCONTENTS

In the aftermath of the 2008 economic crisis, it is not hard to see why some Western political analysts concluded that "the system worked." The worst was avoided: the West and the rest did not plunge headfirst into another Great Depression. The Great Recession did not lead to rapid "de-globalization." Yet if Western democracies were able to avoid the worst, the notion that the system worked overlooks, or downplays, just how unpopular globalism had become *within* Western democracies by 2008. Signs that there was trouble ahead on the domestic front were evident as early as the late 1990s. In the wake of the 1999 Seattle protests, Peter Sutherland, the former head of the WTO, observed that the protests reflected "a fundamental deficit in effective political support for the WTO."[76] The decisive battles were not on the streets, but at the ballot box. It was there that Western voters began registering in ever-increasing numbers their opposition to their governments' deepening commitment to market liberalization and global governance.[77]

End of consensus

That few Western leaders saw it coming is not surprising. For decades after World War II, Western voters had backed liberal internationalist policies, giving policymakers substantial "decision latitude" on foreign policy matters.[78] In most Western democracies, public support for international partnership kept pace with government efforts to expand international markets and promote multilateral cooperation. Scholars wrote of a "permissive mood" or "permissive consensus," where citizens deferred to political elites on matters of economic integration and international governance.[79] Public support for investing in military power was more variable and voluble, due largely to worries about nuclear war (see below). Yet, for the most part, public backing of military spending and preparedness tracked actual government investment in national defense. As Western defense budgets waxed and waned, so, generally, did public support. Even during the widely perceived crisis in Western security in the late 1970s and early 1980s, public support for defense spending was, as one careful study of the period puts it, "largely in tune with the views of governmental elites."[80]

As Figure 2.6 suggests, public attitudes toward the liberal order, and the government elites who championed it, began to change in the 1990s. The figure tracks "voter support" in the EU-15, Japan, and the United States for international partnership and military power from 1950 through 2017. Our voter support estimates are based on Manifesto Project data.[81] We use the Manifesto data to score the extent to which parties run on platforms favoring economic integration and multilateral governance and military spending and preparedness.[82] We then weight those scores by the parties' electoral vote share to estimate the popularity of these foreign policies among a country's voters by year. The party-system averages of such weighted scores provide an estimate of voters' foreign policy positions based on their actual voting behavior—that is, which party platforms they vote for at the polls.[83] These measures do not tell us directly what voters think, but they provide insight into voters' foreign policy preferences, the extent to which they are stable or change over time, and importantly, how closely they parallel their governments' foreign policies.

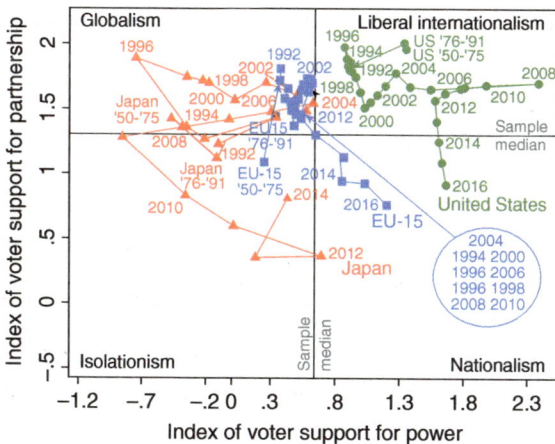

Figure 2.6 Voter support for international partnership and military power by EU, Japan, and United States, 1950–2017

For expositional purposes, we organize the results in Figure 2.6 by time period: with period averages from 1950–1975 and 1976–1991 and annual trends from 1991–2017.[84] The lines demarcating the full-sample medians on each axis provide visual benchmarks for comparing countries and identifying trends. We can see that, relative to the sample median for our twenty-four OECD countries, voter support in the EU-15, Japan, and United States has shifted considerably over time. During the Cold War, voter support for liberal internationalism was clearly stronger in the United States than in the EU-15 or Japan. American voters were more supportive of partnership and power. However, since the Cold War there has been a clear shift in voter sentiment toward nationalism. American, European, and Japanese support for international partnership has decreased, while support for military power has increased. This pattern is particularly clear for the EU-15 and United States, but since 2009, Japanese voters have also moved in the same general direction. Viewed together, Figures 2.4 and 2.6 point to a growing disconnect between governments and voters over foreign policy since the Cold War: with the US, European, and Japanese governments favoring globalism, and American, EU, and Japanese voters, displaying increasing support for nationalism.

To sharpen our understanding of this gap, Figure 2.7 plots Western government and voter support for partnership and power on each dimension, separately. We use again the KOF Swiss Economic Institute's indices measuring government *policy* support for economic and political globalization and SIPRI estimates of military spending as a percent of GDP. Our measure of voter support is based on the same Manifesto data used earlier, though now focusing on the average over-time trends of Western voter support from 1970 through 2017. We display the trends in government policy and voter support on separate scales to better visualize how changes in one compare to changes in the other. The top panel measuring support for partnership essentially capture movement along the vertical axis in the two-dimensional plots above—the extent to which governments and voters favor foreign policy strategies relying on economic integration and multilateral governance. The bottom panel measuring support for power depict movement along the horizontal axis in the two-dimensional plots: the greater government and voter support for defense spending and preparedness in Figure 2.7, the more support for grand strategies that rely on military power in the two-dimensional plots.

We see in Figure 2.7 governments and voters are largely in sync during the Cold War. Western governments invested heavily in foreign policies of

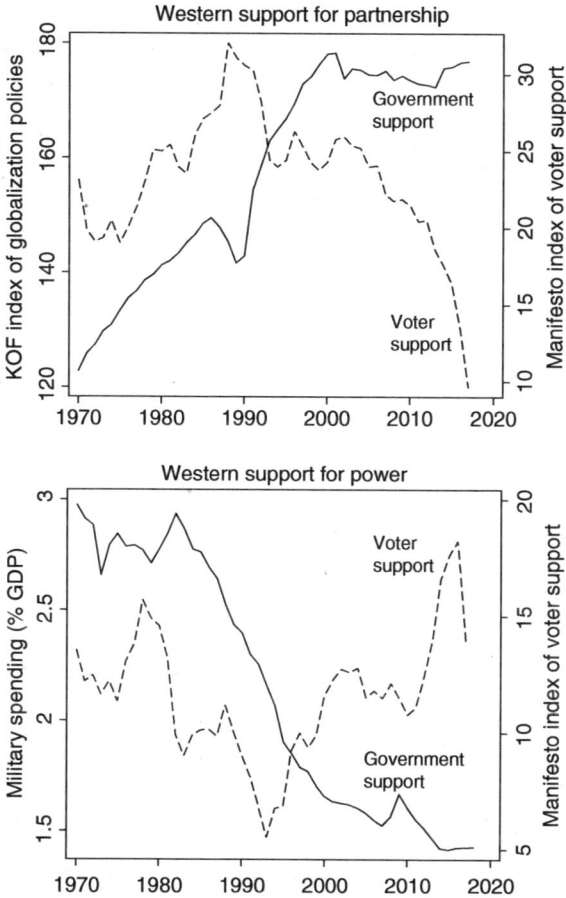

Figure 2.7 Government and voter support for international partnership and military power in Western democracies, 1970–2017

ever-increasing international partnership. Western voters consistently cast their ballots for parties promising to deliver those foreign policies in office. Indeed, Western leaders enjoyed a healthy cushion of support among voters on matters involving economic integration and multilateral governance. This pattern lasted until the 1990s, when public support changed dramatically. While Western government support for economic integration and multilateral cooperation continued to expand, Western voter support dropped sharply in the 1990s and then again in the 2000s. Even as the pace of government support for trade liberalization and institutionalized cooperation slowed in the 2000s, the gap between Western governments' international ambitions and what voters were willing to support continued to widen. Between 1990 and 2017, Western voters' support for political parties running on platforms advocating greater international partnership fell by nearly half. Much of the decline came after 2008, but the widening gap between Western governments and their voting publics was evident well before the financial crisis.[85]

The story is quite different when it comes to the West's commitment to military power, at least since the early 1990s. During the Cold War, Western political leaders who invested in military power did so knowing that public support was less predictable. While Westerners were generally anxious about Soviet power and favored military preparedness, they also worried about the risk of nuclear war.[86] As a result, Western government investment in military power often ran ahead of voters' support for parties running on platforms calling for increased defense spending and military preparedness. However, with the collapse of the Soviet Union the trend lines reversed. Western investment in military power as a share of GDP fell steadily. By contrast, after hitting rock bottom in the 1990s, the voting public's appetite for military spending returned to Cold War levels. Public support for military spending and preparedness intensified following the September 11 attacks, and even more sharply in the 2010s.

These aggregate measures of government and voter support for partnership and power smooth over considerable cross-national variation, of course. The timing and severity of the gaps between Western governments and voters over foreign policy also vary across the West. Yet, as we can see in Figure 2.8, the overall pattern holds for the EU-15, the United States, and, to a lesser extent, Japan. This is especially true of government and voter support for international partnership. In each case, government and voter support for economic integration and multilateral cooperation diverge sharply after the Cold War. This occurs earlier in the EU-15 and the United States, but by the early 2000s, the same pattern is evident in Japan. While European, American, and Japanese government support for international partnership levels off in the post–Cold War era, voter support for government and parties defending these policies steadily declines.

The picture is less clear-cut when it comes to European, American, and Japanese support for investing in military power. In each case, voter support for military spending and preparedness declines after the Cold War before rebounding in the EU and US cases. In US case, the resurgence of support owed partly to lingering concerns about international security, especially

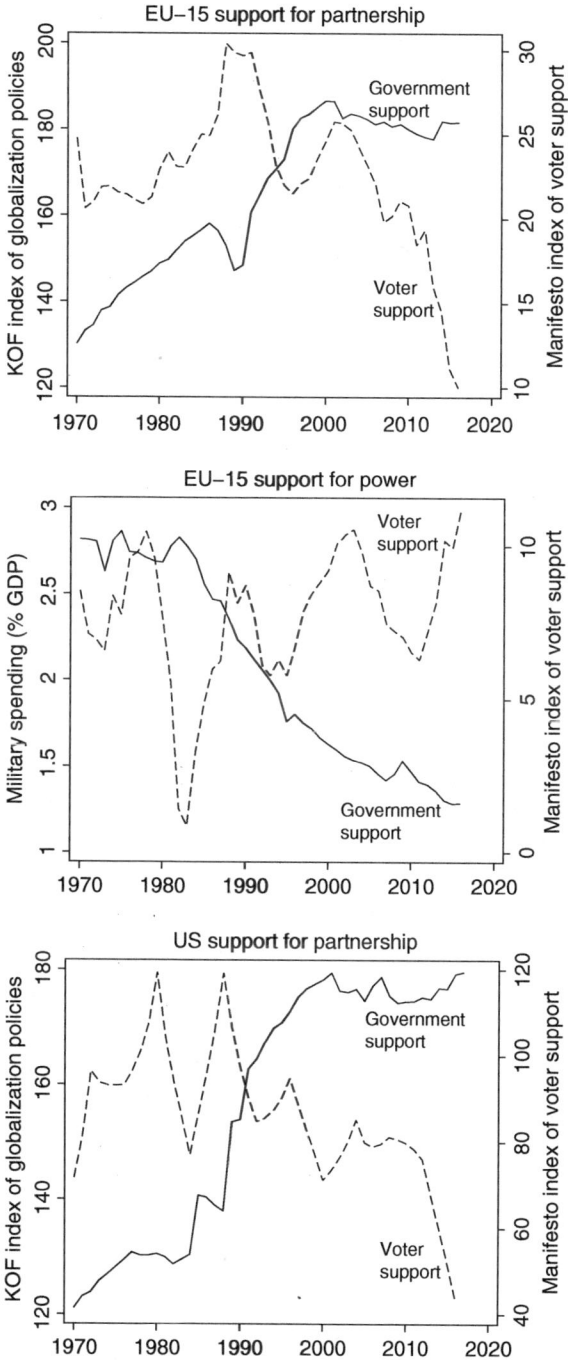

Figure 2.8 Government and voter support for international partnership and military power in the EU, Japan, and United States, 1970–2017

US support for power

Japanese support for partnership

Japanese support for power

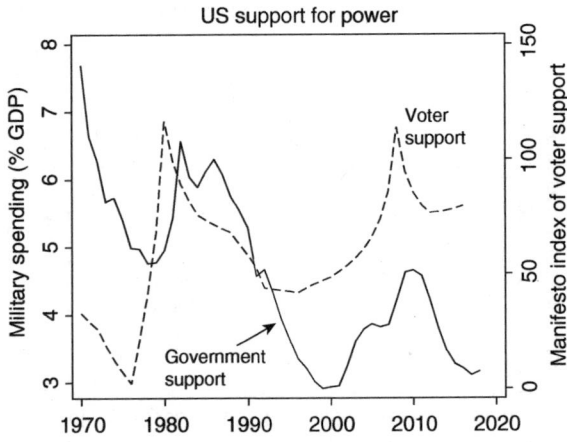

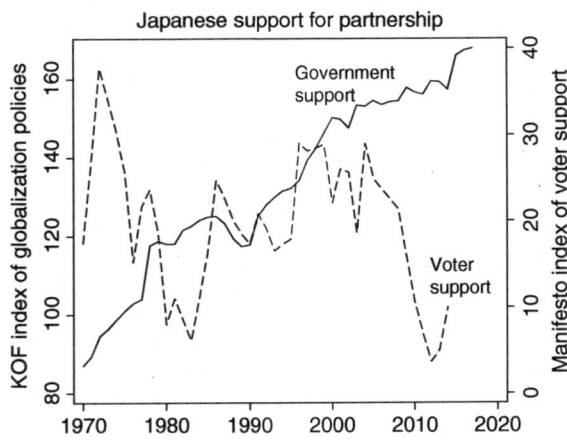

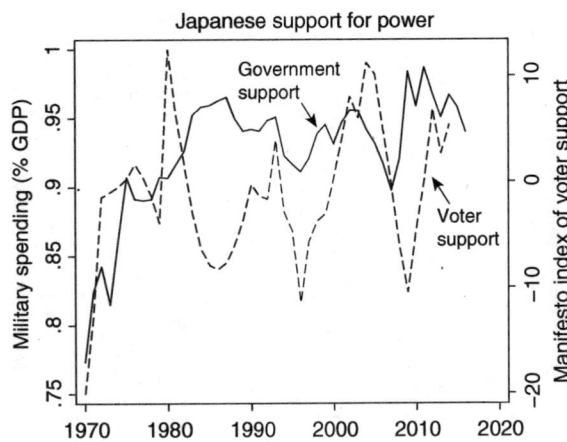

Figure 2.8 Continued

after the September 11 attacks.[87] Continuing voter support for pooling national sovereignty over defense as a means to keep guns-versus-butter trade-offs in check was a factor for many in the EU.[88] In Japan, mounting concerns about China's military buildup and North Korean hostility led to growing support for amending constitutional prohibitions against militarization and expanding the SDF's role to include national security (as well as disaster relief, humanitarian aid, and domestic security).[89] Yet as we show in Chapter 4, the resurgence of voter support for military power also reflects the growing number and strength of anti-globalist, nationalist parties since the Cold War. As these parties gained political strength, the gap between Western governments and voters that took shape in the 1990s widened.

A BRIDGE TOO FAR

In the 1990s, few Western leaders spoke more eloquently about globalism's promise than President Bill Clinton. Speaking before the UN General Assembly in September 1997, Clinton declared: "At the dawn of a new millennium, we can envision a new era that escapes the twentieth century's darkest moments" and "fulfills its most brilliant possibilities." "The forces of global integration are a great tide inexorably wearing away the established order of things."[90] Clinton's optimism about globalism as a bridge to a twenty-first century free of geopolitics and the narrow nationalisms of the past was easily shared by many world leaders sitting in the audience that day, especially those representing the advanced industrialized economies of the West. In the absence of a shared security agenda after the fall of the Soviet Union, Western elites found common purpose in a global agenda calling for the freer movement of capital, goods, and services across national boundaries and greater reliance on multilateral institutions and governance.

The West's turn to globalism would prove a bridge too far. Clinton was right about one thing, though: at the level of government policy, globalism did function as a unifying force in the West. On the one hand, cooperation between Western democracies on trade, security, and other matters continued, and as we have seen, rapidly expanded into new policy domains such as the environment and human rights. On the other hand, Western public support did not keep step with their leaders' efforts to liberalize their economies, delegate more discretionary authority to supranational institutions, and incorporate nations on the periphery of the world economy into their countries' manufacturing supply chains. As we will see, the fact that Western leaders' efforts to promote globalization usually went hand-in-hand with commitments to reform and scale back the welfare state only compounded matters by making it easier for anti-globalists on the left and right to appeal to voters who worried they were being sold a bridge to nowhere.

It would take time before the gap between Western governments and their publics would reach critical proportions, but as we have seen, anti-globalist nationalist sentiment was spreading in the democracies even before the decade of the 1990s was out. The moral of the story is not that domestic politics matter *now*. As we show in Chapters 3 and 4, domestic politics have shaped the political possibilities for liberal international order-building in Western democracies since the very beginning of the postwar era. Forged in an era of superpower rivalry, the postwar liberal order benefited from the backing of Western leaders who saw electoral advantage in a foreign policy strategy that combined partnership and power and that struck a delicate balance between international openness and social protection. That voters backed their governments' foreign policies as long as they did was due in no small part to the depth of Western political leaders' commitment to balancing these conflicting demands and pressures in their national political economies. In the 1990s, this too would change.

3

Roots of Insolvency

Susan Strange, Britain's most influential scholar of world politics in the late twentieth century, was one of globalization's fiercest critics. In a 1997 essay entitled "The Erosion of the State," Strange took exception to a cadre of economists at the time who argued that globalization was "globaloney," a myth or an illusion, and thus of little real consequence to Western democracies. Contemporary globalization, Strange argued, was not their grandfathers' globalization. It was not just the scope and form that differed from earlier versions of globalization, she argued. It was that the globalization of the 1990s was undermining the state as a social safety net and producing "a democratic deficit, not only in Europe, but in America, Japan—the entire globalized economy."[1] Too much authority for managing the world economy was being pooled at the supranational level and delegated to international bureaucrats. Too little thought was being given to how democracies' headlong pursuit of trade liberalization, cross-border investment, and multilateral governance was weakening their capacity "to protect the vulnerable in society." Western leaders, Strange concluded, had to restore "a measure of social justice denied by the market" for those left behind.

Strange's worries about the risks that unbridled globalization posed to democratic solvency were prescient. As we showed in Chapter 2, the insolvency gap between Western governments' international ambitions and what their publics were willing to support steadily worsened over the next quarter-century. Western leaders' growing reliance on economic integration and multilateral governance fueled anti-globalist sentiment and, as we have seen, weakened the liberal order's domestic supports in Western electorates. In this chapter we explain why this happened. We argue that Western governments' turn toward globalism provoked a domestic political backlash because it was stripped of many of the social guarantees and protections that liberal internationalism originally entailed and, importantly, that Cold War geopolitical imperatives reinforced. We show that the stronger Western governments' commitment to social protection, and the more threatening the international environment, the more support liberal internationalism receives from

Geopolitics and Democracy. Peter Trubowitz and Brian Burgoon, Oxford University Press.
© Oxford University Press 2023. DOI: 10.1093/oso/9780197535400.003.0003

parties and voters. This is why political support in Western democracies for the liberal international order ran so strong during the Cold War, and why it has weakened considerably since.

In developing our explanation for the decline of Western support for the liberal order, we focus considerable attention on the collapse of the Soviet Union and its implications for the liberal order. Little has been written about how this international development impacted the internal politics of the two dozen Western democracies who were locked in Cold War with it for nearly half a century. This is not surprising, given the triumphalism that has permeated the topic in Western commentary. However, as we show, the Cold War strengthened national cohesion in Western democracies. It also contributed to the expansion of the welfare state. This matters because the social protections that postwar Western leaders and mainstream parties guaranteed workers were essential to winning their votes. Social protection drew voters into the liberal internationalist fold. Cold War imperatives helped keep them there.

The chapter is organized into three sections. The first section focuses on the relationship between economic openness and social protection. We show that domestic support for liberal internationalism in Western democracies depends in part on the level of social protection they guarantee their citizens. The erosion of social protections in Western democracies since the 1990s helps explain the widening gap between Western governments and voters over foreign policy that we described in Chapter 2.[2] In the second section, we show that geopolitical imperatives reinforced Western governments and mainstream parties' commitment to liberal internationalism during the Cold War. The corollary to this argument is that, in the absence of Cold War pressures, Western domestic support for liberal internationalism weakened. In the third section, we consider why Western governments and leaders did not do more to close the resulting gap with their publics over foreign policy. Was it simply a case of hubris and triumphalism, as some have charged, or does it owe more to changes in the political economies of the advanced industrial nations?[3] We consider several explanations.

POLANYI'S REVENGE

In *The Great Transformation*, Karl Polanyi famously chronicled how globalization in the late nineteenth and early twentieth centuries provoked large-scale social backlashes.[4] Drawing on the economic history of England, Polanyi's study suggested that societies exposed to extensive market liberalization invariably sought to protect themselves by turning to a wide variety of mechanisms ranging from trade protectionism, to capital controls and price-setting mechanisms, to minimum wage laws, workers' compensation, and other forms of "social protection." Polanyi judged these measures of a piece: all part of a society's natural and "spontaneous" effort to shield itself from market forces. If nations experiencing the harshest economic pain were not careful, those efforts to save themselves could metastasize and transform them into illiberal anti-democratic polities, as happened during the interwar years in Germany, Italy, and the Soviet Union. Writing for a broad audience, Polanyi's message was clear. If countries hoped to avoid a recurrence of such calamities, their leaders needed to strike a new bargain between international openness and social protection.

The postwar bargain

In the postwar era, Western leaders sought to strike precisely this balance between market and state.[5] Constructing a liberal international trade and financial order would have to allow governments a substantial degree of social protection in the domestic realm. International openness would have to be harmonized with national autonomy. To be sure, a robust social safety net would not guarantee international order and stability in an anarchical world of states. However, it could cushion the market's most disruptive effects while allowing industrialists, farmers, and workers to reap the rewards of potential export markets and cheaper imports. By taking the hard edge off capitalism, the postwar welfare state could also help strengthen support for liberal internationalism more broadly, among Western publics, and make competing foreign policy strategies of nationalism and isolationism less attractive.

To Western leaders, liberal internationalism and the welfare state were thus mutually supportive.[6] For most voters, the ensuing postwar economic boom was proof enough that the basic formula worked. Across the West, expanded trade drove economic growth, making it easier for Western governments to expand social protections and boost real wages and giving Western voters reason to support closer economic ties within the West. This, in turn, gave Western leaders more latitude to press forward with liberal internationalist policies.[7] Leftist arguments about the evils of capitalism and

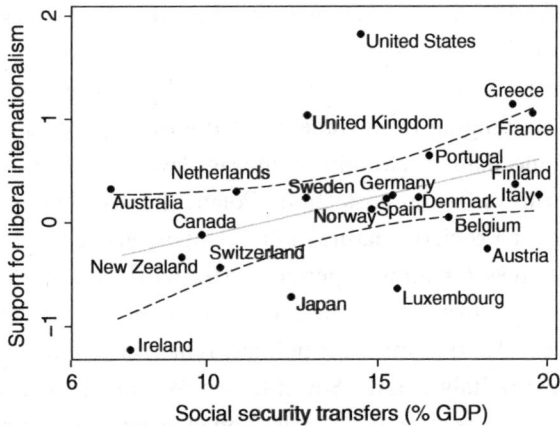

Figure 3.1 Government support for social protection and liberal internationalism by Western democracy, 1970–2017

the American-led postwar order rang hollow at a time when the vast majority of Western workers were benefiting from high rates of growth and much higher unionization rates than today. Right-wing arguments that Western governments harbored wild-eyed "one world" schemes of global government also fell flat politically. Such claims strained credibility in an era when Western leaders turned a blind eye to the many ambitious plans and designs for international federation being advanced by leading international scientists, economists, and public intellectuals.[8]

For decades Western governments maintained this delicate balance between international openness and social protection.[9] Western leaders viewed investing in social protection as an investment in liberal internationalism and international stability. Systematic analysis at the country, party, and voter levels of analysis indicates that they were close to the mark. Starting at the country level, Figures 3.1 and 3.2 show that a country's level of social protection is positively correlated with *partnership* and *power*, individually, and in most cases, our proxy for liberal internationalism: partnership and power combined (*partnership* + *power*).[10] Figure 3.1 provides a descriptive snapshot of the relationship between social protection and liberal internationalism (*partnership* + *power*) from 1970 through 2017 for our sample of Western countries.[11] The solid lines in these and similar figures indicate the direction of the relationship between the variables: in this case, between social transfers and liberal internationalism. The broken lines refer to the tightness of the association, or fit, between the variables. These are set at the

95 percent confidence intervals. If we see that both the upper and lower confidence intervals are positive throughout the distribution, as we do here, then we know with 95 percent confidence that the correlation between the two variables in the figure tends to be positive. In Figure 3.1, we see that on average the higher a country's spending on social protection, the more its government tends to support liberal internationalism.[12]

Figure 3.2 summarizes the results of more systematic analysis of these relationships at the country-year level. Here we consider whether spending on social protection spurs government support for liberal internationalism. We analyze the full country-year variation, with the baseline results focused

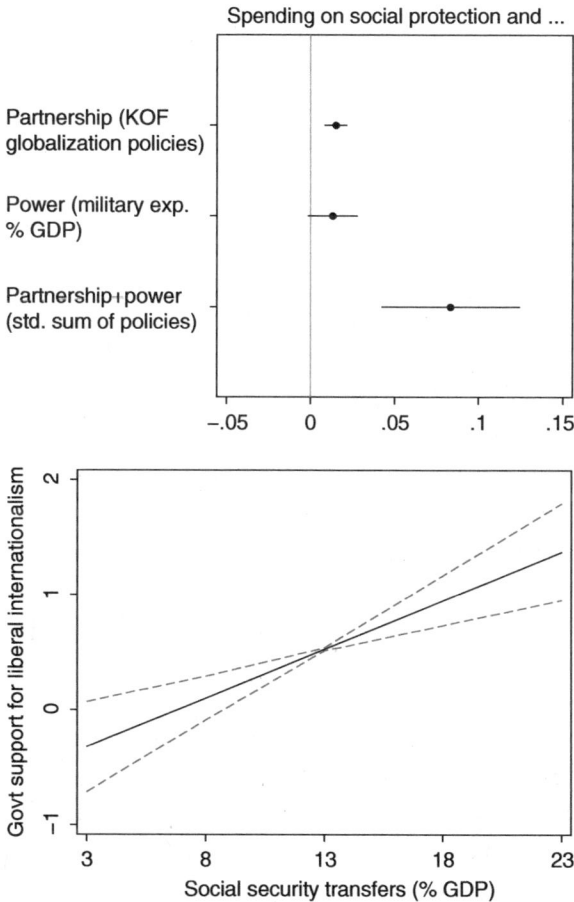

Figure 3.2 Effect of a Western government's spending on social protection on its support for liberal internationalist policies, 1970–2017

on our twenty-four OECD countries. The top panel in the figure summarizes the regression result, where our measure of welfare effort predicts increased government support for liberal internationalism and its component parts, *partnership* and *power*.[13] The results for *partnership* and *partnership + power* are statistically significant and substantively meaningful. The full country-year variation in the West's social security transfers predicts an 8 percent increase in *partnership*, and a 9 percent increase in *partnership + power*. The bottom panel in Figure 3.2 draws out this connection, focusing on the substantive pattern for *partnership + power*. We see clearly that government spending on social protection is positively associated with increased government support for liberal internationalism.[14]

The effects of spending on social protection on Western support for liberal internationalism are also visible when we move to the party level. Figure 3.3 summarizes the results for a range of models measuring the effect of *social protection* in a given country on a given political party's support for *partnership*, *power*, and *partnership + power*. We rely on the same party manifesto data used in Chapter 2, though here, we focus on party-year, which is a more fine-grained unit of analysis. The models are OLS estimates with decade and country fixed effects, and include substantive controls for the effect of globalization flows, level of democracy, unemployment rate, union density, and real GDP growth, as well as individual parties' vote share and left-to-right ideological orientation.[15] These party influences are particularly important to control for here because it is necessary to separate out and isolate the sources of parties' positions on partnership and power from the many other policy stances they take in their electoral manifestos.[16] The top panel in Figure 3.3 reports results averaged across all party families. The bottom panel summarizes the effects of social protection on support for *partnership + power* (liberal internationalism) by party family.[17]

The patterns we see in Figure 3.3 are consistent with our expectations. We see that across the party family spectrum, government spending on *social protection* is associated with high party support for *partnership* and *power*, and with liberal internationalism (*partnership + power*) more generally. The correlation between social protection and partnership here is consistent with a large body of research stretching back to Ruggie's "embedded liberalism" reformulation of Polanyi's argument about the need to balance international markets and social protection. As Ruggie suggested, greater levels of social protection and compensation in the form of unemployment insurance, social services (e.g., health care, housing assistance, child care support), and

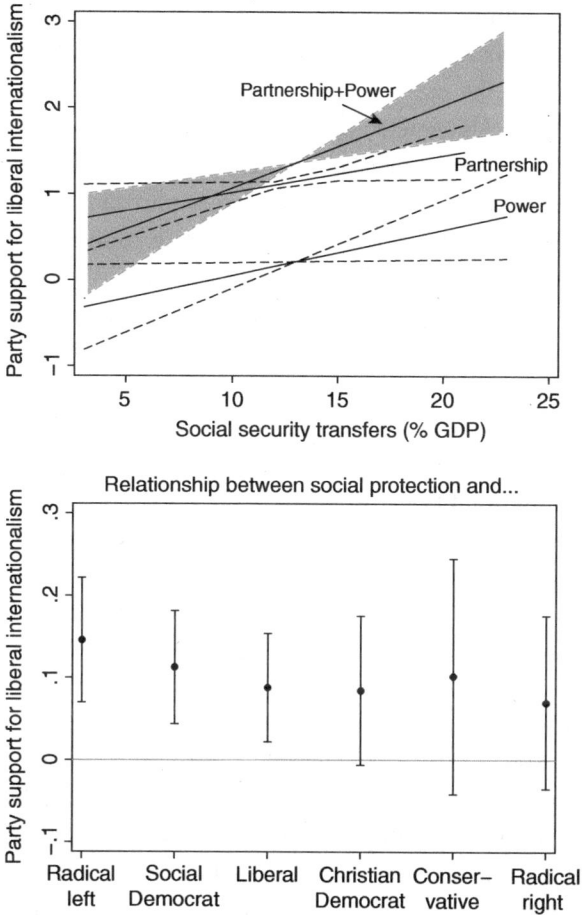

Figure 3.3 Effect of social protection on party support for liberal internationalism by Western party family, 1960–2017

other payments improve the chances that citizens, and their elected representatives, will support international openness and economic integration. This finding is consistent with previous research, including our own.[18]

However, the analysis here goes beyond Ruggie's original formulation and intuition in two important ways. First, we see that the relationship between social protection and liberal internationalism is especially consistent for parties on the left (Social Democrats and radical-left parties), where the confidence intervals do not cross zero. This is striking because one might expect parties of the left, whose working-class voters disproportionately benefit from social spending, to be more skeptical of economic integration and military spending. This suggests that the social protections Western governments put into place in the early postwar decades were especially effective at bringing working-class voters into the internationalist fold. Second, we see that social protection not only leads to increased support for economic integration and multilateralism. It also boosts cross-partisan support for the international security structures and institutions (e.g., military alliances, large armies, military bases) that the United States and other Western democracies put in place and financed to contain Soviet power and ambitions. Put another way, social protection contributed to larger Western geopolitical purposes as well as domestic ends.

This finding squares with a growing body of research on the relationship between the Cold War and the welfare state.[19] It shows that the East-West rivalry was an important factor stimulating the expansion of the welfare state (and not just on the Western side of the Iron Curtain). Whatever its merits as a social policy paradigm, Western leaders came to see social protection as a necessary concession to working-class voters to smooth market capitalism's hard edges, to counter Soviet claims that communism was a "workers' paradise," and to enhance the legitimacy of capitalism in the East-West struggle for dominance. "Western governments were compelled in some way to compete with the Soviet Union ideologically and socially rather than solely in military and political terms," reads an entry in the *Encyclopedia of the Cold War*.[20] Cold War strategic imperatives not only fueled a superpower arms race, they also stimulated an East-West welfare race. As the historian Eric Hobsbawm observed, fear of communism and worries about capitalism's own stability loomed large in the minds of Western policymakers: "Whatever Stalin did to the Russians, he was good for the common people in the West."[21]

Figure 3.4 suggests that Western voters saw it that way too.[22] Here the outcome variable is voter support for *partnership*, *power*, and *partnership + power* (liberal internationalism).[23] To measure voter support, we rely on the vote-weighted party platform measures of voter sentiment that we introduced in Chapter 2.[24] Ideally, we would supplement these indirect voting-based patterns with direct measures of voter sentiment, as we have done in measuring government and party support for partnership and power. However, as noted in Chapter 1, public opinion data on such issues is sporadic and uneven over time and cross-nationally, leaving too many gaps for the country years we are studying. Fortunately, indirect voter-weighted manifesto measures like ours tend to correlate significantly with direct measures

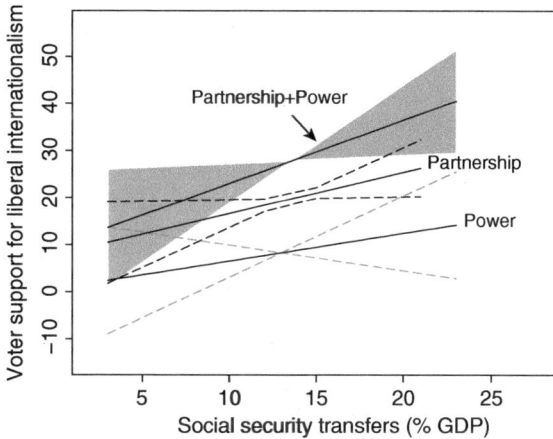

Figure 3.4 Relationship between social protection and voter support for liberal internationalism in Western democracies, 1960–2017

of public opinion.[25] In any event, these measures do tell us which platforms voters actually reward with their ballot choices, whatever their stated sentiment. The explanatory variable, *social protection*, is the same measure used in Figure 3.1.[26]

We see that voters are sensitive to promises of greater (lesser) social welfare. Greater *social protection* is associated with higher support among Western voters for *partnership* and, notably, for liberal internationalism (*partnership + power*) as a whole. The substantive size of the effects in Figure 3.4 are considerable. For instance, a substantial 20 percent of the sample variation in *partnership + power* is "explained" away by the full variation in social transfer spending (explaining from the 52nd to the 74th percentile in *partnership + power*). This result, including its rough magnitude, is consistent with an extensive literature in comparative and international political economy that indicates that governments and parties that provide social policies to mitigate the distributional effects of trade liberalization are rewarded by voters, and conversely, that governments and parties associated with domestic policies that directly or indirectly reduce social protection and welfare compensation more generally, are punished.[27] However, here we show that Western governments' investments in social democracy also yielded international benefits that extended beyond trade. This also helps explain why, when Western governments began reducing their commitments to social protection at the same time that they were increasing their reliance on multilateral institutions as well as international markets, their publics began responding in kind. We turn to this now.

The broken bargain

Western governments' commitment to social insurance, social assistance, and other features of the postwar welfare state began to soften as early as the 1980s. The pace and extent of these cutbacks varied across the West: they arrived earlier and were more draconian in the Anglo-American economies; they came later and with less brute force in many European and Asian economies.[28] In many instances, Western governments did not fully embrace the idea of "welfare state reform" until after the Cold War ended and their economies were under the influence of globalization. With the collapse of the Soviet Union and the spread of liberalism in the former Warsaw Pact countries in Central and Eastern Europe, the Cold War rationale for investing in social protection lost its political potency. America, Britain, France, Germany, and other welfare states began actively looking for ways to reduce the collective costs of welfare while simultaneously lowering barriers to trade, capital, and immigration flows. In the 1990s, the balance between economic integration and social protection shifted decisively toward the market and what became known as "hypergobalization."[29]

Political economists at the time disagreed sharply about the likely impact this shift in Western government policy would have on public support for international openness. Some studies revealed a sharp increase in perceived insecurity and protectionist attitudes among Western citizens who were most exposed to expanded international trade, investment, and immigration as a result of globalization.[30] Other studies yielded evidence that growing exposure to international trade and investment mattered, but painted a mixed picture of the effects of unemployment, inequality, and immigration on public support for globalization.[31] And still other scholarly research suggested that whether an anti-globalist backlash materialized in Western democracies would turn not only on globalization's effects on employment and income. Following Polanyi, Ruggie, and others, their research indicated that it would also depend on Western governments' willingness to invest more resources in social policies and programs to insulate and compensate those workers and sectors most vulnerable to hyperglobalization's disruptive effects.[32]

By this point, Western governments' willingness to make those social investments was thin and, as Figure 3.5 suggests, fell far short of what was needed to address the economic risks and insecurities that working families faced. Figure 3.5 tracks Western governments' investment in social protection from 1960 through 2017. The solid line in the figure represents the raw average of social transfers (as a percentage of GDP). The broken line represents Western governments' social welfare effort, adjusting for the fact that spending automatically increases when unemployment rises.[33] As the solid line in Figure 3.5 shows, welfare spending was very high during the postwar golden age despite the fact that most Western economies were operating at full employment. Since then, social transfers have increased as a share of GDP, in part because of structurally high levels of unemployment in several Western countries. However, when we adjust the social transfer measure for unemployment levels (the broken line in the figure), we see the true effects of Western workers' exposure to higher levels of economic risk stemming from globalization and other market forces (e.g., automation). Even allowing for cross-national variation (workers in some countries are at greater risk than those in other countries), Western governments' commitment to social protection clearly did not match their growing reliance on the market.

Of course, the social bargain that postwar leaders struck with their citizens was not only about the market. It was also about how much

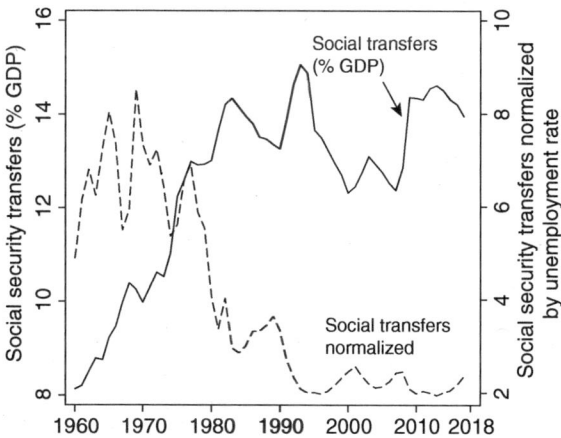

Figure 3.5 Western government investment in social protection for labor force adjusted by economic risk, 1960–2017

authority to delegate and pool in international institutions. As we showed in Chapter 2, the turn toward globalism involved a dramatic increase in the number and type of international bodies.[34] A cornucopia of international and supranational institutions arose to meet a rapidly expanding list of global challenges—terrorism, organized crime, ethnic conflict, and environmental decline, among others. As Jessica Mathews, a leading foreign policy thinker, wrote in 1997, the rapid growth of these institutions was double-edged.[35] On the one hand, they were needed to help solve transnational problems that governments were ill-equipped to address. On the other hand, more international decision-making was certain to stoke public resentment over the loss of national control. At the time Mathews was writing, this was already a potent issue in Europe, where perceptions of "distance" between Brussels and ordinary citizens contributed to the backlash against the Maastricht treaty and the European Union in Denmark and France.[36]

In the years ahead, talk of a "democratic deficit" would become commonplace in Europe. Too much power, globalism's critics charged, was being put in the hands of remote, unelected international bureaucrats making decisions that impacted, often negatively, citizens' lives and livelihoods. Similar concerns were raised in the United States, where a deeply rooted skepticism about international institutions, dating back to Woodrow Wilson's failure to get the League of Nations ratified, resurfaced.[37] In Chapter 2, we saw that Western voters' reservations about international market liberalization and multilateral governance intensified in the years ahead.[38] Opposition was starkest in Europe, but the same steep downward slope in voter support for international openness and institutionalized cooperation was evident in the United States, Japan, and elsewhere.

Political discontent does not arise on its own, of course. It requires politicians and parties to mobilize it. And if there is one thing that Western politicians on the far left and far right became remarkably adept at, it was exploiting working-class frustration and resentment about globalism and the erosion of social protections by fusing the two issues. Among the first to do so were Jörg Haider who led the Austria Freedom Party (FPÖ) from 1986 to 2000 and Jean-Marie Le Pen, the founder and leader of France's *Front National* (FN) from 1972 to 2011. This was no easy feat. For years, both parties depended on the support of small businesses and farmers and steadfastly opposed welfare state spending. In the 1990s, in a bid to win working-class voters, they changed tack.[39] Under Haider's leadership, the FPÖ combined long-standing commitments to low taxes and trade liberalization with "welfare populism" and Euroscepticism.[40] In France, Le Pen did the same, easing up on the party's long-standing anti-tax and anti-government platform in favor of platform planks in support of job security and economic protection. Meanwhile, the FN became one of the EU's staunchest critics, with Le Pen now claiming that European integration was "programmed death" for French sovereignty.[41]

Fusing anti-globalism with social protection was not the only reason the FPÖ, FN, and other right-wing parties started gaining electoral market share in the 1990s. They also leaned heavily on socio-cultural issues (e.g., immigration, law and order, social conservativism) to mobilize voters. Yet voting studies showed that these naked appeals to working-class voters worried about job security and "the loss of national control" paid off at the polls.[42] Enough so that Britain's Nigel Farage, the leader of the far-right United Kingdom Independence Party (UKIP), adopted the continental populist playbook to take things to a new level in British politics. Following a poor showing in Britain's 2010 general election, Farage revamped UKIP's platform by proposing to take funds that the UK contributed to the European Union and use them to improve the country's National Health Service.[43] Farage's bold gambit upended British politics. UKIP came in first in the 2014 EU election with 27.5 percent. More importantly, it forced Conservative Prime Minister David Cameron to promise a referendum on British membership of the EU. Cameron hoped to take the starch out of the so-called "revolt of the left-behinds" that was now wreaking havoc inside his own party. Three years later, Cameron delivered on that promise only to see Farage, along with Boris Johnson and some other prominent Tories, win the referendum that would set Britain on its path to leave the EU.

That same year America's Donald Trump drove the Brexiteers' anti-globalist message home by showing how it could be leveraged to mount a successful insurgency within the liberal order's citadel itself. Lambasting the Washington political class for "worshiping globalism over Americanism," Trump promised to stop the outsourcing and offshoring of US jobs and industry in his run for the presidency against political insider Hillary Clinton. Pledging to withdraw from the twelve-nation multilateral Trans-Pacific Partnership (TPP) that President Barack Obama's administration had signed earlier that year, Trump claimed the treaty would undermine the US economy and independence.[44] Like Farage and Le Pen before him, Trump's broadsides against globalism were paired with a vigorous rhetorical defense of the welfare state. Trump committed to defending popular Social Security and Medicare programs and promised to replace the Affordable Care Act—Obamacare—with a universal health insurance system. Trump's "one-two" combo was effective, especially in the traditional Democratic strongholds of Michigan, Pennsylvania, and Wisconsin, whose industries and workers had been worn down by years of outsourcing and offshoring to China, Mexico, and other destinations for low-cost production, assembly, and supply.[45]

In case after case, the pattern was the same. Parties on the far right campaigned against globalism's costs in economic insecurity and national sovereignty. They urged governments to do more to compensate those harmed by trade liberalization and supranationalism. This, of course, was also true of many parties on the far left. Most rejected the right's incendiary anti-immigration message, but far-left parties also campaigned against hyperglobalization and for expanding compensation and assistance to hard-hit workers, sectors, and communities.[46] The fact that voters rewarded these parties with an increasing share of the national vote revealed just how much the postwar bargain had frayed in Western democracies. Yet, as we have seen, the story of anti-globalism's rise is not only one of popular resentment and grievance bubbling up from below. Political entrepreneurs and parties on the fringes of Western party systems successfully tapped and mobilized this discontent to increase their vote share. That parties on the far left and far right seized on anti-globalism *after* the Cold War ended is no coincidence.

GEOPOLITICS AND DOMESTIC POLITICS

Shortly before the Soviet Union fell, Georgi Arbatov, the éminence grise of Moscow's foreign policy establishment, warned an American audience: "We are going to do a terrible thing to you. We are going to deprive you of an enemy." Arbatov was a seasoned observer of the Western political scene and surely knew that Western unity was not due solely to fears of Soviet communism. Still, Arbatov's claim contained a kernel of truth. For nearly half a century, widespread worries about Soviet communism and the risk of nuclear war made liberal internationalism the strategy of choice in the West's corridors of power and in its courts of public opinion. With the end of the Cold War, these external pressures and influences on domestic politics eased considerably. Security concerns no longer weighed as heavily on voters' minds. Western political leaders and policymakers had more latitude in defining their nation's international interests. So, however, did parties on the far left and far right. As Cold War tensions dissipated, the room for political maneuver in Western democracies expanded.

Cold War constraints

Geopolitics cast a long shadow over the West's politics during the Cold War. Suspicions of Soviet intentions in Europe, Asia, and elsewhere made Western leaders skeptical of schemes for global disarmament and neutralism that were popular on the far left. They were considered too idealistic, too impractical, and too risky. Calls from the far right to "roll back" the Soviet presence in Eastern Europe and rely on nuclear brinksmanship to keep the peace were also rejected as unrealistic or, worse, reckless in a bipolar world where both sides had "the bomb."[47] Isolationism was also a non-starter. American politicians like Senator Arthur Vandenberg, who had advocated it in the face of German and Japanese expansionism in the run up to World War II, now kept the discredited strategy at arm's length. The fear of being second-guessed by political opponents for failing to do enough to contain the spread of communism or, alternatively, being dubbed "trigger happy," forced most politicians into the middle lane. The Cold War thus exerted centripetal pressure on the West's politics.

In the United States, Cold War imperatives pushed Democrats and Republicans toward the bipartisan liberal internationalist center. The two parties often disagreed over how much of the federal purse was needed to contain or balance against Soviet power and what steps needed to be taken to avoid the risk of accidental or inadvertent nuclear war. For example, the Truman, Kennedy, Johnson, and Reagan administrations boosted national defense spending. The Eisenhower, Nixon, and early Carter administrations looked for ways to trim the Pentagon's budget.[48] Yet every administration from Truman's through Reagan's steered clear of strategies that were overly reliant on idealism or realism. Investing in both partnership and power gave them additional leverage against Moscow and limited their political exposure domestically to charges of weakness or recklessness. Presidential hopefuls who strayed too far to the left or to the right—as did George McGovern on the left and Barry Goldwater on the right—paid dearly at the polls.

Geopolitics had a similar effect on West European politics. To be sure, most politicians and parties on the far left and far right flatly rejected liberal internationalism, arguing that it was little more than a stalking horse for US dominance. However, the vast majority of political parties in Western democracies, including socialist parties in Britain, France, Belgium, Holland, Norway, Denmark, and Luxembourg, favored closer transatlantic military and economic ties, and military preparedness, too.[49] Fearing American hegemony, others like West Germany's Social Democratic Party (SPD) and Italy's Socialist Party (PSI) initially resisted and campaigned in favor of a "bridge-building neutralism" in East-West relations.[50] But worries about being judged weak on communism by voters ultimately led the SPD and PSI to put their concerns about American suzerainty aside and embrace Atlanticism. Parties on the center-right, like France's Gaullists, that shared the far left's concerns about Transatlanticism also made their peace with liberal internationalism. On the all-important matter of an independent French nuclear force, they framed the case in terms of collective deterrence and defense against external threats rather than purely in terms of independence from Washington.

In Japan, worries about Soviet ambitions were tempered by fears of entrapment in America's wars in Korea and Vietnam and lingering distrust of the Japanese military.[51] Yet here, too, politicians and parties ignored Cold War exigencies at their peril. Japanese Socialist Party (JSP) elites paid a price for their neutralist position, which "contributed to the party's image as unfit to govern."[52] A large portion of the Japanese public shared the JSP's anti-militarist sensibilities, especially when it came to maintaining firm civilian control over the military. However, that did not mean that they favored unarmed neutrality in the East-West conflict. Opinion polls conducted by *Asahi Shimbun*, one of Japan's largest and oldest newspapers, showed absolute majorities preferring alignment with the United States throughout the 1950s.[53] By contrast, no more than 1 percent of respondents favored aligning with the Soviet Union. Meanwhile, conservative factions inside the ruling Liberal Democratic Party (LDP) that favored a more independent, militaristic approach to Japanese defense ran into strong headwinds within the party.[54] So long as Japanese security was formally tied to the United States, and America and the Soviet Union were locked in the Cold War, LPD leaders had little incentive domestically to buck Washington.[55]

A thaw in the East-West struggle did come, of course. In the late 1960s and early 1970s, Willy Brandt's *Ostpolitik* and Richard Nixon's policy of US-Soviet détente produced understandings about the "two Germanies" and nuclear weapons that eased popular concerns about security. Yet hopes for a more comprehensive, lasting superpower rapprochement came to an unhappy end in the late 1970s and early 1980s. A confluence of events—from Moscow's decision to deploy a new generation of nuclear-tipped missiles in Europe, to the spread of Marxist governments in the Middle East and Africa, to the Soviet military invasion of Afghanistan in December 1979—forced a reckoning. Western voters grew more apprehensive about national security.[56] Western party leaders became more concerned about the credibility of Western security commitments. At a time of heightened anxiety about the possibility of nuclear war and fiscal belt-tightening, there was also political resistance to military build-up. In the late 1970s and 1980s, fears of nuclear war and guns-versus-butter trade-offs figured prominently in party debates about how best to strengthen Western security: should this be done through arms control treaties and confidence-building measures, or by building up the West's offensive nuclear and conventional military capabilities?[57]

It was not until the 1990s, that the strategic imperatives dominating Western political life for over half a century truly disappeared. Without Soviet communism and nuclear Armageddon hanging knifelike over Western polities, Western leaders found themselves with more room to maneuver in foreign affairs, but also with less clarity about which foreign policy strategy—which combination of partnership and power—to place their bets on. When Bill Clinton gushed, "Gosh, I miss the Cold War," he said out loud what many Western leaders at the time were thinking. In a world defined by bipolar superpower rivalry, the international rules of the road were clearer and the task of coalition-building in democracies easier. In the absence of a Soviet-style threat, investing in military power at Cold War levels was less necessary to guarantee security. Defense spending as a percentage of GDP dropped from an average of 2.7 percent in the 1980s to 2 percent in the 1990s, where it would remain for the next twenty years. Defense spending in the United States, UK, and France did edge back up in the 2000s. Yet even in these countries, the share of GDP spent on defense would not return to Cold War levels.

The end of the Cold War also helps explain why the West doubled down on multilateralism. In the 1990s, the prevailing view in Western foreign policy circles was that the international institutions forged in the crucible of the Cold War had worked and could be repurposed to bring other nations and regions into the liberal world order.[58] The initial impulse in America, and Europe too, was to expand existing regional and global institutions in both security and economic cooperation, or use them to devise new ones. In the security realm, NATO was expanded eastward and the role of the Conference on Security Cooperation in Europe was broadened. In the economic area, the GATT was transformed into the WTO, and the European Union and APEC were used to stabilize and integrate emerging market economies in Central and Eastern Europe and the Asia-Pacific region into the advanced world economy. Again, it was Clinton who put Western foreign policy thinking into words. In a 2006 interview, Clinton observed: "I was heavily influenced by the success of the post-World War II and Cold War multilateral organizations. . . . I saw that they worked, and at the end of the Cold War, I saw an opportunity for the first time in history to globalize them in a way that the East-West division had prevented."[59]

In the 1990s, the West's commitment to liberalism and multilateralism was widely seen as its decisive edge in its victory over Soviet communism, the case for globalizing those principles and institutions was a compelling one. John Ikenberry has aptly referred to the process of international consolidation and expansion that followed over the next decade as the "globalization of the liberal order."[60] Western democracies drove economic integration and institutionalized cooperation to new heights. However, the globalization of the liberal order also created problems of governance and legitimacy at home because it was not matched by a comparable commitment to social protection. Instead of expanding the social guarantees that were part and parcel of Cold War liberal internationalism to Western workers, they were reined in. Anti-globalist parties like France's FN, Austria's FPÖ, and later, Germany's *Alternative für Deutschland* (AfD) gained ground by promising not only greater protection from global market forces and supranational institutions but also fewer international security commitments and greater self-reliance in national defense.[61]

In time, the widening appeal of anti-globalism led Western leaders to modulate their own parties' globalist platform planks. In Europe, Conservative and Christian Democratic parties began soft-pedaling trade liberalization, open immigration, and supranationalism, and in some cases actively opposing one or more of the three.[62] In the United States, Donald Trump's 2016 insurgent campaign used anti-globalism to discredit the Republican establishment and, as mentioned earlier, mobilize disaffected white working- and middle-class voters who felt left behind by globalization and the shift to a post-industrial economy.[63] In the Democratic Party, Bernie Sanders came close to defeating the party's establishment candidate, Hillary Clinton, that same year by using trade policy to appeal to those same white working-class voters, along with younger, more educated voters concerned about the effects of globalization on income inequality, climate change, and labor standards.

In Japan, the situation was different. In contrast to Europe and North America, where security constraints loosened, in East Asia they gradually tightened. For Japan, the issue was two-fold: China's rise and North Korea's nuclear and missile defense programs. Heightened concerns about both began registering in Japanese public opinion polls in the late 1990s, along with increasing support for expanding the national defense role of the Japan Self-Defense Forces (JSDF).[64] Prime Minister Shinzō Abe's efforts from 2012 to 2020 to move Japanese policy toward China away from engagement to a more "active balancing strategy" capitalized on this shift in public sentiment, and reinforced it. Under Abe, Japan adopted a larger Indo-Pacific conception of its security interests, invested in even closer security ties with the United States, centralized Japanese security policymaking, and expanded the country's military capabilities. The fact that this more expansive view of Japan's security needs faced little real domestic opposition within the LDP or the country was striking. It was an indication of just how much the political barriers to Japan's security role had come down since liberal internationalism's heyday, when the Yoshida Doctrine held sway.

Threats and politics

We have argued that fears of Soviet communism and nuclear war bolstered Western support for liberal internationalism. They gave most governments, most parties, and most voters reason to support investing in power as well as partnership. To test this argument, we explored whether geopolitical threat correlates positively with government, party, and voter support for liberal internationalism. Our models below rely on the same outcome variables, estimators, and specifications that we used earlier to measure the possible effects of social protection. However, now we consider the relationship between geopolitical threat and support for *partnership, power,* and *partnership + power*. To measure the scope and intensity of *geopolitical threat*, we created a composite index based upon seven different measures of the international security environment for each of the twenty-four OECD countries in our sample.[65] This gives us a scale that runs from low to high for each country.[66] The individual measures that make up this composite index capture different features of a state's "geopolitical threat environment," including how stable its borders and regions are, how territorial or ideological the challenge is, and so on.[67]

The descriptive results for this composite threat measure are summarized in Figure 3.6. It tracks the level of geopolitical threat facing the West in general between 1950 and 2011 (top panel), and for the EU-15, Japan, and the United States individually (bottom panel). Four key patterns stand out in the data. First, we see that there is a secular decline in the level of threat over time, with the average threat level for the full sample of our twenty-four OECD countries falling below zero following the collapse of the Soviet Union, and remaining below that level down to the present era. Second, the

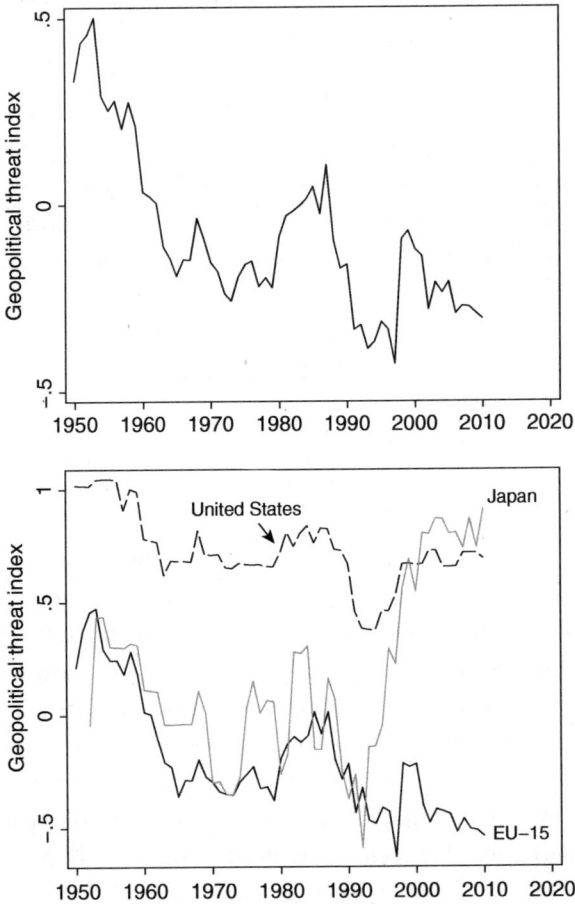

Figure 3.6 Average level of geopolitical threat facing Western democracies, 1950–2011

geopolitical threat scale is sensitive to major developments and events, rising during periods widely considered to be ones of elevated international hostility and great power rivalry (e.g., the Korean War; the "second Cold War" of the 1980s; post-9/11) and conversely, declining during periods of reduced tension, such as the East-West détente of the 1970s and the post-Cold War era. Third, it is evident that threat levels are generally higher for the United States than they are for the European Union and Japan. This is not surprising given America's global forward presence, with roughly 750 overseas military bases in 80 countries and territories.[68] But it does remind us of just how much more global American security commitments are than those of its many strategic allies and partners in Europe and Asia. Finally, we see that the level of geopolitical threat facing the EU-15, Japan, and the United States, individually, drops sharply following the end of the Cold War, although notably in the case of Japan, it begins to rise in the late 1990s.

Figure 3.6 underscores how much the West's strategic environment has changed since the height of the Cold War. It also prompts the question: did support for liberal internationalism in West democracies weaken as the geopolitical threat facing them waned? In Figure 3.7, which covers the 1960–2011 time period for our twenty-four OECD countries, we take a first cut at this question by drawing on a modest cross-section of the period averages from the available data.[69] The figure shows clearly that there is a positive descriptive association between the level of geopolitical threat a country

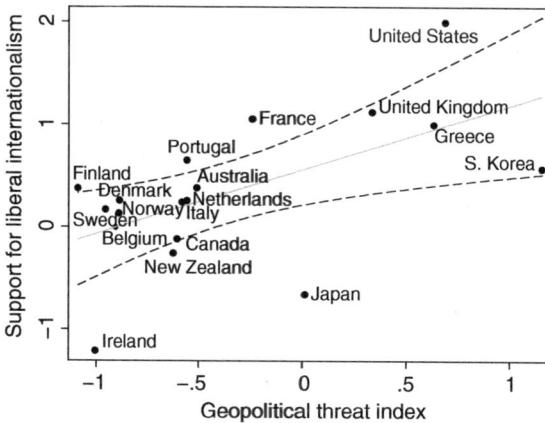

Figure 3.7 Geopolitical threat and Western government support for liberal internationalism by country, 1960–2011

faces on the horizontal axis and its government's support for liberal internationalism (*partnership + power*) on the vertical axis. The positive correlation, which is statistically significant, is in line with what our argument predicts: that Western democracies' commitment to liberal internationalism was driven, in no small part, by the challenge that Soviet power and ambition posed to their security and interests.

The descriptive results reported in Figure 3.7 are based on cross-country averages. To test our argument in a more controlled and systematic way, we expanded the analysis to the country-year level. The regression results are summarized in Figures 3.8 through 3.10.[70] Overall, the analysis provides a good deal of support for our argument. As expected, we see that higher

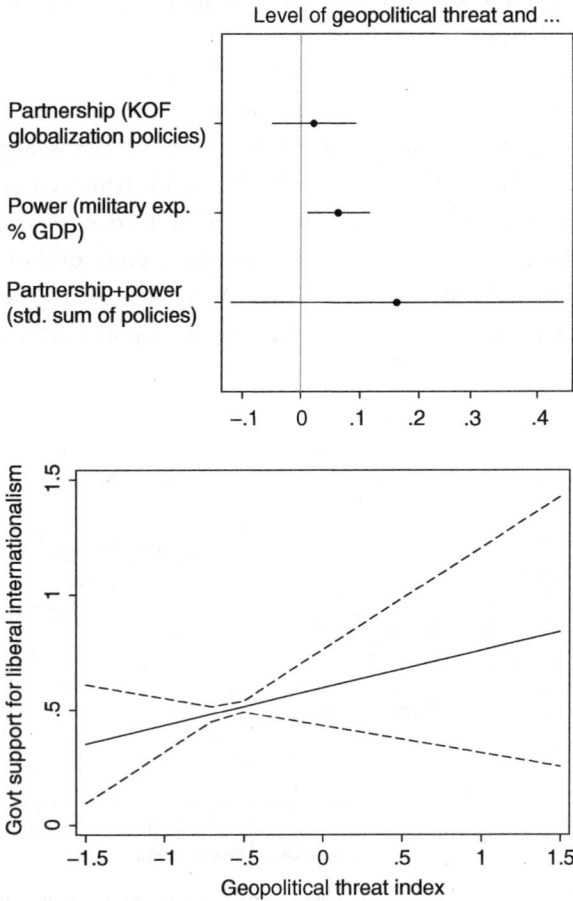

Figure 3.8 Effect of geopolitical threat on Western government support for liberal internationalism, 1970–2017

levels of *geopolitical threat* are associated with increased government and party support for liberal internationalism, though, interestingly, not with voter support. In general, the more challenging a country's international circumstances, the more willing its government and political parties—from left to right—are to invest in power and liberal internationalism (*partnership + power*). This helps explain why liberal internationalism was the strategy of choice in the West during the Cold War. It also helps explain why, in the absence of Cold War imperatives, liberal internationalism has lost domestic political ground to globalism, isolationism, and nationalism. To be sure, *geopolitical threat's* correlation with government policy and party platforms in Figures 3.8 and 3.9 is more modest than *social protection's* impact reported

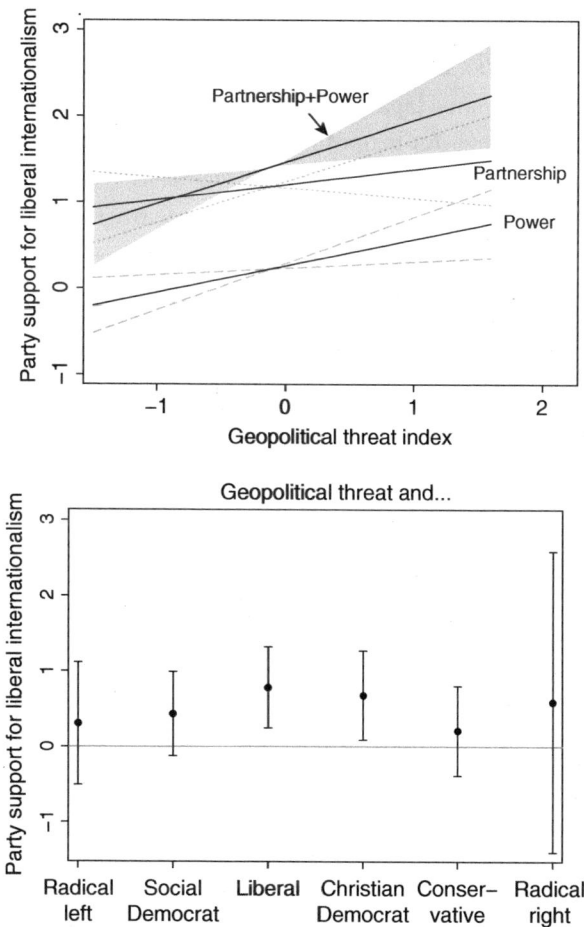

Figure 3.9 Effect of geopolitical threat on party support for liberal internationalism by Western party family, 1960–2015

earlier (Figures 3.2–3.3).[71] However, the overall tenor and direction of *geopolitical threat's* association with Western government and party support are similar.

By contrast, our argument about geopolitical threats gets much less traction when it comes to voters. In Figure 3.10, we see that the level of international security has no significant correlation with voter-weighted party platforms (although *geopolitical threat* almost reaches standard levels of statistical significance for *power*).[72] One possible explanation for this is that government officials and party leaders are more attuned to geopolitics than are voters.[73] Certainly, heads of government have strong electoral incentives to hedge against the risk of foreign policy failure— that is, the risk of being blamed by their partisan rivals for failing to correctly read the international security environment.[74] As we have seen, during the Cold War such concerns weighed on political leaders in the United States, Germany, Japan, and other Western democracies. Another possible reason is that our geopolitical threat scale does not fully capture well-documented public anxieties during the Cold War about the risk of catastrophic nuclear war.[75] The various threat measures that make up this scale focus on geopolitical risk (e.g., territorial expansion), as opposed to existential risk (e.g., public fears of "nuclear winter" in the 1980s). While the two are related, they are not the same. As we showed in Chapter 2 (Figures 2.7 and 2.8), public support for defense outlays during the Cold War rose sharply during periods, like the late 1970s, of heightened concern

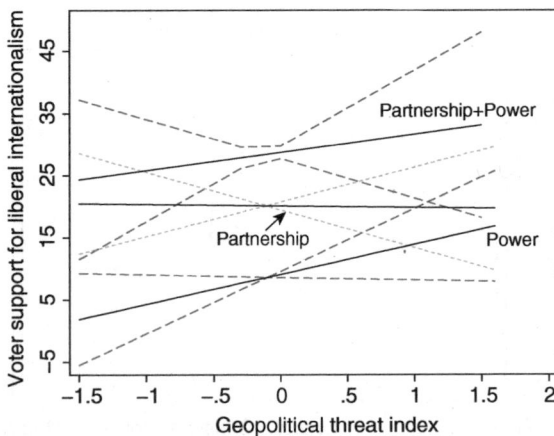

Figure 3.10 Relationship between geopolitical threat and voter support for liberal internationalism in Western democracies, 1960–2017

over Soviet ambitions. Conversely, public support for military spending dropped sharply during periods of heightened fears of nuclear war, such as the early 1980s.

FAILURE TO ADJUST

Much has been written about globalization and its economic, political, and social consequences. Much less has been written about why political leaders did not do more for those that globalization was leaving behind.[76] In the face of a mounting anti-globalist backlash, one might have expected Western leaders to trim their international sails, expand social safety nets, and redesign international institutions to make them more responsive to the demands of national electorates. As we discuss in Chapter 4, there was some movement by Western governments along these lines. The breakneck pace of trade liberalization and multilateral cooperation began to slow even before the 2008 economic crisis. In some OECD countries (e.g., Ireland, Italy, Norway), welfare generosity and other social protections also increased. Yet Western leaders did not actively look for programmatic ways to close the ends-means gap. Western government efforts to liberalize trade and capital markets continued to outpace Cold War levels and, in most cases, government support for social protection or other measures of social policy generosity stalled or declined, as it did in Denmark, Germany, the Netherlands, and Sweden.

Some theories

Why didn't Western leaders do more to close the gap over globalism? Why didn't they take steps to address the concerns of populists before the anger and resentment over globalism reached crisis proportions? Some scholars and analysts attribute the failure to political arrogance, elitism, and "groupthink." These factors may help explain why Western leaders embraced globalization and supranationalism in the 1990s, but they are less helpful in explaining why, in the face of mounting political resistance, self-interested elected leaders did not balance their support for globalization and multilateralism with greater investments in social protection and compensation. Fortunately, existing theories of international and comparative politics suggest several candidate explanations for Western democracies' failure to adjust.

One plausible explanation is "financialization," and the growing influence of international financial and corporate interests over political deliberation and deal-making in Western capitals—a shift that many scholars argue was in full swing by the 1990s.[77] There is an extensive literature on this topic, but the crux of the argument is that, as Western leaders became more dependent on these financial and corporate interests for holding on to power, political parties were transformed from postwar "catch-all" or "big tent" parties that sought to win the "median voter" by providing public goods into "cartel parties" that focused on richer "median" voters by letting markets and central banks set policy. In short, Western leaders became less focused on mass electorates, and more responsive to the needs of high-flying internationalist business interests.

A related explanation emphasizes the effects of Western leaders' growing reliance on international institutions. They argue that Western governments have become more responsive to the expectations of unelected international technocrats than to the needs of their own citizens.[78] This is not simply due to "multilateral overreach" where, in the natural course of carrying out their duties, the policymakers and technocrats that staff these institutions have gradually expanded their authority.[79] The deeper problem is that Western leaders *intentionally* "outsourced" decision-making authority to these international bodies to shield themselves from voters over politically sensitive redistributive issues like trade liberalization.[80] Needless to say, this strategy did not depoliticize these issues. However, that was not considered a sign of the strategy's flaws and shortsightedness, but rather, further evidence of popular democracy's ineffectiveness in responding to the *global* forces of science, technology, and modern capitalism. The more domestic pushback there was, the more policy needed to be "rescued" from politics.

There is also the declining influence of labor in national political economies to consider. Many scholars have argued that the secular decline of the manufacturing sector in Western economies, and the center-right's efforts to undercut labor's bargaining power, made it easier (safer, politically) for political leaders to cater to pro-globalization interests and ignore or soft-pedal working-class interests.[81] By the 2000s, the attack on labor that began under Margaret Thatcher and Ronald Reagan in the 1980s, and then spread to other advanced industrialized economies, had reached a point where unions no longer had sufficient leverage over labor markets to act as a political check on financial and business interests, and political leaders aligned with them. Between 1980s and 2010, average OECD union density—a standard measure of union political strength based on union workers as a proportion of civilian employment—dropped by more than ten percentage points.[82]

Gauging the gap

To gauge the weight of these possible explanations for why Western government policies' have consistently outstripped voter support since the end of the Cold War, we empirically explored several possible predictors of the gap. To assess the impact of international financial interests *and* supranational institutions on Western policymaking, we rely on the KOF Swiss Institute's indices for de facto globalization. These include de facto *economic globalization, political globalization,* and KOF's composite *all globalization* index.[83] We measure *union strength* using a standard measure of union density: union members as a proportion of civilian employment. We control for democratic representativeness (Polity-IV *democracy* score and *voter turnout*), political orientation (*left-right platform* position and *right-party* percentage of cabinet posts), and economic performance (*unemployment rate* and *GDP growth*).[84] The outcome variable (*government-voter gap*) measures the extent to which a given Western government and its voters converge (diverge) in their support for international partnership between 1970 and 2017.[85] We focus here on international partnership because, as we showed in Chapter 2, this is where Western governments have consistently run ahead of voters since the end of the Cold War.[86]

Figure 3.11 summarizes the key results.[87] We see that our three measures of *de facto globalization,* which plausibly capture the size and influence of international business and financial interests in Western capitals and Western leaders growing reliance on supranational institutions, tend to be positively and significantly associated with our outcome of interest: the gap between governments and voters over international partnership. Figure 3.11 captures the substantive size of these associations: the outcome variable (*government-voter gap*) is always on the same scale and the panels display the full-sample variation for each KOF de facto globalization measure.[88] The broadest conception of globalization (*all globalization*; top panel) has the strongest association with the solvency gap. *Economic globalization* (middle panel) and *political globalization* (bottom panel) have more modest associations, though

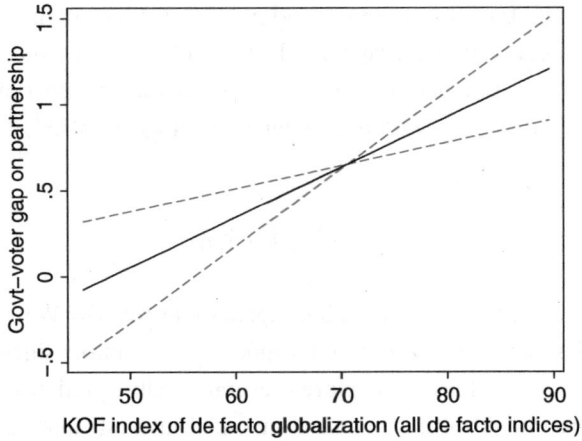

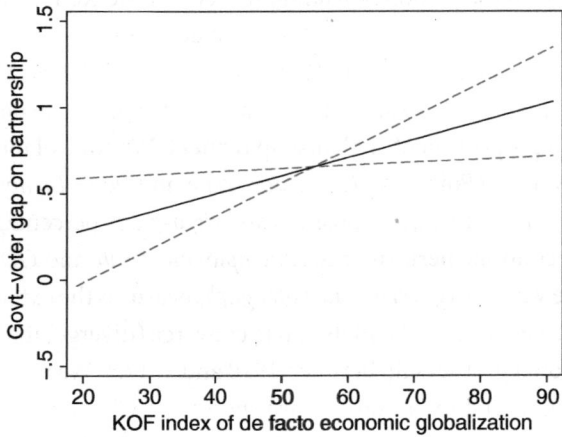

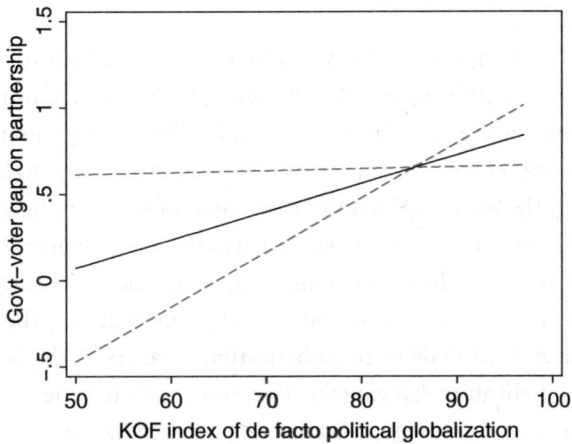

Figure 3.11 Relationship between globalization and government-voter solvency gap over international partnership in Western democracies, 1970–2017

still substantively as well as statistically significant.[89] The pattern suggests that the de facto political and economic faces of globalization are complementary and cumulative. The full variation of each de facto globalization measure predicts roughly 45 percent of the variation in the *government-voter gap* with respect to international partnership (predicting a shift from roughly the 25th percentile to roughly the 70th percentile).[90]

The full results (reported in Table B.5, Appendix B) also indicate that *party vote share average* is a negative predictor of the solvency gap. This is consistent with the idea that political systems with parties that are more dependent on international financial and business interests, or governments that have delegated a great deal of decision-authority to supranational institutions, or both, might be less responsive to what voters want. As expected, *union strength*, our measure of labor's political and organizational strength, is negatively associated with the solvency gap, but is not statistically significant in most specifications. The other controls have little or no effect, though more right-oriented party systems tend to be associated with greater insolvency. All told, the patterns suggest that Western leaders are increasingly responsive to internationally oriented interests, and have a freer hand to do so, domestically. It is here, in the shifting balance of international and domestic power, that the failure of Western political leadership lies.

MIND THE GAP

In the two decades following the publication of Susan Strange's writings about globalization, Western public support for economic integration and multilateral institutions faded. As we have seen, one critical reason is that Western governments' commitment to social protection did not keep up with their efforts to liberalize markets and expand the authority of international institutions. Coming on the heels of the neoliberal reforms of the 1980s, Western governments' commitment to social democracy weakened in the 1990s as the East-West conflict came to an end. Free of Cold War geopolitical rivalries and tensions, Western leaders and voters no longer felt as compelled to uphold liberal internationalism. Western leaders saw political advantage in moving toward globalism. Western voters moved in the opposite direction, with growing numbers seeing greater promise in the anti-globalist agendas and foreign policies that populist and nationalist parties were offering.

It took time for the West's turn to globalism to produce a backlash. Looking back, it is also clear there was also no single defining moment when the tide of Western political support for the liberal order turned. The 2003 invasion of Iraq, the 2008 financial crash, and the 2015 Syrian refugee crisis are often singled out as inflection points. Certainly, each contributed to the widening democratic solvency gap between Western governments and their publics over international openness and cooperation. However, the downward spiral in domestic support began well before the Iraq War, and it has continued to widen with each passing year since then. And it did not occur on its own. Since the 1990s, populist and nationalist politicians have actively mobilized globalism's discontents by speaking to Western publics' fears and interests. Mainstream political leaders did remarkably little materially to offset and counteract those attacks.

The failure of Western democracies to close this ends-means gap sheds new light on how and why the liberal international order fractured. Writing in the early 1990s, many international relations scholars and foreign policy analysts predicted that in the absence of geopolitical imperatives, the West would quickly divide and splinter over security and economic issues.[91] Without a common enemy to unite them, Western democracies strategic and commercial interests would diverge. This did not happen. The liberal order did not devolve into rival trading blocs. NATO did not collapse. Friends did not become foes. What did happen is that Western foreign and domestic policy diverged. This has proved enormously costly for Western democracies, internationally as well as domestically. We turn to these issues now.

4

Reaping the Whirlwind

In 1949, historian and New Dealer Arthur Schlesinger Jr. published *The Vital Center*, a best-selling call to arms. Writing in the shadow of the Cold War, Schlesinger saw a vibrant liberal political center as the West's best defense against the spread of Soviet-style communism or a possible resurgence of the laissez-faire capitalism that could result in depression and war. Though writing principally for an American audience, Schlesinger's assessment of the international predicament and domestic challenges facing the United States in the late 1940s echoed public fears and anxieties in Britain, France, Germany, and other Western democracies. With memories of war and democracy's failings in the interwar years still rife, Western voters from all strata of society and every class favored political moderation and consensus-building over ideological fervor, economic volatility, and political extremism. For the vast majority of Western voters, mainstream parties— Christian Democratic and Social Democratic, Conservative and Liberal— offered the best hope for guaranteeing protection from Soviet ambitions and market forces.

For much of the past seventy-five years, mainstream political parties were the bedrock of the Western liberal international order. As the vital center, they were not only a bulwark against political extremism from the political left and political right during the Cold War. Mainstream parties were also the building blocks upon which the West's shared commitment to the liberal international order rested. Western leaders could advance internationalist policies, knowing that those policies rested on sturdy foundations in national party systems. This is no longer the case. While most mainstream parties continue to back the liberal order, their political capacity to support and promote it has weakened considerably. Over the past thirty years, insurgent parties have made inroads on both right and left in one democracy after another. Political authority has fragmented and coalition-building has become more difficult. Even in two-party systems like the United States and Britain, anti-globalist movements have made it harder for leaders to govern

Geopolitics and Democracy. Peter Trubowitz and Brian Burgoon, Oxford University Press.
© Oxford University Press 2023. DOI: 10.1093/oso/9780197535400.003.0004

effectively, eroding international confidence in their commitment to the liberal order.

In this chapter, we focus on the decline of the West's vital center and consider its international implications. We show three things. First, we show that, in contrast to the Cold War, when party democracy and liberal order were mutually reinforcing, today, the fragmentation of Western party democracies is making it harder for Western leaders to mobilize domestic support for liberal order-building. Second, we show that, while many factors have contributed to party fragmentation, Western governments' turn to globalism in the 1990s played a pivotal role by handing insurgent parties a potent issue to mobilize disenchanted voters. There is great irony here because one reason Western leaders turned to globalism was to shore up their electoral bases. Finally, we show that this process of domestic political fragmentation has not only reduced the latitude Western leaders have in foreign policymaking. It has also weakened core features of the liberal international order itself.

In developing these arguments, we build on the analysis in Chapter 3 by showing that Western leaders' political ambitions have contributed to this downward spiral between party democracy and liberal order. In the 1990s, in an effort to expand their parties' support base, Western leaders on the center-left as well as the center-right upended the delicate balance between international openness and social protection that their postwar predecessors had set, by slowing the growth of the welfare state while liberalizing international markets. While this "double move" succeeded in greatly expanding the liberal order, it came at the cost of working-class support for mainstream parties themselves. As we showed in Chapter 3, parties on the far left and, especially, the far right responded by using anti-globalism to appeal to disaffected voters. In this chapter, we show that their efforts paid off at the ballot box. Parties campaigning against trade liberalization and multilateral governance succeeded in expanding their share of the national vote at the expense of the vital center, and the liberal order.

THE VITAL CENTER

During the Cold War, Social Democrats, Liberals, Christian Democrats, and Conservatives found common ground in liberal internationalism. In contrast to the interwar years, when established Western parties fanned the flames of nationalism and international disorder, mainstream parties acted as a break on domestic jingoism, xenophobia, and revanchism and as a guardian against foreign intimidation and subterfuge. The leaders of mainstream parties were well placed in the highest reaches of national government to frame public debate, influence foreign policymaking, and keep nationalist and populist pressures in check. Even in Europe, where communist parties were competitive, mainstream parties dominated Western electorates, capturing between 75 and 85 percent of the national vote between 1950 and 1991.[1] Their dominance all but guaranteed broad and consistent domestic support for Western governments' foreign policies aimed at checking Soviet ambition and promoting closer economic ties within the West. At the same time, Western governments' commitment to the liberal order was a source of domestic support. Western leaders could advance liberal internationalist foreign policies, confident that political parties representing different regions, classes, and ideologies would support them.

Cold War consensus

That support took different forms in different countries and party systems. In America's two-party system, liberal internationalism was backed by both of the country's two major parties and by major segments of business, labor, and agriculture.[2] Democrats' and Republicans' shared power base in postwar America's internationally competitive industrial financial centers of the urban Northeast gave them a strong incentive to work together to rebuild the world economy and defend it against potential military and political threats in Europe and Asia. Democrats from the agrarian South and trans-Mississippi Republican West, whose commodity producers stood to benefit from freer trade, also favored liberal internationalism. To be sure, partisan politics did not stop at the water's edge. Democrats and Republicans frequently disagreed over the size of the defense budget and the amount of foreign aid. Yet these partisan divisions were sporadic and transitory. On the core features of liberal internationalism—the need for freer trade, the importance of security alliances, the role of international institutions—bipartisan consensus was the norm in the United States during the Cold War.[3]

In Europe's multiparty democracies, liberal internationalism garnered support from both sides of the left-right ideological divide. Under the leadership of Christian Democrats and Conservatives, who largely dominated party politics in the 1950s, Western European countries joined NATO, rearmed militarily, and took the first steps toward political confederation and an integrated common market.[4] Some center-left parties like West Germany's Social Democratic Party (SPD) and Italy's Socialist Party (PSI) initially opposed the center-right's liberal internationalist agenda. However, by the early 1960s they too had come around to supporting European integration and NATO membership, even if military rearmament remained an issue for many on the center-left.[5] Conservatives in Britain and France who worried about liberal internationalism's sovereignty costs sought to assert some control or impose limits, but did not reject it outright. French Conservatives sought to impose control by making a Paris-Bonn axis the central coordinate of any move toward European unity. British Conservatives approved European unity so long as it did not require Britain to be "in Europe" or jeopardize the UK's nascent "special relationship" with the United States.[6]

In Japan, the ruling Liberal Democratic Party (LDP) favored what might be characterized as liberal internationalism *lite*.[7] Guided by the skillful leadership of Shigeru Yoshida, postwar Japan adopted a Western-oriented foreign policy that relied on US security guarantees, homeland defense, and foreign markets. The LDP rejected substantial military rearmament in favor of cheaper Self-Defense Forces (SDF) and relied on state-led development of the civilian economy instead of the market. Under the so-called Yoshida Doctrine, successive Japanese governments accepted infringements on national sovereignty, most notably in the form of continued American military bases and forces on Japanese soil. Japan's status as a "semi-sovereign nation" was a price that most members of the LDP were willing to pay if it meant greater access to US markets and technology, and did not require the party to sacrifice its support coalition of industry and farmers—the so-called coalition of "steel and rice"—on the altar of free trade.[8] To bolster broader public support for aligning with America in the East-West struggle, mainstream conservatives committed to forgoing nuclear weapons and arms exports and to a narrowly prescribed regional security role for Japanese military forces.

Western support for liberal internationalism did not mean unanimity, of course. In the United States, progressive Democrats initially favored closer cooperation with Moscow and opposed military spending and the use of military force in distant lands.[9] In the early postwar years, Republicans on the far right—Fortress America and America-First regionalists—opposed strengthening transatlantic ties. In Western Europe, Atlanticism also sparked fierce resistance on the fringes of French, German, and Italian party politics, and debate over East-West neutrality was a staple of party politics in smaller states such as Austria, Sweden, and Switzerland, that traditionally favored foreign policies of neutrality and restraint.[10] On the far left, communist parties campaigned for disarmament. Most were also hostile to European integration.[11] Parties on the far right generally shared the far left's reservations about Transatlanticism. However, they had few qualms about investing in military power and were occasionally willing to accept some form of loose European confederation to counterbalance American as well as Soviet power and influence on the Continent.

In Japan, the Japan Socialist Party (JSP) opposed liberal internationalism, as did conservative factions within the LDP. Parties on the left favored a progressive "mixture of pacifism, isolationism, and idealism."[12] They preferred "unarmed neutrality" to rearmament and alignment with the United States and, in the case of the Japanese Communist Party (JCP), dissolution of the SDF and peace with the Soviet Union and China.[13] Japanese communists and socialists saw unarmed neutrality and breaking up Japan's large industrial financial conglomerates (Zaibatsu) as the best ways to guarantee Japanese security and prosperity and prevent a revival of Japanese militarism and prewar political repression.[14] Japanese security, many argued, could be best guaranteed through security treaties with Moscow and Beijing and making the East Asia–Pacific region a denuclearized zone. Ultra-right conservatives within the LDP shared the ultra-left's concerns about preserving national autonomy. However, they saw military power and repealing Article 9 of the Constitution prohibiting military rearmament as the best way to make Japan less dependent on the United States and less vulnerable to Soviet and Chinese ambitions.[15]

In the West, the critical dividing line over foreign policy was thus between the parties in the vital center and parties on both the far left and far right. This can be seen plainly in Figure 4.1. The figure is based on party platform data drawn from the Manifesto Project Data.[16] Here we use it to identify, summarize, and compare political parties' foreign policy preferences. We use Manifesto variables that include a pro and con position taken on issues relevant to our two key foreign policy dimensions: international partnership and military power.[17] We use these measures to locate party families in each of the twenty-four OECD nations in our sample on each foreign policy dimension from 1950 to 1975.[18] Each dot in the space represents a party family per country-year.[19] Mainstream parties are color-coded in blue; radical-left parties are labeled in green; radical-right parties in red. To provide reference points, we set the axes in Figure 4.1 (and subsequent two-dimensional

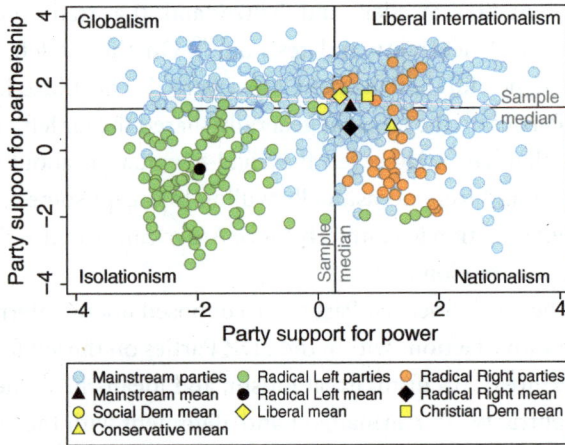

Figure 4.1 Party support for international partnership and military power in Western democracies, 1950–1975

plots in this chapter) using the full sample medians on each dimension from 1950 through 2018. These median values roughly correspond to the values demarcating the four quadrants in Figure 1.2 in Chapter 1: globalism (high partnership, low power); liberal internationalism (high partnership, high power); isolationism (low partnership, low power); and nationalism (low partnership, high power).[20]

As we see in Figure 4.1, mainstream parties were liberal internationalism's staunchest supporters in the postwar era; parties on the far left and far right, dedicated opponents. Most mainstream parties ran on party platforms advocating liberal internationalism and, as a result, we see that the means for each of the mainstream party families are located in, or in the case of Social Democrats and Conservatives, close to, quadrant 2. Mainstream parties show comparatively little support for strategies of isolationism (quadrant 3) or nationalism (quadrant 4). As one might expect, Social Democratic parties are less supportive of defense spending, military preparedness, and the use of force than Conservative parties. As a result, there is a fair amount of dispersion along the horizontal axis (military power) among mainstream parties in the liberal internationalist quadrant. There is less dispersion or variation among mainstream parties along the vertical (international partnership) axis—that is, on matters having to do with international trade, European integration, and multilateral cooperation.

Most radical-left parties cluster on the left side of the space and, especially, in the lower-left quadrant (isolationism). Radical-right parties are concentrated on the right side of the space. Most are located in the bottom-right nationalist quadrant, though some are in the upper-right, liberal internationalist quadrant. These alignments are not surprising. Parties on the far-left championed disarmament and generally opposed European integration.[21] Radical-right parties were more divided than the far left on the issue of European integration: for some parties on the right, some form of European confederation was preferable to US hegemony. Some far-right parties also supported trade liberalization. However, most ultra-right parties ran on party platforms that strongly favored containing the Soviet Union and investing in national military power; hence, their location on the right side of the figure. Last, we see in Figure 4.1 that there were relatively few radical-right parties, as most reactionary movements from the interwar years had collapsed.

In Western democracies, the level of mainstream party support for liberal internationalism was impressively strong. It also proved resilient, despite repeated challenges. The most serious of these was the crisis of the 1970s, when the postwar compromises between left and right frayed. While parties on the center-left urged governments to double down on Keynesianism by expanding government spending and market regulation, parties on the center-right called for political retrenchment, privatization, and market liberalization, or what came to be known as "neoliberalism." At first, the political fight tilted in the center-left's favor. Center-left parties held or gained ground in national elections in Austria (1975), Britain (1974), the Netherlands (1972), and West Germany (1976).[22] In time, however, the balance of power shifted to the center-right. Popular dissatisfaction with the status quo and pressure from powerful business interests propelled Conservatives to victory in Britain (1979), the United States (1980), and Germany (1983). As Margaret Thatcher, Ronald Reagan, and Helmut Kohl began experimenting with different combinations of neoliberal economic policies, competitive pressure on other Western governments to follow suit intensified. Even France's François Mitterrand's socialist government (1981–1995) found it necessary to pivot toward greater market liberalization.

For all the churn in Western party systems during the 1970s and 1980s, mainstream parties continued to dominate the political landscape. As Figure 4.2 indicates, they also remained firmly in the liberal internationalist camp.

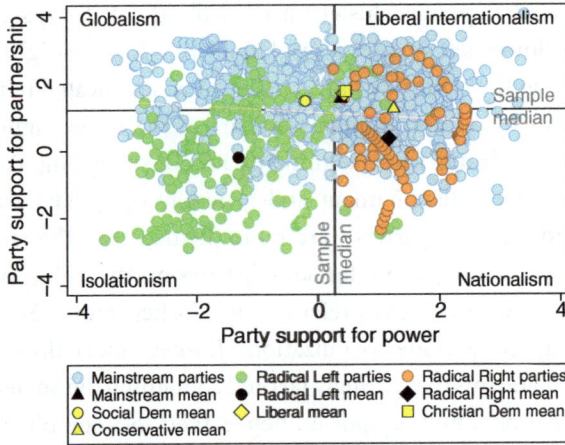

Figure 4.2 Party support for international partnership and military power in Western democracies, 1976–1991

Mainstream parties remain liberal internationalism's strongest supporters between 1976 and 1991; radical-left and radical-right parties, ardent foes. Center-left and center-right parties continue to cluster heavily in the upper-right, liberal internationalist quadrant. Radical-left and radical-right parties still clustered on the left and right sides of the space, respectively. Most far-left parties continued to campaign on platforms urging disarmament and protectionism and for the most part, opposed multilateralism as a means to make progress on issues high on their agenda (e.g., the environment; human rights). Radical-right parties' foreign policy platforms also did not change much. Some far-right parties, such as Austria's FPÖ, continued to cluster in the upper-right quadrant.[23] Other far-right parties, like France's FN, began to drift toward the lower-right nationalist quadrant.[24] In the 1990s, this trend would accelerate.

Custodians of the order

During the Cold War, the mainstream parties that made up Schlesinger's vital center were the liberal order's custodians. Lying between voters and governments, they acted as critical intermediaries, shaping and aggregating voters' foreign policy preferences in the electoral arena and translating that support into programmatic policy. The relative strength of center-left and center-right parties varied within Western democracies, as did the depth of their support for military spending and preparedness. However, the degree of continuity and robustness of their foreign policies to party and party-coalition turnover was striking. International commitments undertaken by center-right governments were upheld by center-left governments when political power shifted hands, and vice versa. As a general rule, the larger mainstream parties' share of the national vote, the stronger Western governments' commitment to liberal internationalism.

Figures 4.3 and 4.4 provide empirical support for this claim.[25] These models focus on the relationship between party strength and government policy, taking into account how factors shaping government policies favoring international partnership might be related to government policies involving increased military power.[26] We measure *partnership* using the KOF globalization policies index used in Chapter 3. Again, *power* refers to defense spending as a percentage of GDP. *Partnership + power* is the same composite measure for liberal internationalism we used in Chapter 3.[27] We use national vote share—a standard measure of party influence—to measure party strength in each of the following five party categories: *mainstream vote share* (the combined vote share of Social Democratic, Liberal, Christian Democratic, and Conservative parties), *radical-right vote share* and *radical-left vote share* (their respective share of the national vote), *total radical vote share* (the combined radical party vote share) and *net mainstream vote share* (the vote share for mainstream parties minus the vote share for all radical parties combined).[28]

Figure 4.3 summarizes the basic direction and significance of the associations between party family vote shares and government support for *partnership* (top panel), *power* (middle panel), and *partnership + power* (bottom panel). Each panel summarizes the results for these country-level outcome variables. The black dots in the figures represent coefficients for the predicted associations between party family vote share and our outcomes of interest: partnership, power, and partnership and power combined. The bars summarize the 95 percent confidence interval of the estimates (with estimates meeting the threshold of statistical significance when the bars do not cross zero). We see that each of the key patterns summarized in Figure 4.3 is in the predicted direction. The two models measuring the effect of *mainstream party vote share* and *net mainstream vote share* with *partnership*, *power*, and *partnership + power* have a significant positive correlation. By contrast, the three models measuring the effect of *radical-right vote share*,

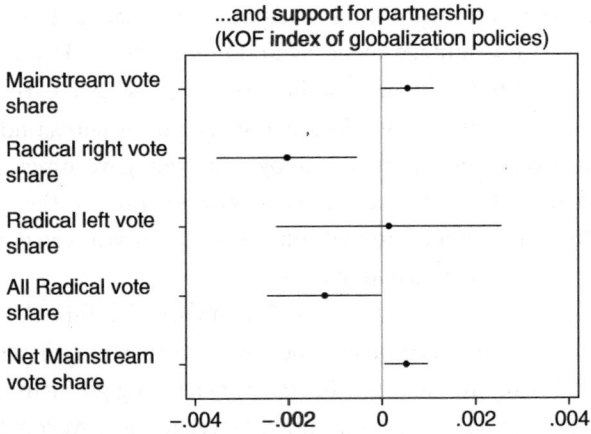

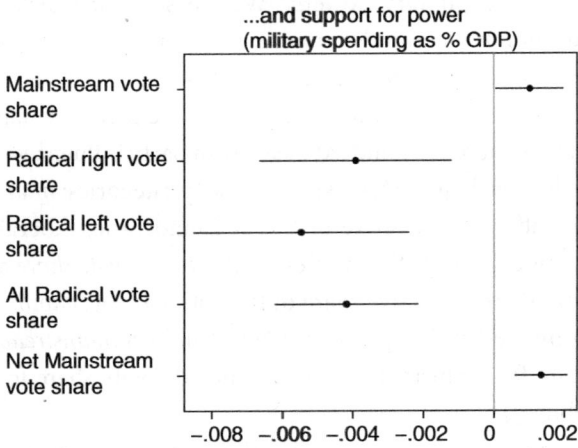

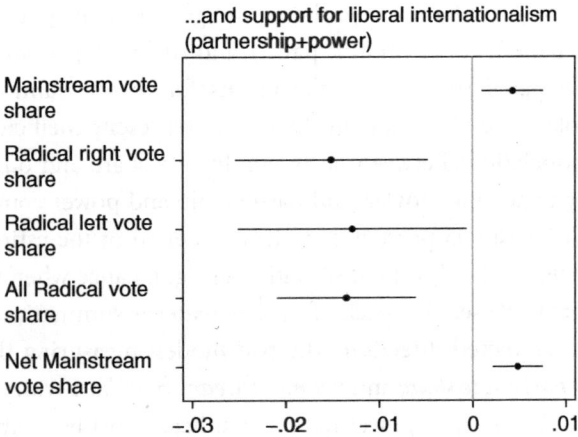

Figure 4.3 Effect of party vote share on government support for international partnership and military power in Western democracies, 1970–2017

radical-left vote share, and *combined radical vote share* are all strongly negatively correlated with government support for each of our outcome variables.

Figure 4.4 summarizes what these patterns mean substantively. Each panel displays the counterfactual predicted levels of government policy support for *partnership + power* as a function of the full sample variation of (a) mainstream party vote shares (top panel) and (b) all radical-left and radical-right party vote shares (bottom panel). The vertical axis for both models is the same.[29] Again, the solid lines in the figures refer to the direction of the regression line capturing the two-way association between the variables on

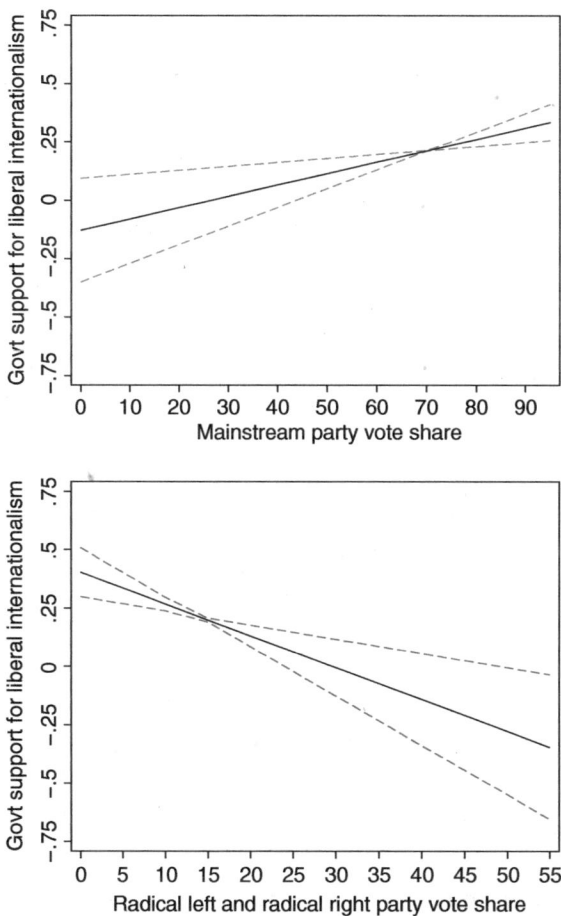

Figure 4.4 Relationship between mainstream and radical party strength and government support for liberal internationalism in Western democracies, 1950–2017

the horizontal and vertical axes. The broken lines refer to the consistency or tightness of the fit between these two variables with 95 percent confidence. As the top panel makes clear, the larger the mainstream parties' national vote share, the more likely Western governments are to invest in partnership and power—that is, in liberal internationalism. In the bottom panel, we see that the greater the radical parties' vote share, the less likely Western governments are to invest in liberal internationalism. Notably, the positive effect of mainstream party strength is marginally smaller than the negative effect of radical party strength. This is captured in Figure 4.4, where we see that the full sample variation of mainstream vote share predicts a smaller swath of variation in liberal internationalism (top panel) than does the sample variation in radical party vote share (bottom panel). These are substantial associations. The variation in radical party vote shares predicts between 20 and 30 percent of the variation in government policies of *partnership + power*.[30]

The West's double commitment to partnership and power distinguished liberal internationalism from other foreign policy strategies on offer, and mainstream parties from their competitors on the far left and far right. However, as the analyses in Figures 4.3 and 4.4 make clear, it was mainstream parties' strength at the ballot box during the Cold War, especially relative to the radical parties, that enabled Western leaders to put liberal internationalism on a stable footing as the West's strategy of choice.[31] This point is often forgotten or glossed over in accounts of the liberal order's formation after World War II and its subsequent amplification and elaboration in the decades that followed. It was a time when party politics in Western democracies was remarkably stable or "frozen," as Seymour Lipset and Stein Rokkan put it in their classic 1967 cross-national study of party democracy.[32] A hidden source of Western strength during the Cold War, the party alignments that Lipset and Rokkan identified would remain in place until it ended.

THE GREAT UNWINDING

In the 1990s, Western party systems began to unwind. Parties on the center-left and center-right started losing vote share at a slow but accelerating pace to insurgent parties on the far left and far right. Scholars of comparative politics have written extensively about the decomposition of the West's postwar party systems and its implications for democratic governance. Much less has been written about how the West's turn to globalism in the post-Cold War era contributed to the fragmentation and disruption of Western party systems or on its implications for Western solidarity and international influence. In Chapter 3, we showed how Western democracies' failure to maintain adequate levels of social compensation at a time of rapid economic integration stoked anti-globalist sentiment among voters and created opportunities for parties on the far left and far right to make political hay. In this section, we show that insurgent parties capitalized on those opportunities by using anti-globalism to chip away at mainstream parties' vote share and political power.

Working-class blues

When the Cold War ended, the parties that made up the vital center continued to dwarf their rivals. Mainstream parties continued to win the lion's share of the national vote and, as a result, retained control of the pivotal foreign policymaking positions in national governments. Between 1976 and 1991, mainstream parties captured nearly 80 percent of the popular vote, on average; lower than the share they received during the postwar era, but not significantly so. As Figure 4.5 indicates, thirty years later, the situation looks quite different. Since the Cold War, mainstream parties' share of the national vote has dropped by a full 15 percent of the total vote—averaging only around 65 percent of the vote by the late 2010s. In some countries, the drop was sharper still. For example, in the 1990 German election, Social Democrats and Christian Democrats received

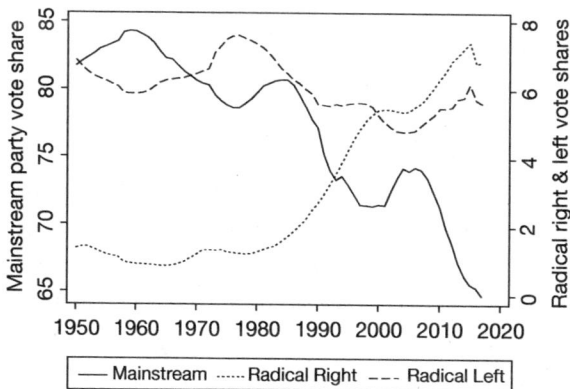

Figure 4.5 Average vote share by party family in Western democracies, 1950–2017

over 70 percent of the vote. In the 2021 election, together they received just under 50 percent.[33]

Mainstream parties have not only lost vote share. Over the past thirty years, Western government majorities have become smaller and Western electorates have become more disjointed and volatile.[34] The erosion of the mainstream parties' dominance in Western governing majorities is evident in the data. Since 1991 the percentage of cabinet portfolios held by main-stream parties dropped from a Cold War average of almost 50 percent to just 30 percent during the 2010s.[35] As shared governments have become more commonplace in the West, the process of putting them together and keeping them together has become more complex and taxing. A two-party system like America's is spared the trials and tribulations of coalition government, but worsening polarization in the United States has also made it more difficult for Republicans or Democrats to build winning coalitions to enact national legislation. Twenty years ago, Congress passed 225 laws in a year. In 2020, it passed only twenty-eight laws.[36]

Many factors have contributed to the electoral decline of mainstream parties, from technological change, to secularization, to generational change, to mass immigration, to income inequality.[37] However, a strong case can be made that Western governments' turn toward globalism after the Cold War played a decisive role. In the heady days of Western triumphalism over capitalism and open economies, Western leaders on the center-left did not only see globalization as a strategy to expand the liberal order, internationally. They also saw it as a means to boost their parties' political fortunes, after a decade or longer languishing in the political wilderness while center-right parties set the policy agenda. Bill Clinton's New Democratic agenda, Tony Blair's "New Labour," Lionel Jospin's *réalisme de gauche* (left realism), and Gerhard Schröder's "Agenda 2010" were cut from the same neoliberal cloth, and under the influence of globalization, driven by the same political imperative to make the center-left more competitive electorally.

During the Cold War, center-left leaders relied on the support of working-class voters to win elections. The viability of that electoral strategy depended greatly on the manufacturing sector's vitality in Western economies. For decades, that was a safe bet. However, over time center-left leaders found it increasingly difficult to win national office relying principally on blue-collar votes.[38] The secular decline of the manufacturing sector in Western economies, and the concomitant rise of the service sector, led Social Democratic leaders in the 1990s to adopt more pro-globalization policies in hopes of winning over service-sector voters who benefited from cheaper goods and services increasingly provided by imports and low-wage immigrant labor.[39] In effect, center-left leaders began trading a large part of their traditional older working-class political base that was being hurt by hyperglobalization to win over younger, educated, middle-class voters who benefited from market liberalization and supported multilateral cooperation. By one estimate, in 1980 Social Democratic parties mobilized roughly twice as many working-class voters as middle-class voters. By 2010, the proportions were roughly the reverse.[40]

In Europe, Social Democratic and socialist leaders had already begun changing course when they agreed to the creation of a single market in the 1980s. In the 1990s, they abandoned what remained of their long-standing commitment to independent, *national* roads to social democracy by embracing economic and monetary union.[41] The 1992 Maastricht treaty, formally establishing the European Central Bank and a common European currency, ruled out the kind of national autonomy that center-left parties once insisted upon to protect their working-class constituencies from market forces. Britain's Labour Party, at most a reluctant supporter of earlier efforts to promote European economic integration, set aside its "ancient enmity" toward market liberalization and threw in its lot with the new European Union. As Donald Sassoon puts it in his magisterial history of the European Left, Maastricht "decreed that inflation, and not unemployment, was the main enemy. This was now fully accepted by the Labour Party and by all other European socialist parties."[42]

In the United States, Clinton and other New Democrats broke with Democrats from the aging Rust Belt cities of the Northeast on globalization as well as on welfare policy, and aligned with conservative Republicans.[43] Clinton embraced trade liberalization and pushed for the NAFTA regional trade pact (1994), the GATT agreement creating the WTO (1994), and granting permanent normal trade relations (PNTR) to China (2000). These agreements angered labor and other Democratic constituencies (e.g., environmental groups, human rights NGOs), and put Clinton at odds with many traditional Democrats in Congress.[44] But free trade deals helped Clinton and the New Democrats earn the support of fast-growing high-tech and service sectors, as well as their voters.[45] These sectors were not strongly attached to the Republican Party, and they were a huge potential source of votes and money. Liberal, redistributive Democratic programs could not win over this new class of voters and investors. What could help move them into the

Democratic column were cheaper imports and the promise of greater access to foreign markets and investment opportunities.[46]

In Japan, globalization also weakened old party alignments and led to new domestic alliances. In the early 1990s, the coalition of "steel and rice" fractured, sending the conservative LDP to its first electoral defeat in nearly four decades. While the LDP soon regained power, its defeat ushered in a host of institutional reforms that led to a more competitive, fluid party system.[47] Urban and middle-class voters previously frozen out of party politics by the dominant LDP's fealty to farmers were now an object of political mobilization drives. In 2001, Junichiro Koizumi, a political maverick, captured the LDP's presidency and Japan's premiership, campaigning on a neoliberal platform targeting these voters.[48] Koizumi's platform of "reform, with no sacred cows" took aim at the protection of inefficient sectors like agriculture while offering neoliberal policies like lower taxes, privatization (e.g., postal service), and cuts in pork barrel spending to woo new voters.[49] Stealing a page out of the US and EU playbook, Koizumi sought to strengthen Japan's economic ties to other countries in the region through "open regionalism."[50]

In the 1990s, center-left as well as center-right parties in Western democracies saw political advantage in promoting globalization and its domestic corollaries: lower corporate taxes, tighter fiscal policy, fewer government regulations, trimmed down welfare states, and weaker trade unions. This trend continued though the 2000s as the balance of power in America, France, Germany, and other Western democracies shifted from the center-left to the center-right.[51] Under Germany's Angela Merkel, France's Nicolas Sarkozy, and America's George W. Bush, multilateralism and intergovernmentalism remained the preferred mode for global economic cooperation. The same was true of the Democratic Party of Japan (DPJ), which came to power in 2009, and the LDP's Shinzo Abe, who returned to power in 2012.[52] Both continued to pursue FTAs with other nations and backed the multilateral negotiations that culminated in the 2016 Trans-Pacific Partnership Treaty (TPP).[53]

Figure 4.6 summarizes the party alignments in Western democracies over foreign policy during these years. We see that most center-left and center-right parties continue to cluster in quadrant two (liberal internationalism). However, many mainstream parties also now cluster in quadrant one (globalism). When compared to Figures 4.1 and 4.2, the most significant change in the behavior of mainstream parties is their movement up the vertical axis, indicating greater support for economic integration and institutionalized cooperation. Center-left and center-right parties are now on average more

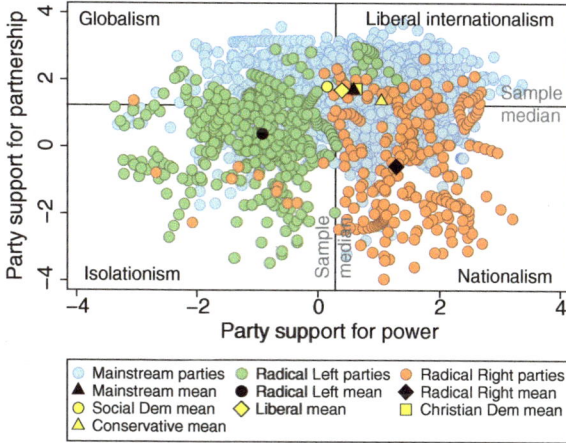

Figure 4.6 Party support for international partnership and military power in Western democracies, 1992–2018

deeply committed to partnership than they were during the Cold War (and far more than parties on the radical left and, especially, the radical right). By contrast, there is little sustained change in mainstream party family support for military power. As during the Cold War, the more conservative the mainstream party family, the more likely it is to urge increased military spending and preparedness.

The shift in mainstream parties' support for globalization is easier to see in Figure 4.7. It tracks the mean position of each mainstream party family, as well as the mean location of radical-left and radical-right parties from 1950 through 2017. In the case of mainstream parties, we see gradual movement up the vertical axis. This is clearest in the case of Social Democrats, but we see the same upward drift in the mean position of Conservatives and Liberals (though not Christian Democrats). To be sure, the upward shift in overall mainstream party support for market liberalization and institutionalized cooperation is not as dramatic as the overall movement toward market-favoring change in Western government foreign policy that we described in Chapter 2. This is not surprising, however. Party manifestos can tell us something important about what parties promise voters, but they are an imperfect guide to what their leaders actually do once in office. As the analysis in Chapter 3 showed, one important reason for the divergence between government policy and party platforms on trade liberalization and international institutions is that Western leaders have become overly responsive to

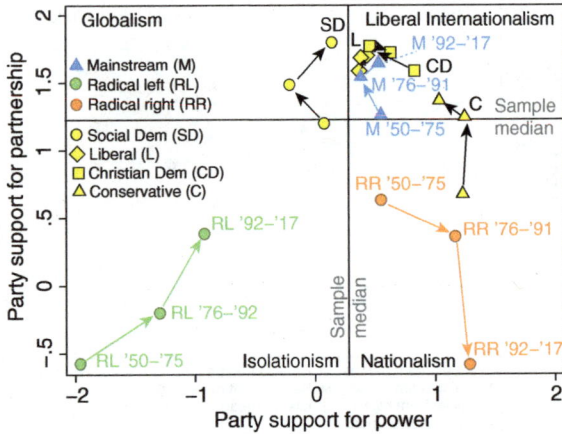

Figure 4.7 Average party family support for international partnership and military power in Western democracies, 1950–2017

the market-oriented views and expectations of international business and international technocrats—far more than voters anticipate, based upon their party's election platforms.[54]

Things fall apart

The most significant post-Cold War changes to Western party platforms in the area of foreign policy were those that radical-left and radical-right parties put before voters.[55] Throughout the Cold War, parties on the far left ran for election on platforms with foreign policy planks favoring disarmament, East-West neutrality, and in most cases, trade protection. As we have seen, these parties generally gravitated toward the lower-left isolationist quadrant, opposing government investment in both military power and international partnership. Radical-right parties were less of a single mind. While they agreed that governments should spend more on national defense, they were less united over how much international partnership was enough. Most radical-right parties opposed free markets and international institutions. Others viewed open markets as a means to combat socialism at home and saw institutionalized cooperation as a means to dilute American power and influence. During the Cold War (Figures 4.1 and 4.2), some radical-right parties thus aligned with Conservative parties in the upper-right liberal internationalist quadrant. Others gravitated to the bottom-right nationalist quadrant.

In the 1990s, many radical-left parties began combining traditional calls for defense cuts and disarmament with a greater willingness to work through international institutions. Parties that once viewed international institutions as inherently elitist and undemocratic, now argued that international institutions could play a valuable role in mounting effective, democratic responses to transnational challenges such as climate change, human rights, and social justice.[56] Speaking for many on the left, Mary Kaldor argued that global institutions could be reimagined to help "civilize globalization."[57] No longer laboring under the weight of the Cold War, political parties on the far left certainly had more political room to reposition themselves for such a mission. Figure 4.7 captures this movement in the foreign policy orientation of parties on the far left from the lower-left quadrant toward the upper-left quadrant (globalism). As a result, a growing number of these parties can now be found just above or just below the horizontal axis in Figure 4.6.

The far left's willingness to campaign for institutionalized cooperation and global governance had its limits though. First, as Figure 4.6 indicates, most radical-left parties continued to oppose trade liberalization and supranationalism; the vast majority were still located in the bottom-left isolationist quadrant. This included newer left-wing populist parties in Spain, Greece, and Italy which were hard-hit by the Eurozone crisis of the early 2010s. Podemos, Syriza, and other parties on the far left all sharply contested EU-backed austerity programs and rules and made the case for democratizing decision-making in Brussels. The radical left's increased support for partnership also did not translate into increased support for the WTO or multilateral trade initiatives. In Europe, parties on the far left opposed the Transatlantic Trade and Investment Program (TTIP). They argued that the negotiations were too secretive, and that the agreement lowered EU food, auto, and environmental standards, while threatening local jobs and wages by giving foreign companies unfair advantages.[58] Similar arguments were made against the TPP in Australia, New Zealand, and other Pacific nations.[59]

The post–Cold War era also led radical-right parties to reposition themselves on foreign policy. As discussed in Chapter 3, those radical-right parties that once favored free and open trade began reversing course in the 1990s, combining calls for tighter restrictions on trade, outsourcing, and immigration with their traditional support for military preparedness.[60] They also stepped up their attacks on supranational institutions like the European Union and the WTO, whose rules, regulations, and decision-making processes, they argued, infringed on national sovereignty.[61] We see in Figures 4.6 and 4.7 that parties on the far right now clustered heavily in the bottom-right nationalist quadrant. Older radical-right parties such as France's FN and the Denmark's DPP, which sometimes aligned with liberal internationalist parties in the past, were now squarely in the nationalist fold.[62] So were newer far-right parties like Britain's UKIP and Germany's AfD.[63] Still vociferous backers of military power and strength, after the Cold War radical-right parties also became ardent foes of international partnership.

They also became deft practitioners of wedge politics. As discussed in Chapter 3, radical-right parties were actively using anti-globalism as early as the 1990s to mobilize voters no longer strongly aligned with Social Democratic parties and to put Conservative and Christian Democratic parties on the political defensive.[64] By the 2010s, campaigning against trade liberalization and supranational institutions had become an effective strategy for winning over working-class voters, especially in regions that were severely impacted by globalization and falling behind economically.[65] In the run-up to the Brexit referendum, UKIP's Nigel Farage made gains with the so-called "left behind" in Northern and Eastern England's aging Rust Belt cities and towns by fusing the explosive issue of immigration with opposition to EU membership. In 2017, Marine Le Pen ran for the French presidency merging the FN's long-standing opposition to mass immigration with a new "strategic plan for reindustrialization" aimed directly at regions of France's north and east hard-hit by globalization.[66]

Their efforts did not catapult them into national government, but they did succeed in putting mainstream parties on the defensive and, importantly, capturing a larger share of the electorate. Indeed, the more issues of trade liberalization and supranationalism were debated, the more radical-right parties stood to benefit. Evidence for this can be found in more detailed quantitative analysis of whether a given party's platform position on international partnership and military power before a national election improves or hurts its performance (vote share) in the election. Our baseline models in Figures 4.8 and 4.9 pool all parties, countries, and years in the Manifesto Project data (1950–2017), and control for all party families, decades, and country fixed effects. We also control for a given party's other manifesto positions on a left-versus-right ideological scale to better isolate the possible electoral effects of its stance on partnership and power.[67] We expected that, all things being equal (e.g., in the absence of a corollary commitment to expand social protections), parties that were more supportive of international

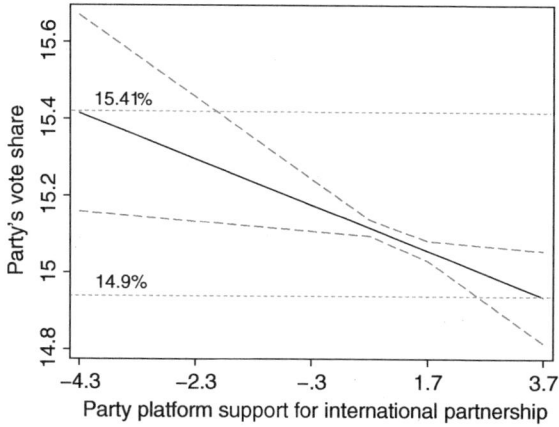

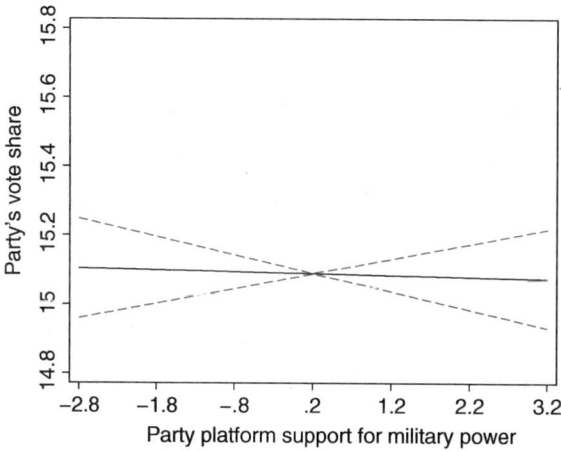

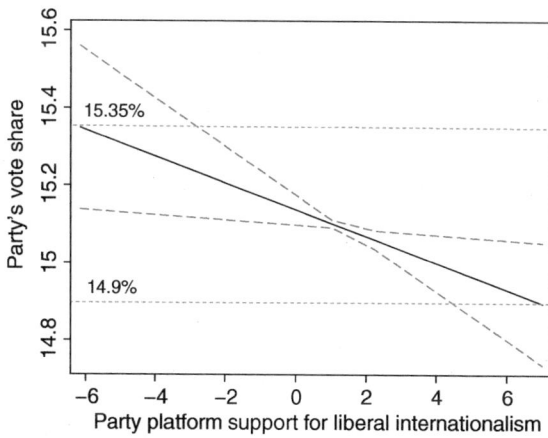

Figure 4.8 Relationship between party support for international partnership and military power and electoral success in Western democracies, 1960–2017

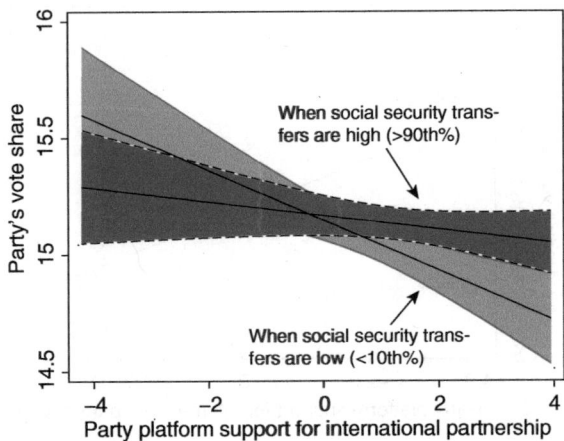

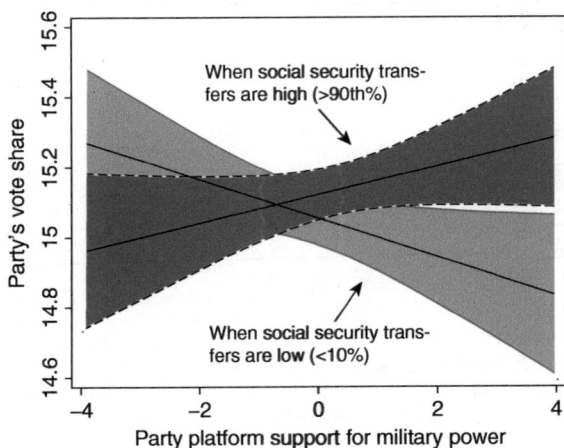

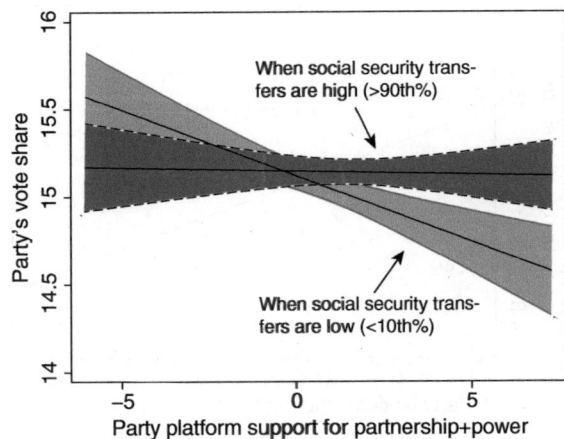

Figure 4.9 Relationship between social protection, foreign policy, and party vote share in Western democracies, 1950–2017

partnership would be punished at the ballot box, while parties more opposed to partnership would be rewarded.

This is, in fact, what we see in Figure 4.8. While there is low correlation between a given party's support for military spending and preparedness (*power*; middle panel) and that party's share of the national vote (*party vote share*) in the ensuing election, a party's support for trade, international institutions, and multilateralism (*partnership*; top panel) correlates significantly and negatively with its subsequent electoral performance. In general, parties supporting *partnership* lose votes. By contrast, opposing *partnership* increases their *vote share*. This pattern applies for the entire 1950–2017 time period, but, notably, the electoral rewards for parties opposing partnership have increased since the end of the Cold War.[68] This same pattern is evident for liberal internationalism (*partnership + power*; bottom panel), but does not hold up for party support of *power*.

Figure 4.9 takes things a step further by considering how sensitive the correlations reported in Figure 4.8 are to the presence or absence of social protection. In Chapter 2, we showed that voters are more inclined to support liberal internationalism when social protections are robust, as they were during the Cold War in the advanced industrialized economies. Here, we consider whether this commitment to social democracy made voters more likely to vote for parties supporting liberal internationalism. To answer this question, we interacted *social protection* with liberal internationalism (*partnership + power*; bottom panel) and *partnership* (top panel) and *power* (middle panel), separately.[69] The model is based on the same specifications as the models in Figure 4.8, though now we add these interactive terms. Figure 4.9 compares the counterfactual results, with two schedules in each of the three panels: a light-shaded schedule, where the level of social protection is modest (at the sample's 10th percentile of social protection); and a dark-shaded schedule, where social protection is strong (at the sample's 90th percentile).[70]

The results we see in Figure 4.9 are clear-cut. In countries where social protection is robust, parties running on platforms favoring partnership and power do not pay an electoral price. Indeed, parties calling for increased military spending and preparedness gain vote share, provided strong social protections are in place. By contrast, in countries where social protection is modest, a party running on the same liberal internationalist platform can expect to experience a sharp decline in its vote share, all else equal. These results are consistent with an extensive literature in comparative and international political economy that shows that governments and parties that act to mitigate the uneven distributional effects of economic openness are rewarded by voters, while those that do not are punished at the ballot box.[71] However, the results in Figure 4.9, show that this holds for military spending as well. This suggests that voters are sensitive to guns-versus-butter trade-offs, and that all things being equal, prefer both. More broadly, the analysis here indicates that political parties investing in partnership or power will suffer at the polls unless liberal order-building and social protection go hand-in-hand.

It is here, at the intersection of international and domestic politics, that Western governments, and the mainstream parties leading them, lost their way and opened the door to populist and nationalist parties once on the fringes of party democracy. To be sure, the factors mentioned earlier, such as automation, mass migration, economic inequality, have also contributed to the rise of radical-right parties and the decline of mainstream parties. A case can be made that many of these are having effects picked up in our measures. It is also important to bear in mind that while statistically significant, the negative correlation between *partnership* (and *partnership + power*) and *party vote share* are modest, with the full sample variation in Figures 4.8 and 4.9 predicting no more than a 0.7 percent shift in vote share. All of that said, the results reported in Figures 4.8 and 4.9 are robust to a number of model specifications.[72] The results are also consistent with country-level aggregate analyses that show that the size of the gaps between governments and voters over foreign policy correlate positively with radical parties' electoral success and negatively with mainstream party performance at the polls.[73] Minimally, what these results tell us is that liberal order-building no longer affords mainstream parties the electoral advantages it once did, and that radical-right parties have found a powerful weapon in anti-globalism to challenge the authority of Western democracies' vital center.

A DECLINING ASSET

For decades international relations scholars largely took Western democracies' legitimacy and capacity to govern themselves as givens. The main focus was on how rapid international changes were impacting the liberal order: how shifts in the balance of power, technological change, and environmental degradation affected the willingness and ability of states to open their economies and to cooperate multilaterally.[74] International relations scholars had much less to say about how changes in the distribution of political authority and power *within* countries affect the possibilities for cooperation between them. Political polarization and democratic backsliding in the West has exposed the limits of viewing the liberal order as though it is suspended above domestic politics. As we have shown, party democracy has shaped the possibilities of international cooperation between Western governments since the inception of the postwar liberal order. In this section, we consider how the erosion of political authority in Western democracies is impacting the liberal order today.

Western power and influence

During the Cold War, party democracy was a force multiplier for Western governments in international politics. The stability, legitimacy, and effectiveness of the mainstream parties that made up the vital center was a source of Western strength and international influence. Western leaders had little reason to worry that party and party-coalition turnover in the two dozen democracies that formed the core of the liberal order would lead those governments to renege on international commitments undertaken by their predecessors, or at least far less than they do today. This did not mean that mainstream parties within Western democracies were always in agreement with one another, or that elections never produced foreign policy reversals. Social Democrats emphasized liberal internationalism's commitment to partnership; Conservatives, put the accent on power. But in general, alternation in power between the mainstream parties did not bring radical shifts in governments' commitments to partnership and power. Indeed, scholars have argued that the robustness of foreign policy commitments to democratic deliberation and party turnover within Western democracies was a critical source of their international credibility.[75] At a time of great anxiety about Soviet ambitions and the risk of nuclear war, party democracy was a foreign policy asset, bolstering Western collective purpose and resolve and strengthening the liberal order's domestic foundations.

Western democracies did not always see eye-to-eye, of course, and liberal order-building did not move in a straight line. There were setbacks and inconsistencies (e.g., high tariffs on agricultural goods, France's 1966 decision to opt out of NATO's integrated military command). Fears of American domination and abandonment were never very far from the surface in Europe or Asia.[76] Yet by working within multilateral institutions, Washington was able to reassure its allies that it would wield its immense power in concert with them rather than use it to reap unilateral advantage. The fact that both of America's major political parties publicly backed these commitments to managed openness, multilateral cooperation, and the common defense was a constant source of reassurance too. Among other things, it signaled a high degree of consistency in US foreign policy. Former Secretary of State Dean Acheson once referred to bipartisanship as the "oil of national government."[77] By signaling American purposefulness and reliability, party cooperation over foreign policy also lubricated the wheels of Western cooperation.

This was also true of the West's many multiparty democracies and coalition governments. There, too, political stability was an international asset. Whatever policy differences American policymakers had with their European and Asian counterparts, they had little reason to think that the foreign policy pendulum would swing dramatically when a center-left coalition replaced a center-right coalition, or vice versa. As we have seen, liberal internationalism enjoyed the unstinting support of the many mainstream parties that governed in Europe and Asia during the Cold War. Broad-based domestic support was not a substitute for Western governments' directly signaling their commitment to liberal internationalism by negotiating down tariff barriers or agreeing collectively to increase their share of the common defense. But it did underscore multiparty democracies' *capacity* to make good on these commitments, and that was no small thing in a world where East and West seized every international opportunity to claim that their political model was best.

Often derided as volatile, dysfunctional, and ineffective today, Western democracies were seen differently in the age of party democracy. Party democracy was a source of Western international attraction. West Germany and Japan were proof that ideological extremism could be tamed, and for the many countries that wanted "in" to the liberal order, that democracy could deliver the goods. For political elites in the developing world, the liberal order's promise of economic growth and advancement may have been its main attraction. But the democratic make-up of the polities driving the liberal order forward did not go unnoticed by their citizens. Between the early 1980s and the early 2000s, the proportion of democratic countries in the world more than doubled.[78] Of course, many of the countries that were part of this "third wave" of democratization and liberal constitutionalism never fully crossed the democratic threshold. Others did democratize only to revert to autocratic rule. Yet the sharp rise in democratization reminds us that Western democracies have not always been on the political defensive, internationally.

The price of fragmentation

To better understand the international effects of Western democracies' political fragmentation, we developed a model focusing on three key features of the liberal order. These are the degree of international openness, the amount of multilateral regulatory and adjudicatory authority, and the extent to which non-Western countries align themselves with Western democracies. If party democracy contributed to the expansion of the liberal order, we would expect party fragmentation to result in less international openness among Western democracies, less delegation and pooling of authority by Western and other international states to multilateral institutions, and less willingness by non-Western states to align with Western democracies in international bodies.

To test these arguments, we rely on three quantitative measures. The first is KOF's (2021) de facto index of economic, political, and sociocultural globalization among Western democracies.[79] We treat this index as a proxy for the degree of Western international openness. The second is Hooghe et al.'s (2018; 2020) Measure of International Authority (MIA). We use this measure to gauge the level of authority delegated, pooled, and vested by states in international governmental organizations with strong Western membership. Our third measure uses Voeten et al.'s (2009) UN voting agreement (or similarity) scores to measure how much non-Western countries vote with Western democracies on General Assembly roll call votes.[80] We measure party fragmentation using Rae's (1968) popular index of *legislative* fractionalization of the party system.[81] We take each of these measures of the liberal order in turn, starting with the effects of party fragmentation on international openness.

International openness

Figure 4.10 tracks the level of international openness based on KOF's most comprehensive measure of globalization. It measures actual economic, political, and sociocultural globalization flows at the country level for our sample of twenty-four OECD nations from 1970 through 2018. We see clearly that globalization steadily increased from the early 1970s until the mid-2000s, when it slowed and leveled off. The trend here closely parallels the steady

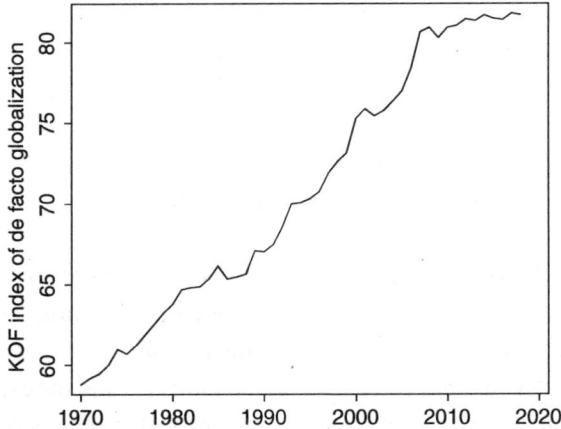

Figure 4.10 Average level of globalization among Western democracies, 1970–2018

increase in Western government *policies* promoting economic and political globalization that we described in Chapter 2 (see Figure 2.7). However, Figure 4.10 is tracking the *actual* flow of goods, services, and peoples across national boundaries, participation in peacekeeping operations, and the spread of human rights, civil liberties, and culture. That these two indicators have moved roughly in parallel since the 1970s, when the time series begins, is not surprising. Policy change is expected to lead to changes in trade behavior, currency flows, migration patterns, and so on.

In Figure 4.11 we summarize the main result of a regression analysis estimating the effects of Western party fragmentation on international openness. Here, we regressed models of KOF de facto globalization on five-year lagged moving averages of parliamentary fractionalization. The models include a range of substantive controls (level of democracy, voter, turnout, GDP growth, union density, openness, social transfers, and unemployment rate), and "dummy" variables for time and country.[82] As is clear from the negative slope of the line and its confidence intervals, party fragmentation does result in less international openness. The negative correlation is significant in substantive terms too. We see that the full sample variation in party-system fragmentation predicts about 30 percent of the sample variation in globalization flows (between roughly the 30th and the 60th percentile in the full sample distribution of the KOF index of de facto globalization). As Western democracies have become more fragmented and volatile, the pace of international integration has slowed.

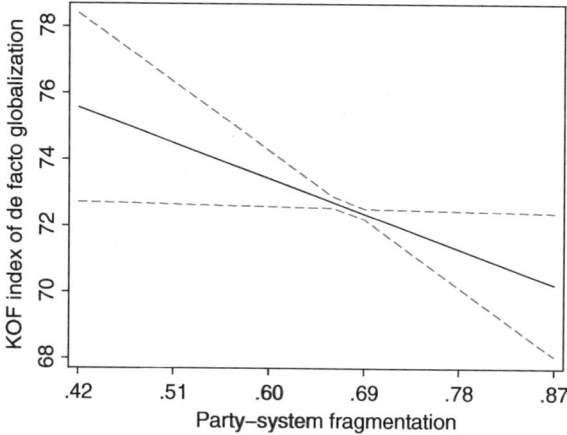

Figure 4.11 Relationship between domestic political fragmentation and globalization, 1970–2018

Global governance

If globalization has slowed in the face of Western domestic fragmentation, efforts to expand multilateral governance have stalled outright. Figure 4.12 tracks the growth of international authority from 1950 through 2019 for twenty-five international organizations where Western democracies are active members.[83] We use the MIA database's three scales to capture differences in the scope, form, and level of authority states lodge in international governmental institutions.[84] These include the extent to which states *delegate* authority to international institutions, jointly *pool* authority in international organizations, and international bodies have the authority to *resolve* or settle disputes among their member states. We see in Figure 4.12 that, after a relatively brief increase in the 1990s, the amount of international authority in two of the three indicators levels off in the 2000s, with little subsequent growth in international intergovernmental authority over the next two decades.

In estimating the association between party-system fragmentation and international authority, we focus on how strongly an international institution's authority in a given year correlates with its authority in the preceding year.[85] The results of the time series analysis are summarized in the top panel in Figure 4.13.[86] They offer considerable support for our argument. The more Western party systems fragment in a given year, the less authority Western governments are willing to delegate or pool in international institutions, on average. The relationship between party-system fragmentation and international dispute settlement is also negative. However, it is not

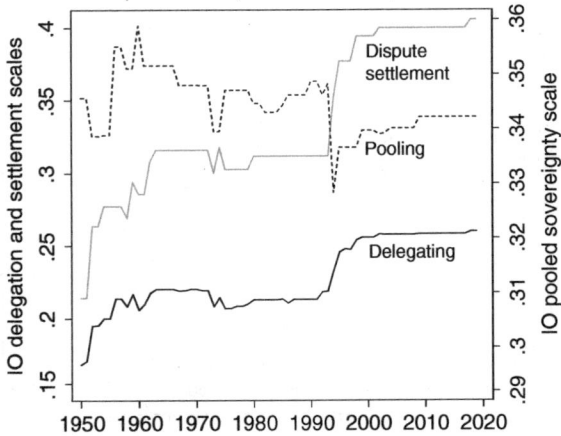

Figure 4.12 Average level of decision-making authority exercised by international organizations (IOs), 1950–2019

statistically significant. Finally, we see that party fragmentation also significantly correlates with a composite measure combining the three MIA scales. Thus, in three out of four measures of international authority, we see the expected effect or association.

The substantive meaning of the results is also summarized in Figure 4.13 (bottom panel). It focuses on the results for delegating and pooling international authority. We can see from the negative slopes (including the upper and lower confidence intervals) that fragmentation of Western party systems has a substantially large as well as statistically significant correlation with governments' willingness to delegate and pool authority in multilateral institutions. Based on the first-differences of the variables, we see that the full variation in party fragmentation is associated with a major portion of the sample variation in the annual delegation and pooling of authority: for delegation, roughly the 15th percentile to the 80th percentile and, for pooling, roughly the 3rd percentile to the 78th percentile. These patterns are also evident in our composite measure.[87]

Aligning with the West

Our final test focuses on the extent to which states align with Western democracies in multilateral institutions. We consider how often states vote with the West in the UN General Assembly. Of course, the UN is only one international organization of import and much of the negotiation in the run-up to public votes on UN resolutions takes place behind closed doors.

Nevertheless, UN General Assembly voting provides a useful way to uncover latent voting blocs and political alignments and to test theories about the conditions under which they form. Our interest here is in determining the extent to which Western democracies' governing effectiveness has burnished or tarnished their international reputation and standing. We cannot test this directly, but voting behavior in the UN General Assembly provides an indirect method for assessing the relationship between political fragmentation within Western democracies and the "Western model's" attractiveness internationally.

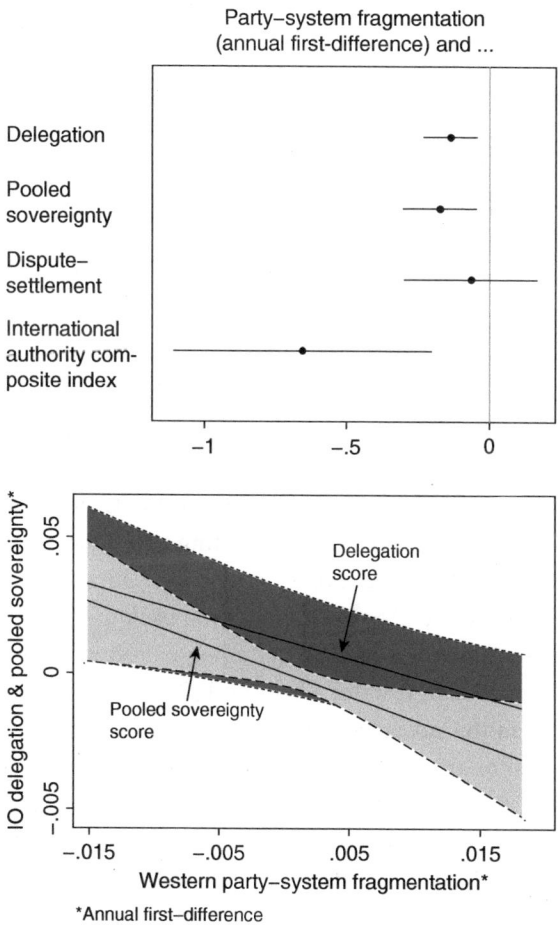

Figure 4.13 Effect of domestic political fragmentation in Western democracies on IO decision-making authority, 1960–2018

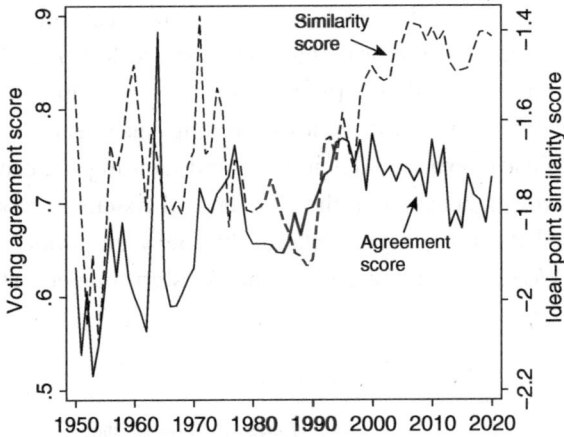

Figure 4.14 Level of voting similarity between Western and non-Western countries in UN General Assembly, 1950–2020

Figure 4.14 tracks the level of voting similarity between Western and non-Western states between 1950 and 2020 using two separate but related measures: "voting agreement" and "ideal-point similarity."[88] The first is simply the share of all votes cast by our sample of twenty-four Western states that are in agreement with non-Western states.[89] The "ideal-point similarity" index is based on a model of similarity of broader voting patterns in a given year (here recalculated for similarity between Western and non-Western states). We see that ideal-point similarity between Western and non-Western countries has increased considerably since a low point in the 1970s and 1980s. The trend is more stable over time when using the voting agreement measure, though here, too, since the 1990s the level of voting agreement between the West and the rest is above the historic norm dating back to the 1950s. However, by either standard we see a marked softening in voting "likeness" between Western and non-Western states since the 1990s. The pattern is evident by the early 1990s in the voting agreement index, and by the mid-2000s using the ideal-point similarity measure.[90]

Did political fragmentation within Western democracies contribute to this leveling off in voting likeness between the West and the rest? In Figure 4.15, we summarize the results of a regression analysis of the relationship between party fragmentation and UN voting similarity between Western and non-Western states.[91] We expect the pattern of voting agreement and ideal-point similarity to be negatively correlated with party fragmentation, even

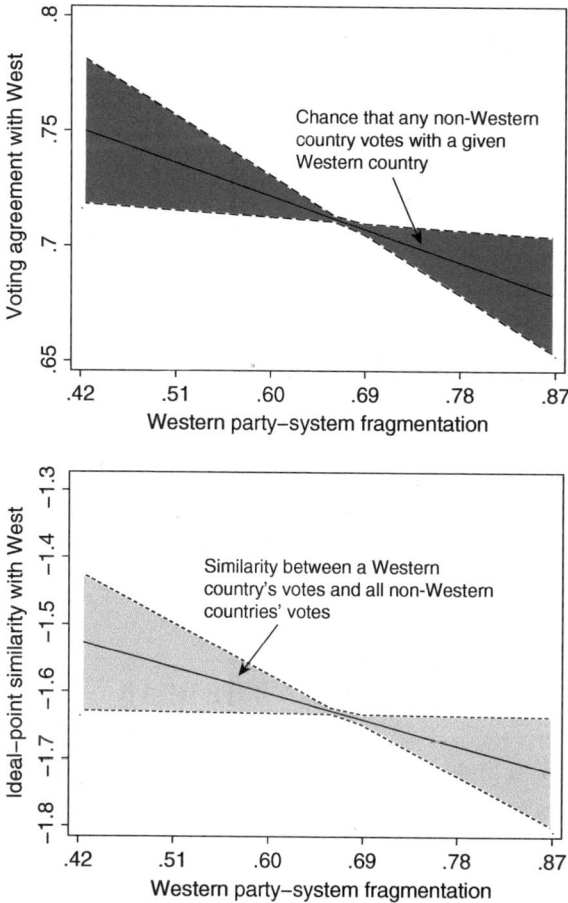

Figure 4.15 Relationship between domestic political fragmentation in Western democracies and voting similarity with non-Western countries in the UN General Assembly, 1960–2018

after controlling for the influence of other factors.[92] The top panel shows the results for the basic "voting agreement" scores. We see that higher party fragmentation does, in fact, result in lower rates of agreement between Western and non-Western countries. The correlation is statistically significant, and the substantive associations are quite substantial. The full sample variation in fragmentation "explains" roughly 35 percent of the variation in UN voting agreement (from the roughly 25th to 60th percentiles in the sample distribution of non-Western agreement). In the bottom panel, we see the same negative pattern for ideal-point similarity, even if it is less significant, statistically and substantively. In both cases, party system fragmentation in a given Western country decreases voting likeness with non-Western countries.

Taken together, these patterns suggest that as Western democracies have become more politically divided and volatile, they have lost some of their international luster as models of good governance. Of course, other factors (e.g., China's growing influence in Africa, Latin America, and other world regions; the West's ill-conceived military interventions in the Middle East in the 2000s) have undoubtedly contributed to the softening in voting correspondence between Western and non-Western states. We have only scratched the surface. Additional research on this issue is needed. But this much is already clear: the political fragmentation disrupting Western democracies today is taking a toll on international openness, international authority, and international affinity with the West. At a time when illiberal powers are challenging the liberal international order from the outside, Western democracies are suffering from what Abraham Lincoln, in another context, famously called "the fire in the rear."[93]

THE FIRE IN THE REAR

The 1990s were a high-water mark for the West's confidence in itself. Many commentators viewed the collapse of the Soviet Union and communism in Eastern Europe as a victory for liberalism and open economies.[94] The end of the Cold War, they argued, represented the permanent victory of liberal democracy and capitalism over the forces of illiberalism and nationalism. Great hopes were pinned on the new European Union's communitarian spirit, the promise of a more open, integrated world order that included China, the former communist countries of Central and Eastern Europe, and other emerging economies, and America's capacity to consolidate, protect, and extend democracy and markets across the globe.

Today, those Western visions of the future look dated and off-target. Western prognosticators significantly underestimated the extent to which nations outside the Western-led system would resist efforts to globalize liberal norms, laws, and institutions. They also greatly overestimated Western democracies' political capacity to support such a far-reaching global agenda. In the absence of a renewed commitment to social democracy, Western governments' turn toward globalism after the Cold War weakened the liberal order's vital center by giving insurgent parties and movements a potent wedge issue to peel off disillusioned voters and put mainstream parties on the political defensive. As support for the vital center declined, and Western democracies became more fragmented, disjointed, and volatile, the liberal order itself has fractured.

New fault lines have emerged over how best to tame the disruptive forces of globalization and to guarantee international security in a world rapidly devolving into competing power centers. Western political fragmentation and volatility have also exposed new vulnerabilities, as illiberal states have sought to capitalize on these divisions by stoking nationalism and fomenting unrest within the West. Once mutually reinforcing, party politics and liberal order are now pulling Western democracies in opposite directions. This brings us to the West's current predicament. Given the intensity of the domestic pressures now confronting Western democracies, any hope of bringing international ends and domestic means back into balance must start from within. The West must find ways to renew the liberal order's domestic purposes and legitimacy. We take up this issue in the next chapter.

5

Bridging the Gap

Writing in the midst of World War II, Walter Lippmann argued that the key to successful international statecraft involves keeping ends and means in balance. "In foreign relations," Lippmann wrote, "a nation must maintain its objectives and its power in equilibrium, its purposes within its means and its means equal to its purposes." When nations fail to balance international commitments and national capabilities, Lippmann added, they "will follow a course that leads to disaster."[1] International relations scholars and foreign policy analysts often equate Lippmann's means to military and economic capabilities, but as Lippmann himself argued, a country's *political* "solvency" is often more critical to effective statecraft than its material means.

Today, Western democracies are suffering from a "Lippmann gap."[2] A large gulf has opened up between Western governments' internationalist ambitions and their domestic political capacity to support them. Donald Trump's presidency, Britain's decision to leave the European Union, and the spread of anti-globalist parties and movements in Europe are the most visible signs of this gap. Yet, as we have shown in this book, today's anti-globalist backlash represents an intensification of a process that has been gathering strength in Western democracies for three decades now, unbowed by terrorism, pandemic, or war. The many commentators who view Russia's invasion of Ukraine as a watershed moment in the reaffirmation of the Western alliance may be proven right in time, but if so, it will be because Western leaders capitalized on the moment by rebuilding the domestic foundations of the liberal international order.

As we have seen, the erosion of domestic support for the liberal order in Western democratic polities took shape in the aftermath of the Cold War, and at the height of Western optimism about the future. In the ensuing years, as Western leaders deepened their nations' commitment to economic integration and institutionalized cooperation while loosening long-standing social protections, domestic support for these foreign policies weakened. Once a wellspring of domestic consensus and coalition-building, foreign policy became a source of political disruption and fragmentation within the West.

Geopolitics and Democracy. Peter Trubowitz and Brian Burgoon, Oxford University Press.
© Oxford University Press 2023. DOI: 10.1093/oso/9780197535400.003.0005

Mainstream parties lost ground to parties on the far left and especially to the anti-globalist right. The gap between Western governments and voters over foreign policy continued to widen. Today, the domestic political foundations of the Western liberal international order are a pale shadow of what they were at the height of the Cold War. The West overreached.

The West's failure to keep international ends and domestic means in balance is not a classic case of imperial overreach. The anti-globalism roiling the advanced democracies is not a backlash against far-flung empires, bloated military establishments, or endless wars on the periphery. It has more to do with Western leaders' overreliance on global markets and international institutions than with war and military expansion. As we have shown, since the end of the Cold War, Western governments failed to maintain high levels of social protection to compensate for the disruptive effects of capitalist growth in an era of hyperglobalization. This eroded public confidence in the liberal order and created opportunities for new politicians and new parties to win over disaffected and angry voters. Freed of Cold War imperatives, nationalist parties in Western countries turned liberalized trade, European integration, and national sovereignty into potent wedge issues against mainstream political leaders and parties.

This has proved costly for the West, domestically as well as internationally. Domestically, the fragmentation of Western party systems made it harder for Western governments to marshal the political power and authority required to deliver on issues their citizens care most about. This fuels voter dissatisfaction which, in turn, leads to greater fragmentation, paralysis, and dysfunction. Internationally, domestic fragmentation has slowed the pace of liberal order-building and eroded confidence in the West. China and Russia have been quick to seize on the erosion of support for Western international leadership to promote alternative, illiberal visions of politics and society and to test Western resolve. Many factors contributed to Putin's invasion of Ukraine, but one was surely the belief that Western democracies were too internally divided and polarized to respond collectively and programmatically.

In this concluding chapter, we discuss the implications of Western overreach, and the strategies now on offer to bring ends and means back into balance. We begin by summarizing our main findings on how Western governments' approach to international order-building has changed over the past seventy-five years and how this resulted in the anti-globalist backlash we see across the West today. We compare and contrast our analysis of Western overreach, anti-globalism, and political fragmentation to other explanations.

Finally, we conclude by discussing the implications of our findings for restoring Western solvency. We consider three paths Western democracies are being urged to follow, and assess their advantages and disadvantages in light of our analysis of the liberal order.

PARTNERSHIP AND POWER

All foreign policy strategies involve choices. Leaders must decide how much to rely on partnership, and how heavily to invest in power. They must decide how much to subordinate national autonomy to international markets and pooled sovereignty, and how much to spend on military power (guns) versus on domestically oriented policies and programs (butter). International relations scholars and foreign policy analysts writing about world politics and foreign policy typically focus on one dimension or the other: on partnership, or on power. There are obvious economies in doing so. Yet, as we have shown, widening the field of vision to include *both* of these key dimensions of international statecraft in a single framework offers real payoffs. We have used this framework to track the evolution of the liberal order from its postwar inception to the current crisis, and to test our arguments about the origins, timing, and extent of Western overreach across twenty-four OECD countries and four hundred political parties.

From virtuous to vicious cycle

The Western-led liberal order has changed in far-reaching ways since its inception seventy-five years ago. During the Cold War era, the United States, Europe, and most of the rest of the OECD shared a vision of international order-building that rested on a robust commitment to both international partnership and military power. At once liberal and realist, the Western-led order balanced the demands of geopolitics and social democracy, and international openness and national autonomy. The social democrats, liberals, Christian democrats, and conservatives that dominated Western governments advanced liberal internationalist policies knowing that those policies would enjoy broad public support and, in turn, pay electoral dividends for them. For over half a century, what was good for liberal internationalism was good for party democracy, and vice versa.

The Western liberal order that took form in the postwar era was not a monolith, of course. Western democracies did not move in lockstep. At any given time, there was significant cross-national variation in levels of government support for partnership and power along the liberal order's Atlantic and Pacific axes, and across party families within the liberal order's many democracies. Western leaders combined partnership and power in varying ways, and to varying degrees, due to differences in their country's geopolitical, domestic, and historical circumstances. Yet to an extent that even the most optimistic postwar planners did not anticipate, the Western liberal order became more open, integrated, and institutionalized. America, Britain, France, West Germany, and most other Western democracies all came to display a level of commitment to partnership and power that sharply distinguished the West from the rest, and that would endure through the Cold War.

What seemed to many like a virtuous cycle between foreign policy and party democracy in Western democracies did not last. The first cracks in liberal internationalism's domestic foundations appeared in the 1980s, when Western governments' turn to neoliberalism in response to the crisis of the 1970s set in motion forces that would weaken the liberal order's party foundations. However, it was not until the Cold War ended that the virtuous cycle between foreign policy and party democracy broke down. In the 1990s, Western governments shifted from a strategy of liberal internationalism that combined power with partnership, to a strategy of globalism that relied increasingly on market forces without corresponding investments in social protections and economic security for their citizens.

Domestic support did not keep stride, however. As we have seen, that support has eroded most starkly in the European democracies, but similar patterns emerged in America, Japan, and in most OECD countries. Across the West, a gap opened up between governments and voters over globalism. Anti-globalist parties successfully exploited these gaps. Support for radical left and radical right parties grew steadily in the 2000s, and then swelled in the wake of the 2008 financial crisis. At the same time, globalism became a source of contestation and division within mainstream parties themselves. The Tea Party faction of the Republican party in the United States and the Brexit faction within Britain's Conservative party broke with the majority over foreign policy.

By the time Donald Trump launched his campaign for the presidency in 2015, the virtuous cycle between foreign policy and party democracy in Western democracies had broken down. Parties and candidates that actively campaigned on the anti-globalist platforms of protectionism, Euroskepticism, and "taking back control from unelected bureaucrats" in Brussels and foreign policy establishments were rewarded by voters. Those that called for expanding and deepening institutional ties lost ground, fragmenting the liberal order's domestic foundations and reducing the political room that Western governments have to make foreign (and domestic) policy. Early hopes that Western democracies' response to the COVID-19 pandemic would foster greater international cooperation were frustrated. Most Western countries responded by entrenching themselves behind their borders and engaging in vaccine nationalism.[3]

Sources of Western anti-globalism

What explains the politicization of foreign policy in Western democracies? How did foreign policies that were once widely accepted by Western voters become political lightning rods? We have argued that our understanding of these questions can be significantly enhanced by considering how international and domestic politics interact to shape the possibilities for foreign policy consensus and fragmentation. As we have shown, since the inception of the Western-led system in the early postwar era, the level of democratic support for liberal international order-building among its member states has been conditioned by two key drivers: the level of geopolitical threat or risk facing Western democracies, and the extent to which Western governments are committed to providing social protection and welfare support for their citizens.

During the Cold War, geopolitical imperatives were a source of political consensus within Western democracies, and between them. For Western governments, a common strategy that relied on military rearmament, military alliances, and economic integration offered the best hope for promoting economic growth and prosperity for their citizens and limiting or containing the political impact of Soviet power and communism in Europe and East Asia. For Western voters, this liberal internationalist agenda was vastly preferable to foreign policy strategies being advanced by parties on the far left and the far right that were considered too soft on communism, or too belligerent and thus too risky in the superpower bipolar nuclear age. For mainstream parties, whose electoral strength in the postwar era depended on their ability to secure broad cross-class support, a strategy that combined partnership and power was not only considered wise statecraft, it was good politics too. A foreign policy strategy that relied solely on one or the other risked alienating center left or center right voters. In short, liberal internationalism was a Goldilocks solution: just the right mix of liberalism and realism, integration and autonomy, and partnership and power.

Cold War imperatives gave Western governments and voters reason to support liberal internationalism. So did the generous social protections that were part and parcel of the postwar welfare state. The nature of these social protections and welfare provisions varied across the OECD, but the different types of welfare models—social democratic, Christian democratic, and liberal—shared common values of full employment, social security, and increasing social equality. The idea that governments were responsible for balancing free markets and economic security was widely accepted, as was the principle that wealth should be redistributed from those that benefited the most from greater economic growth to those who did not. These social bargains limited how far Western governments could open up their economies to trade and capital flows, or transfer decision-making authority to international bodies. They also helped cushion the free market's disruptive effects, while allowing industry, workers, and farmers to reap the benefits of increased exports and imports. Mainstream parties' commitment to these social bargains and understandings secured the votes of critical working-class voters during the Cold War who might otherwise have backed parties on the far left.

Consensus did not mean unanimity within or between the liberal order's members, and every crisis generated new predictions of imminent Western decline. During the Cold War, the most serious test of Western democracies' commitment to liberal internationalism was the crisis that unfolded in the 1970s. The end of the postwar boom and the rise of US-Soviet strategic parity raised new doubts at the elite and mass levels about the postwar liberal order's ability to continue delivering prosperity and security. A rift opened between center left and center right parties over its causes and how best to restore growth and enhance security. The crisis was ultimately resolved in the 1980s on terms favorable to the center right. Center left parties began shifting course, moving toward the right. International markets were liberalized, security alliances were strengthened, and social protections were reined in. Political allegiances and alignments that had defined Western party democracy for decades frayed, but they did not unravel. The center held.

In the 1990s, the political opportunity structure favoring liberal internationalism over other foreign policy strategies changed. The collapse of the Soviet Union removed one of the central justifications in Western democracies for investing in power as well as partnership: the need to contain Soviet power on the Eurasian landmass and protect the free flow of economic activity along the liberal order's Atlantic and Pacific axes. The end of the Cold War also weakened a key rationale for social protection: the need to offer working-class voters an alternative to state socialism and unrestrained capitalism. Even before the Berlin Wall fell in 1989, the postwar balance between international openness and social protection was shifting in favor of the former. This continued in the 1990s. In an effort to win support of the most globalized (pro-globalization) sectors of business and capital and attract younger, educated, middle-class voters who benefited from globalization and supported multilateral cooperation, Western leaders on the center left and center right prioritized market liberalization and institutionalized cooperation. In the 2000s, this globalizing trend gathered momentum.

Western leaders' efforts to globalize the liberal order after the Cold War succeeded in expanding the web of international institutions and making national borders more porous. But it also spurred political fragmentation within Western democracies. Political ideologies and alignments frozen by the bipolar Cold War conflict thawed. Foreign policy strategies sidelined and shunned by Western leaders during the long East-West struggle gained a new lease on political life. As popular fears of communist expansion and nuclear Armageddon receded, Western voters were more willing to take a chance on parties advancing foreign policy platforms that were once considered beyond the pale. At a time when Western governments were retrenching politically, working-class voters and members of the new precariat certainly were not at a loss for reasons to buck mainstream parties.

In response, parties on the far left and far right began to reinvent and reposition themselves. On the far left, parties combined traditional calls for trade protection, defense cuts, and disarmament with transnational issues such as social justice, climate change, and social regulation, relaxing their opposition to all forms of multilateral cooperation. On the far right, long-standing commitments to laissez-faire capitalism were jettisoned in favor of antiglobalism and social protection in hopes of broadening their appeal to the growing ranks of disenchanted working-class voters and the structurally unemployed. As pressure mounted on their flanks in the ensuing years, center left and center right parties have increasingly looked for ways to incorporate key elements of the far left and far right's agenda. Center left parties have become increasingly Green in hopes of winning over younger, educated voters. Center right parties have become more nationalist and nativist, and in many cases more protectionist. At the height of the Cold War, parties on the center left and center right had more in common with each other than they did with the parties further toward the political extremes. Today, in many cases, this is no longer true.

DEMOCRACY AND FOREIGN POLICY

For three decades, domestic opposition to globalism has been building in Western democracies. Understanding anti-globalism's roots is important for several reasons. For one thing, it reminds us how different the path to the West's present predicament is from the one that international relations scholars and foreign policy analysts envisioned in the Cold War's aftermath. Visions of the liberal order's future ranged from liberals who believed democracy and free markets had permanently triumphed over the forces of illiberalism and nationalism, to realists who predicted heightened economic and strategic competition between Western democracies as the imperatives of international anarchy reasserted themselves. If liberals overestimated democracies' immunity to illiberalism and nationalism, realists underestimated the extent to which increasing economic integration and interdependence would be a primary cause of nationalism's revival. What both missed was the extent to which the liberal order's trajectory would be determined by politics *within* the Western democracies.

The politics of overreach

This book is predicated on the argument that our understanding of the origins, consolidation, and retreat of the liberal order can be deepened by taking into account domestic politics. Most accounts of the liberal order's evolution are pitched at the international level—at the level of state-to-state relations. States' geopolitical circumstances do tell us a great deal about their foreign policy choices. During the Cold War, the presence of a common threat had a disciplining effect on politics within Western democracies. However, Western governments' foreign policy choices are also shaped and influenced by similarities in their domestic makeup and political circumstances (e.g., class composition, social commitments). The liberal order arose in an age of Cold War *and* social democracy. Twin pressures—one international, the other domestic—reminded Western leaders of the need to balance international integration and national autonomy, free markets and social protection, foreign and domestic policy.

With the end of the Cold War, Western leaders were under less pressure to keep international ends and domestic means in balance. The collapse of the Soviet empire opened up new international markets for Western capital while reducing the strategic impetus for welfare-state growth at home. The ongoing erosion of the manufacturing sector in Western economies, and the rapid expansion of service sectors and knowledge-based economies, led mainstream parties to put their hand on the scale in favor of globalization and younger, educated middle-class voters who benefited from market liberalization and supported multilateral cooperation. The end result was the growing mismatch between Western international ambitions and the domestic capacity to sustain these ambitions. This is what we have described and documented in this book.

This explanation of Western overextension differs from those who attribute it to political leaders' overreliance on military power. Many international relations scholars and foreign policy analysts argue that America's and, more generally, the West's failed efforts to use war to promote democracy and other ends in Afghanistan, Iraq, and elsewhere fueled nationalism abroad and eroded public trust at home.[4] There is no doubt that the heavy cost in blood and treasure of the failed wars in the Middle East eroded public confidence in Western political elites, to say nothing of the anger and resentment they generated in countries at the receiving end. However, as we have seen, Western publics' disenchantment with foreign policy set in well before their governments began putting "boots on the ground" in the Middle East. Moreover, since the 1990s, Western governments' investment in partnership has been of greater concern to voters, including American voters, than has investment in military power. It has also been costly for mainstream parties at the ballot box. Radical parties have enjoyed more success campaigning against free trade and supranationalism than against defense spending and military preparedness.[5]

Sources of fragmentation

There is a large and growing literature on the effects of globalization on Western party democracy. Numerous cross-national and country-specific studies by economists and political scientists indicate that globalization's uneven domestic economic effects have taken a heavy toll on mainstream parties in recent decades.[6] Economic and social dislocations, especially in hard-pressed manufacturing regions, have made it easier for populist and nationalist politicians to use trade, Euroskepticism, and immigration to exploit voters' economic and social anxieties. Our analysis of the party and electoral consequences of the West's turn to globalism is consistent with these findings. We have shown that Western party fragmentation has increased since the end of the Cold War, and that increasing opposition to the liberalization of international markets and the transfer of national sovereignty to international institutions is one key reason. Anti-globalist parties have gained national vote share by attacking mainstream parties for outsourcing jobs to lower-wage producers like China and Eastern Europe, and for transferring too much discretionary power to supranational institutions such as the European Commission and the WTO.

We have seen too that Western democracies' vulnerability to the siren calls of nationalism and isolationism depends partly on the strength of their commitment to social protection. In general, voters' support for mainstream parties rises when government spending on social security and other welfare entitlements increases. Decline in such spending is one reason that support for mainstream parties has fallen in most Western democracies since the 1990s. This is when many OECD countries began reducing spending on income maintenance. Western governments' commitment to social protection did not keep stride with their efforts to liberalize international markets and expand the scope of international rule through trans- and supranational institutions. Instead of taking steps to shore up domestic support for liberal international order-building, Western leaders' austerity programs made it easier for populist and nationalist politicians to use protectionism, Euroskepticism, and nativism to increase their parties' share of the national vote.

Our analysis breaks new ground by demonstrating the critical role that the Cold War, the Soviet collapse, and geopolitics more generally have played in shaping the domestic politics of liberal order-building across the West. We have shown that the disappearance of a common geopolitical threat after the Cold War expanded the domestic political playing field for political parties on the far left and right that had been marginalized during the Cold War, and that refused to subordinate local grievances and claims to wider post–Cold War international geopolitical logics. This finding is also consistent with work by political scientists who have shown that the end

of the Cold War weakened mainstream parties' support for social protection, and for the welfare state more generally, in Western democracies.[7] For
much of the Cold War, the rivalry between the capitalist West and the Soviet
bloc encouraged both sides of the East-West divide to spend unprecedented
sums on social welfare to demonstrate the superiority of their "system" and
to gain popular support and legitimacy in the struggle. With the end of the
Cold War, an important strategic impetus for Western welfare state growth
disappeared.

The analysis also sheds new light on the fragmentation of Western party
systems. Much of the current debate among scholars specializing in comparative party politics is focused on whether economic or cultural causes
best explain the decline of mainstream parties and the concomitant rise of
populist and nationalist parties. This analytic distinction has its limits. The
differences between explanations that stress the consequences of globalization, technological change, and economic inequality on those "left behind"
and "cultural backlash" theories that emphasize parochialism, nationalism,
and nativism as drivers are often overdrawn. Both explanations point to
voters' feelings of social marginalization and their resentment against political elites, government bureaucracies, and "foreigners."[8] Moreover, political
discontent does not find its fullest political expression on its own. The story
of anti-globalism's rise since the end of the Cold War is not only one of popular demands for social redress. It is also about how political entrepreneurs
and parties on the fringes of Western party systems successfully tapped and
mobilized popular discontent.[9]

The politics of anti-globalism can be read as a textbook case of how parties
and party leaders actively try to mobilize and demobilize voters to gain and
hold on to power. As the ties between mainstream parties and working-
class voters frayed in the 1990s, parties on the far left and especially the far
right sought to capitalize on this opening by using anti-globalism to reach
out to these newly unattached voters. In the case of radical right parties, it
meant abandoning long-held laissez-faire platform positions concerning
international trade in favor of economic nationalism and protectionism.
Meanwhile, in a world where the West faced no peer challenger, voters were
more open and amenable to radical parties' foreign policy appeals. In hind-
sight, it is clear that Western leaders seriously misjudged this electoral threat.
By doubling down on globalization while they were putting the brakes on the
growth of the welfare state and eliminating legislation favorable to unions,
political leaders fed a slow-burning fire. Western democracies have paid a

heavy price for the failure of their leaders to keep international ends and domestic means in balance.

DRIFT OR MASTERY

Can Western leaders bring foreign and domestic policy back into balance? Is it possible for Western governments to renew their commitment to the liberal order without fueling further division within their societies? In this concluding section, we consider three strategies for easing this tension and bridging the gap between international ends and domestic means. Discussion around these choices is already underway. One option is for Western democracies to scale back international commitments to keep the West's international expectations in line with what domestic politics will currently allow. A second approach is to use Great Power confrontation with China and Russia to rekindle Western solidarity and revive domestic support for liberal internationalism. A third strategy is to attack the ends-means problem from the domestic side by investing in a strategy of economic renewal, and thereby gird the West for the return of geopolitics.

Strategic retrenchment

The idea that Western democracies can bring international ends and domestic means back into equilibrium through strategic retrenchment is an alluring one. The argument is especially well-rehearsed in the United States, where an entire school of thought—the "restraint" school—calls on America to reduce its international commitments in Europe, Asia, and elsewhere.[10] Made up of conservative libertarians, anti-imperialist progressives, and balance-of-power realists, the restraint coalition claims that the mainstream foreign policy establishment's preoccupation with promoting "liberal hegemony" has led America astray. Under the guise of liberal order, Democratic and Republican presidents alike have invested far too much blood and treasure in parts of the world that are not vital to America's core national interests. This encourages wealthy allies to free ride on US military might and engage in "reckless driving."[11] It also fuels insecurity among states who are suspicious of US and Western motives. "Restrainers" argue that Putin's invasion of Ukraine was the direct result of American and European efforts to expand NATO into Russia's Near Abroad.[12] The United States, restrainers argue, would be better served by a strategy of "off-shore balancing," where American power is reserved for rare occasions when regional balances of power fail and an onshore US military presence is needed to check an aggressor and restore stability.[13]

A strategy dedicated to reeling in US security commitments is guaranteed to set off alarm bells among America's allies in Asia and Europe. Restrainers acknowledge this, but they contend that weaning allies off the "American pacifier" will force them to take more responsibility for their own security. Meanwhile, restrainers argue that it will reduce the risk that Washington is inadvertently drawn into regional disputes that have little bearing on America's national security, and provide cost savings that might be invested in butter or used for debt reduction. Many American strategists disagree, arguing that a strategy of restraint is neither safer nor cheaper, and risks throwing the baby out with the bathwater. They argue that America's strategic alliances and forward presence in Europe and Asia strengthen regional stability, and are cheaper to maintain than to rebuild once dismantled.[14]

Whatever its geopolitical advantages, a strategy of restraint stands little chance of success domestically. One takeaway from our comparative analysis of Western democracies' foreign policies since World War II is that grand strategies are only as stable and durable as the domestic political foundations they rest on. "Ends-against-the-middle" ideological coalitions like the restraint coalition, which straddle positions on the far left and the far right, are inherently unstable and invariably short-lived.[15] Indeed, such coalitions are rare in Western democracies, and rarer still in two-party systems. Trump's America First strategy, which crudely aped many of the restrainers' core strategic arguments, failed to win broad-based support not only because of presidential incompetence. It also ran up against the limits of security policies that appeal only to ideological extremes. Bipartisan consensus may not be a political prerequisite for programmatic foreign policy change in the United States, but foreign policies that appeal to a broad cross section of voters are a prerequisite for durable, programmatic shifts.[16]

Practical politics aside, restrainers have also misdiagnosed America's ailments. As we have shown, the erosion of domestic support for the liberal order is not unique to America, or due to its overreliance on military power, however misguided. It stems from the abandonment of managed trade, the fraying of the social safety net, and overreliance on multilateral governance. Like their Western counterparts, America's leaders began betting too heavily on the beneficial effects of trade liberalization and multilateral institutions, and became too inattentive or indifferent to the political risks of scaling back the welfare state. As Western governments invested in ever greater economic integration and pooled more and more authority in multilateral institutions, Western voters balked at the rising costs in national sovereignty and their own economic insecurity. In short, restrainers are prescribing the wrong medicine for the patient. American and other Western publics are not clamoring for fewer security commitments abroad. They are demanding greater economic security at home.

Cold War 2.0

If America and other Western democracies cannot bridge the ends-means divide by pulling back internationally, perhaps they can do so through Great Power competition. This is the view of a growing number of policymakers, political analysts, and pundits who see geopolitical rivalry with China and Russia as a way to increase domestic buy-in and support for international order-building.[17] By harnessing the geopolitical tensions to the cause of global activism, the argument goes, Western democracies can drive domestic social transformation, much as they did during the postwar boom that began in the early 1950s. Already political analysts are drawing stark parallels between a "new axis of autocracy" led by China today and the threat posed by the former Soviet Union and its allies in the 1950s.[18] The thinking is that worries about China's growing power might reinforce Western solidarity and keep nationalist pressures in check domestically, just as the Soviet challenge had during the Cold War.

Can a strategy that makes China enemy No. 1 close the solvency gap? Would such a strategy pitting democracies against autocracies foster greater social coherence and common purpose in the West? Yes, up to a point. Foreign threats can boost domestic solidarity. History is full of examples of this dynamic.[19] Indeed, we have shown that the Soviet threat played a critical role during the Cold War in marginalizing liberal internationalism's domestic opponents. Yet the Cold War analogy must be handled with care.[20] As we have shown, Western solidarity did not rest solely on shared concerns about Soviet power and intentions, and the West's *trente glorieuses* owed more to the expansion of international trade than to military spending. Western democracies also found unity and common purpose in embedded liberalism. Social democracy was not sacrificed to fight communism during the Cold War. In the absence of a similar commitment to domestic renewal and inclusive growth, strategies aimed at isolating and "othering" China or other illiberal states are unlikely to generate the broad based domestic buy-in needed to sustain a containment-like Western strategy.

The nature of the geopolitical challenge posed by illiberal powers like China and Russia today is also different. The Soviet Union was a hardened, ideological adversary. The pervasive fear of communism in the West compelled political elites to strike the class compromise between capital and labor that was a hallmark of embedded liberalism.[21] During the Cold War, Western elites had to demonstrate that capitalism was every bit communism's match, and more, by offering workers greater economic security, equality, and opportunity. This critical social dimension of the Cold War rivalry for "hearts and minds" is missing today. China can attract other countries, including many in the West, by offering aid, technology, and infrastructure, but it has no comprehensive, alternative vision to offer the outside world. As diplomatic historian Melvyn Leffler puts it, "Beijing today may disparage Western democracy and tout socialism with Chinese characteristics, but all the world can see that it has embraced a capitalist mentality and nationalist ethos."[22]

Playing the China card to draw Western democracies together is not a sure thing either.[23] Western democracies are growing increasingly anxious about China's strategic ambitions in Eurasia and along the maritime "string of pearls" stretching from the Chinese mainland through the Strait of Malacca to the Horn of Africa. However, those worries are not equally shared by Western governments. Some Western capitals worry more about Beijing's geopolitical ambitions than others—concerns are greater in Washington than in Berlin, and in Tokyo than in Seoul. As a result, Western governments differ on how best to deal with China. Most of America's allies favor some mix of "carrots" and "sticks" or "hedging," hoping to maintain access to China's markets and labor along with the security and protection that American power affords. For most Western democracies, dealing with China is thus a mixed sum, not a zero-sum, game. Here, too, the Cold War analogy breaks down.

During the Cold War, Western security and economic policy toward Moscow were both committed to the same strategic objective: containing Soviet power. Geopolitics and geo-economics were joined up. Since the end of the Cold War, however, the security and economic dimensions of grand strategy have grown increasingly disjointed. One key reason for this was the

West's deliberate policy of promoting China's steady growth and integration into the world economy on the assumption that, as the rewards of trade and economic development spread through society, Chinese leaders would find it hard to resist pressures to liberalize socially and to cooperate with the West on security as well as economic matters. However optimistic that strategy may appear today, China's outsized role in the global economy now makes isolating it a tough sell within the West, let alone in the Global South, where Beijing has a strong economic as well as diplomatic presence.

At a time when economic growth itself has become a planetary threat due to environmental unsustainability, a strategy that aims to isolate China is also dysfunctional. This is not only because China is now the world's largest carbon emitter whose actions will decide a large part of the climate future. It is also because Western democracies are *internally* divided over the China challenge. In the United States, where talk of a "bipartisan consensus" against China is commonplace, there are divisions within America's political parties and among the wider public.[24] The same is true in other Western countries such as Germany and France, where mainstream parties find themselves at odds over China with parties on their left and right, respectively.[25] This could change, of course. Much depends on Beijing's behavior, including how firmly it allies with Russia and other autocratic powers and how aggressively it acts toward its Asian neighbors or repressively within its own borders. Yet it also depends on whether Western parties and interests that see advantage in a strategy of domestic renewal are able to build broad-based domestic coalitions to move their progressive agenda forward with agreement on China.

Domestic renewal

Proponents of domestic renewal argue that Western democracies must return to their postwar roots—to the compromise of embedded liberalism—if they hope to close the Lippmann gap between ends and means.[26] At the heart of the postwar compromise was a progressive grand bargain between capital and labor that ensured crucial domestic support for liberal order-building for decades to come. However, when Western governments turned to neoliberalism in the 1980s and 1990s, and broke the bargain their predecessors had struck between growth and equity, domestic support weakened. Market liberalization created new, sharper divisions between winners

and losers in Western societies, and heightened the distinction between traditional blue-collar workers and the rapidly expanding pool of immigrant
labor joining the labor force. In short, rising economic insecurity and inequality eroded the liberal order's legitimacy within Western democracies.
If Western governments want to restore the liberal order's social purposes,
renewal's proponents argue, they must revitalize their commitment to social
democracy.

Our analysis provides empirical support for this interpretation of the predicament Western democracies now find themselves in. As we have shown,
as government support for social protection weakened, so did domestic support for liberal order. Yet our analysis has also highlighted the pivotal role that
parties have played as intermediaries in this process, from brokering the initial compromise of embedded liberalism, to its subsequent breakdown over
the turn to neoliberalism and globalism in the 1980s and 1990s, to the anti-
globalist backlash roiling Western democracies today. By bringing political
parties into the analytic frame, we have underscored the extent to which the
social bargain underlying the liberal order is contingent on party democracy.
As mainstream parties' willingness to support social protection and economic inclusiveness wavered, so too did voters' enthusiasm for international
openness, institutionalized cooperation, and multilateral governance. Once
dismissed as a problem of little strategic significance, the widening chasm
between Western governments and their voters is now a source of Western
international weakness and vulnerability.

Geopolitics can help bridge this ends-means gap, as it did during the long
Cold War. But alone it cannot restore the liberal order's legitimacy. If Western
leaders hope to rebuild popular support for the liberal order, they must attack
this ends-means problem "from the inside out"—that is, from the domestic
rather than the international side.[27] In eras like the present, when traditional
foreign policy remedies (e.g., trade liberalization) have fallen into disfavor
and the domestic coalitions long associated with those foreign policies have
fragmented, political leaders must find new arguments about the necessity of
international openness and institutionalized cooperation and forge new domestic bargains and political alliances to support them. Policy requires politics. This is the crucial takeaway from our analysis of seventy-five years of
liberal order-building by Western democracies. Today, as in earlier periods
of intense debate and conflict in Western democracies over the proper balance between foreign and domestic policy, these struggles will be shaped and
influenced by political parties competing for electoral advantage.[28]

What precise shape these political arguments and party alliances might take is unclear. Much will depend on the ability of political leaders to reimagine the relationship between foreign and domestic policy and reconnect policies in the international realm to recognizable benefits at home. Western democracies cannot return to the early decades of the postwar liberal order, but they can look for new ways to renew and update their commitment to inclusive growth and economic security for their citizens. This will require innovation in domestic growth regimes centering on strategic localization of productive activities, investment in human capital, quality-of-life supports, and environmental sustainability. Some of these processes are already underway in some progressive internationalist policy initiatives within the OECD. Yet given the depth of the anti-globalist backlash, far more is needed if Western democracies hope to close the solvency gap. By rebuilding support for the liberal order from the inside out, such a strategy of renewal would also put Western democracies on a stronger footing to compete geopolitically in a world where international power and authority are increasingly contested. To paraphrase Lippmann, Western democracies' international purposes would once again be within their domestic means, and their means equal to their purposes.

Appendices

APPENDIX A

Summary statistics for country-year and party-year analyses.

Table A.1 Country-year summary statistics for Western democracies, 1960–2017.

Variable	Obs	Mean	Std. Dev.	Min	Max
Government support for *partnership*: KOF index of globalization policies	1,049	5.06	0.18	4.36	5.27
Government support for *power*: Military spending (% GDP) (logged %)	1,158	1.12	0.36	0.29	2.31
Partnership + Power (standardized sum of policies)	1,005	0.28	0.84	−2.80	2.16
Mainstream party vote share	1,225	76.21	15.49	9.56	99.62
Radical right party vote share	1,225	3.47	6.20	0	30.76
Radical left party vote share	1,225	6.07	7.10	0	44.88
All radical party vote share	1,225	9.55	9.77	0	55.48
Net mainstream vote share	1,225	66.67	22.85	−29.46	99.62
Party-system fragmentation (Rae-legislative fragmentation)	1,195	0.68	0.11	0.35	0.89
Party platform support for *partnership* (mean)	1,225	1.12	0.77	−1.86	2.73
Party platform support for *power* (mean)	1,225	0.25	0.66	−2.20	2.81
Party platform support for *Partnership + Power* (mean)	1,225	1.37	1.05	−2.42	4.82
Manifesto index of voter support for *partnership*	1,225	24.90	22.66	−49.41	119.41
Manifesto index of voter support for *power*	1,225	11.14	17.59	−27.90	116.54
Manifesto index of voter support for *partnership + power*	1,225	36.05	34.47	−45.87	235.95
Manifesto index of voter support for *partnership* (normalized)	1,225	1.32	0.83	−2.0	2.90

(*continued*)

Table A.1 Continued

Variable	Obs	Mean	Std. Dev.	Min	Max
Manifesto index of voter support for *power* (normalized)	1,225	0.50	0.60	−1.40	2.53
Social transfers (% GDP)	1,193	12.44	3.97	3.80	22.79
Geopolitical threat index	840	−0.53	0.61	−1.47	1.05
Government-voter gap: *partnership*	1,049	0.61	0.56	0	2.58
Government-voter gap: *power*	1,158	0.36	0.50	0	2.84
KOF index of political globalization flows (de facto)	1,049	83.71	13.47	38.51	97.72
KOF index of globalization flows (de facto)	1,049	70.37	10.65	45.71	90.69
Voting agreement in UNGA	989	0.73	0.10	−0.26	0.88
Voting agreement of non-West in UNGA	989	0.71	0.10	0.23	0.89
Ideal-point similarity in UNGA	989	−1.49	0.42	−3.27	−0.69
Ideal-point similarity of non-West in UNGA	989	−1.63	0.46	−3.50	−0.596
Right government cabinet share	1,194	38.08	32.23	0	100
Democracy score	1,134	9.70	1.33	−6	10
Party vote share average	1,225	19.46	9.49	6.97	49.77
Voter turnout	1,195	78.01	13.07	39.77	95.72
Union density	1,157	40.80	19.65	7.63	93.65
Unemployment rate	1,195	5.44	3.79	0	23.13
GDP growth	1,182	3.03	1.79	−4.94	10.34
Left-to-right platform average	1,225	−5.59	10.97	−38.58	45.68
Effective number of parties	1,195	3.48	1.30	1.54	8.74

Table A.2 Party-year summary statistics for Western democracies, 1950–2018.

Variable	Obs	Mean	Std. Dev.	Min	Max
Party platform support for *partnership*	6,871	1.16	1.34	−4.29	4.06
Party platform support for *power*	6,871	0.18	1.21	−3.67	3.58
Party platform support for *partnership + power*	6,871	1.34	1.89	−6.17	7.46
Manifesto index of voter support for *partnership*	6,871	20.79	32.63	−113.82	161.20
Manifesto index of voter support for *power*	6,871	7.76	24.77	−108.41	160.45
Manifesto index of voter support for *partnership + power*	6,871	28.55	47.16	−113.82	289.00
Vote share	6,879	15.44	13.86	0	57.71
Vote share (moving-average)	6,879	15.63	13.94	0	56.16
Social transfers (% GDP)	6,868	13.10	3.76	4.32	22.79
Geopolitical threat index	5,595	−0.11	0.59	−0.91	2.35
Party families (1–7)	6,879	3.55	1.90	1	7
Democracy	6,542	9.82	0.71	1	10
KOF de facto globalization	6,313	4.28	0.15	3.86	4.51
Military expenditures (logged)	6,639	0.64	0.49	−0.82	2.14
Unemployment rate	6,879	6.02	4.11	0	26.17
Left-to-right platform (adjusted)	6,871	−2.70	19.74	−74.30	78.85
Decades	6,879	5.62	1.49	3	8
Country code	6,879	33.47	17.62	11	71

APPENDIX B

Detailed statistical results for regression estimations.

Table B.1 Government support for international partnership and military power as a function of social security transfers and geopolitical threat in Western democracies, 1970–2017 (summarized in main text, Figure 3.2 and Figure 3.8).

	(1) Govt. support for *partnership*	(2) Govt. support for *power*	(3) Govt. support for *partnership + power*	(4) Govt. support for *partnership*	(5) Govt. support for *power*	(6) Govt. support for *partnership + power*
Social transfers (% GDP)	0.015***	0.013	0.086***	0.015***	0.013*	0.086***
	(0.003)	(0.007)	(0.019)	(0.003)	(0.006)	(0.017)
Geopolitical threat	0.014	0.066*	0.132	–0.01	0.076*	0.127
	(0.035)	(0.03)	(0.145)	(0.038)	(0.037)	(0.152)
Democracy level	0.005	–0.026	–0.054	0.011	–0.028**	–0.039
	(0.009)	(0.017)	(0.043)	(0.006)+	(0.009)	(0.035)
Trade openness	0.001	–0.001	0	.0004	–0.002	–0.002
	(0.001)	(0.002)	(0.006)	(0.001)	(0.002)	(0.005)
Avg. vote share	–0.003	0.005	0.006	–0.001	0.006	0.008
	(0.003)	(0.004)	(0.016)	(0.002)	(0.004)	(0.014)
Voter turnout	–0.001	0.002	–0.006	–0.001	0.001	–0.009
	(0.002)	(0.004)	(0.012)	(0.002)	(0.003)	(0.010)
Union density	–0.004*	–0.001	–0.019*	–0.004**	–0.001	–0.016*
	(0.001)	(0.002)	(0.008)	(0.001)	(0.002)	(0.007)

	(1)	(2)	(3)	(4)	(5)	(6)
Unemployment rate	0.002	0.001	−0.001	0.0002	−0.002	0.002
	(0.004)	(0.005)	(0.018)	(0.003)	(0.003)	(0.015)
GDP growth	0.001	−0.016	−0.026	0.004	0.004	0.023
	(0.005)	(0.013)	(0.03)	(0.004)	(0.009)	(0.029)
Constant	5.059***	1.629***	2.054	5.041***	1.692***	1.843
	(0.199)	(0.366)	(1.103)	(0.2)	(0.297)	(1.038)
Country dummies	Yes	Yes	Yes	Yes	Yes	Yes
Decade dummies	Yes	Yes	Yes	Yes	Yes	Yes
R-squared	0.897	0.917	0.899	0.897	0.874	0.879
Observations	698	822	698	793	793	793

(1) and (4) DV = Government policy support for international *partnership* (KOF index of globalization policies)

(2) and (5) DV = Government policy support for military *power* (military spending, % GDP)

(3) and (6) DV = Government policy support for *partnership* + *power* (standardized sum of government policy support for *partnership* and for *power*)

Models (1)–(3) are OLS coefficients and robust-cluster standard errors (in parentheses) clustered by country. Models (4)–(6) are seemingly unrelated regression with OLS coefficients and robust-cluster standard errors (in parentheses) clustered by country. Decade and country fixed effects included but not shown.

*** p<0.001, ** p<0.01, * p<0.05, + p<0.1 (two-tailed)

Table B.2 Party platform support for international partnership and military power as a function of social security transfers in Western democracies, 1960–2017 (summarized in main text, Figure 3.3).

	(1)	(2)	(3)	(4)	(5)	(6)
	Party Platform partnership	Party Platform power	Party Platform partnership + power	Party platform partnership	Party platform power	Party Platform partnership + power
Social security transfers	0.043*	0.053*	0.096**	0.043	0.017	0.059
	(0.019)	(0.024)	(0.029)	(0.028)	(0.031)	(0.048)
Radical-left (RL)	−1.12***	−0.9***	−2.02***	−0.981*	−2.20***	−3.18***
	(0.152)	(0.199)	(0.256)	(0.457)	(0.395)	(0.676)
Social Democratic (SD)	0.396	−0.121	0.275	0.025	−0.448	−0.423
	(0.192)	(0.163)	(0.296)	(0.455)	(0.501)	(0.66)
Liberal (L)	0.73***	0.382*	1.112***	0.539	0.196	0.735
	(0.171)	(0.143)	(0.211)	(0.444)	(0.292)	(0.512)
Christian Democratic (CD)	0.709**	0.421**	1.13***	0.847	−0.057	0.79
	(0.194)	(0.138)	(0.252)	(0.521)	(0.477)	(0.765)
Conservative (C)	0.544*	0.782***	1.326**	0.411	0.354	0.765
	(0.249)	(0.178)	(0.38)	(0.596)	(0.417)	(0.832)
Radical-right (RR)	−1.039**	0.981***	−0.058	0.043	−0.224	−0.181
	(0.273)	(0.146)	(0.349)	(0.819)	(0.524)	(0.807)
Social security × RL				−0.01	0.097**	0.087
				(0.034)	(0.029)	(0.048)
Social security × SD				0.03	0.024	0.053
				(0.028)	(0.035)	(0.045)
Social security × L				0.015	0.014	0.029
				(0.034)	(0.02)	(0.04)

	(1)	(2)	(3)	(4)	(5)	(6)
Social security × CD				−0.01	0.035	0.025
				(0.041)	(0.031)	(0.055)
Social security × C				0.01	0.032	0.043
				(0.048)	(0.031)	(0.07)
Social security × RR				−0.076	0.087*	0.011
				(0.06)	(0.039)	(0.055)
Democracy level	0.115	0.156	0.27	0.119	0.144	0.263
	(0.092)	(0.092)	(0.166)	(0.095)	(0.09)	(0.167)
Trade openness	0.005	0.008**	0.013**	0.005	0.008***	0.014**
	(0.004)	(0.002)	(0.004)	(0.004)	(0.002)	(0.004)
Unemployment rate	−0.016	−0.044**	−0.06*	−0.013	−0.043*	−0.057*
	(0.017)	(0.015)	(0.022)	(0.016)	(0.016)	(0.022)
Avg. vote share	0.006	0.018***	0.025**	0.006	0.018***	0.025**
	(0.006)	(0.004)	(0.008)	(0.007)	(0.004)	(0.008)
Left-right platform	−0.014***	0.01**	−0.005	−0.015***	0.01**	−0.005
	(0.003)	(0.003)	(0.003)	(0.003)	(0.003)	(0.003)
Constant	−0.847	−2.595*	−3.442*	−0.892	−2.004	−2.896
	(0.912)	(0.979)	(1.579)	(1.026)	(0.996)	(1.692)
Country dummies	Yes	Yes	Yes	Yes	Yes	Yes
Decade dummies	Yes	Yes	Yes	Yes	Yes	Yes
R-squared	0.397	0.462	0.461	0.401	0.47	0.463
Observations	6935	6935	6935	6935	6935	6935

(1) and (4) DV = Party platform support for international *partnership*

(2) and (5) DV = Party platform support for military *power*

(3) and (6) DV = Party platform support for *partnership* + *power*

Models are OLS coefficients and robust-cluster standard errors (in parentheses) clustered by country. Decade and country fixed effects included but not shown.

*** p<0.001, ** p<0.01, * p<0.05

Table B.3 Manifesto index of voter support for international partnership and military power as a function of social transfers and geopolitical threat in Western democracies, 1960–2017 (summarized in main text, Figure 3.4 and Figure 3.10).

	(1)	(2)	(3)	(4)	(5)	(6)
	Voter support: partnership	Voter support: power	Voter support: partnership + power	Voter support: partnership	Voter support: power	Voter support: partnership + power
Social security transfers	0.88*	0.591	1.348*			
	(0.393)	(0.546)	(0.568)			
Geopolitical threat				−0.483	4.144+	2.375
				(2.768)	(2.679)	(4.286)
Radical-left	−8.336**	−7.44**	−13.843***	−8.113*	−8.842**	−14.952**
	(2.481)	(2.188)	(3.556)	(2.958)	(2.421)	(4.069)
Social Democratic	8.491*	−11.732***	−3.088	8.541*	−12.261***	−3.493
	(3.181)	(2.573)	(3.929)	(3.622)	(2.656)	(4.418)
Liberal	4.413*	3.188	6.862*	4.403	3.304	6.983*
	(2.027)	(1.915)	(2.425)	(2.561)	(2.275)	(2.936)
Christian Democratic	7.682**	2.775	8.615**	6.35**	1.859	6.063*
	(2.232)	(2.029)	(2.928)	(2.034)	(1.993)	(2.841)
Conservative	3.429	14.403***	16.718**	4.164	15.252***	18.065**
	(3.815)	(3.531)	(5.068)	(4.045)	(3.906)	(5.524)
Radical-right	−11.821***	7.379***	−5.243	−10.277***	7.228**	−4.144
	(2.384)	(1.817)	(2.609)	(2.602)	(2.165)	(2.679)
Democracy level	3.085**	1.908	5.164*	2.329*	2.691	4.551*
	(0.874)	(1.534)	(1.851)	(0.856)	(1.546)	(1.79)

	(1)	(2)	(3)	(4)	(5)	(6)
Past globalization flows	-36.212		-68.243*	-22.406		-32.383
	(19.657)		(24.17)	(23.908)		(28.128)
Past military spending		-4.759	-5.854		-2.089	-2.641
		(5.353)	(7.08)		(5.048)	(8.47)
Unemployment rate	-0.184	-0.589	-0.584	0.286	-0.327	-0.115
	(0.352)	(0.309)	(0.435)	(0.372)	(0.315)	(0.5)
Avg. vote share	1.429***	0.821***	2.3***	1.436***	0.787***	2.271***
	(0.155)	(0.112)	(0.185)	(0.162)	(0.115)	(0.201)
Left-right platform	-0.135**	0.083*	-0.011	-0.132*	0.057	-0.026
	(0.044)	(0.039)	(0.049)	(0.052)	(0.042)	(0.055)
Constant	109.085	-26.642	216.267*	69.491	-29.925	88.163
	(80.287)	(16.19)	(98.898)	(98.392)	(14.614)	(119.57)
Country dummies	Yes	Yes	Yes	Yes	Yes	Yes
Decade dummies	Yes	Yes	Yes	Yes	Yes	Yes
R-squared	0.601	0.465	0.657	0.598	0.462	0.645
Observations	6077	6935	6077	5164	5976	5164

(1) and (4) DV = Manifesto index of voter support for international *partnership*

(2) and (5) DV = Manifesto index of voter support for military *power*

(3) and (6) DV = Manifesto index of voter support for *partnership + power*

Models are OLS coefficients and robust-cluster standard errors (in parentheses) clustered by country. Decade and country fixed effects included but not shown.

*** p<0.001, ** p<0.01, * p<0.05

Table B.4 Party platform support for international partnership and military power as a function of geopolitical threat in Western democracies, 1960–2015 (summarized in main text, Figure 3.9).

	(1) Party platform: partnership	(2) Party platform: power	(3) Party platform: partnership + power	(4) Party platform: partnership	(5) Party platform: power	(6) Party platform: partnership + power
Geopolitical threat	0.156	0.42**	0.576**	0.34	-0.328	0.667*
	(0.137)	(0.115)	(0.167)	(0.20)	(0.159)	(0.26)
Radical-left	-1.109***	-0.971***	-2.08***	-1.143***	-0.955***	-2.098***
	(0.176)	(0.212)	(0.276)	(0.177)	(0.222)	(0.299)
Social Democratic	0.365	-0.199	0.166	0.311	-0.168	0.143
	(0.209)	(0.173)	(0.319)	(0.19)	(0.181)	(0.308)
Liberal	0.72**	0.325	1.045***	0.758***	0.289	1.047***
	(0.2)	(0.165)	(0.237)	(0.166)	(0.185)	(0.221)
Christian Democratic	0.664**	0.349*	1.013**	0.652**	0.374*	1.026**
	(0.197)	(0.149)	(0.268)	(0.188)	(0.165)	(0.276)
Conservative	0.583*	0.758***	1.341**	0.565*	0.768***	1.333**
	(0.265)	(0.193)	(0.412)	(0.243)	(0.196)	(0.4)
Radical-right	-0.935**	0.936***	0.001	-1.01*	1.025***	0.015
	(0.297)	(0.157)	(0.381)	(0.403)	(0.191)	(0.438)
Social security × RL				-0.273	0.047	-0.226
				(0.171)	(0.258)	(0.367)
Social security × SD				-0.208	0.082	-0.125
				(0.173)	(0.208)	(0.312)
Social security × L				0.211	-0.201	0.01
				(0.215)	(0.282)	(0.335)

	(1)	(2)	(3)	(4)	(5)	(6)
Social security × CD				0.053	0.075	0.128
				(0.189)	(0.217)	(0.314)
Social security × C				-0.664**	0.351	-0.313
				(0.203)	(0.23)	(0.345)
Social security × RR				-0.233	0.298	0.065
				(0.867)	(0.374)	(1.036)
Democracy level	0.101	0.19*	0.291*	0.099	0.191*	0.289*
	(0.064)	(0.077)	(0.118)	(0.066)	(0.077)	(0.114)
Trade openness	0.007	0.01*	0.017*	0.007	0.011**	0.017*
	(0.007)	(0.004)	(0.008)	(0.007)	(0.004)	(0.008)
Unemployment rate	0.011	-0.021	-0.01	0.012	-0.022	-0.01
	(0.017)	(0.019)	(0.027)	(0.018)	(0.019)	(0.028)
Avg. vote share	0.006	0.018**	0.024*	0.006	0.018**	0.024*
	(0.007)	(0.005)	(0.009)	(0.006)	(0.005)	(0.008)
Left-right platform	-0.014***	0.009*	-0.006	-0.014***	0.008*	-0.006
	(0.003)	(0.003)	(0.003)	(0.003)	(0.003)	(0.003)
Constant	-0.357	-2.418**	-2.775*	-0.338	-2.43**	-2.768*
	(0.64)	(0.816)	(1.176)	(0.639)	(0.809)	(1.113)
Country dummies	Yes	Yes	Yes	Yes	Yes	Yes
Decade dummies	Yes	Yes	Yes	Yes	Yes	Yes
R-squared	0.393	0.457	0.454	0.406	0.462	0.456
Observations	5976	5976	5976	5976	5976	5976

(1) and (4) DV = Party platform support for international *partnership*

(2) and (5) DV = Party platform support for military *power*

(3) and (6) DV = Party platform support for *partnership + power*

Models are OLS coefficients and robust-cluster standard errors (in parentheses) clustered by country. Decade and country fixed effects included but not shown.

*** p<0.001, ** p<0.01, * p<0.05

Table B.5 Analysis of government-voter solvency gap over international partnership in Western democracies, 1970–2017 (summarized in main text, Figure 3.11).

	(1)	(2)	(3)	(4)	(5)	(6)
	Govt.-voter gap over partnership	Govt.-voter gap over partnership	Govt.-voter gap over partnership	Govt.-voter gap over partnership	Govt.-voter gap over partnership	Govt.-voter gap over partnership
De facto all globalization	0.017***	0.026***				
	(0.005)	(0.008)				
De facto economic globalization			0.005***	0.01**		
			(0.002)	(0.004)		
De facto political globalization					0.007	0.015**
					(0.006)	(0.007)
Left-to-right	0.013***	0.004	0.016***	0.004	0.012**	0.005
	(0.003)	(0.006)	(0.004)	(0.006)	(0.005)	(0.006)
Platforms		-0.007		0.001		-0.008
		(0.021)		(0.02)		(0.022)
Democracy level	-0.01		0.003		0.012	
	(0.057)		(0.061)		(0.056)	
Right government	0.001	-0.002	0	-0.002	0	-0.001
	(0.001)	(0.001)	(0.001)	(0.001)	(0.001)	(0.001)
Avg. party vote share	-0.028***	-0.006	-0.029***	-0.004	-0.03***	-0.004
	(0.003)	(0.015)	(0.004)	(0.015)	(0.004)	(0.016)
Voter turnout	-0.004	0.015	-0.005*	0.014	-0.004	0.012
	(0.003)	(0.01)	(0.003)	(0.011)	(0.003)	(0.009)

	(1)	(2)	(3)	(4)	(5)	(6)
Union density	−0.001	−0.007	0	−0.009*	0	−0.006
	(0.004)	(0.004)	(0.004)	(0.005)	(0.004)	(0.004)
Unemployment Rate	0.009	0.009	0.011	0.014	0.002	0.016
	(0.008)	(0.014)	(0.008)	(0.012)	(0.011)	(0.012)
GDP growth	−0.03	0.001	−0.036*	−0.007	−0.02	0.002
	(0.022)	(0.014)	(0.021)	(0.015)	(0.017)	(0.017)
Constant	0.728	−2.11*	1.555**	−0.623	0.897	−1.607
	(0.662)	(1.16)	(0.717)	(0.872)	(0.706)	(1.056)
Country dummies	No	Yes	No	Yes	No	Yes
Decade dummies	No	Yes	No	Yes	No	Yes
R-squared	0.461	0.628	0.435	0.622	0.428	0.624
Observations	934	934	934	934	934	934

(1)–(6) DV = *Government-voter gap over international partnership*

Models are OLS coefficients and robust-cluster standard errors (in parentheses) clustered by country. Decade and country fixed effects included but not shown.

*** $p<0.001$, ** $p<0.01$, * $p<0.05$

Table B.6 (a–e) Government support for international partnership and military power as a function of mainstream and radical party vote share in Western democracies, 1970–2017 (summarized in main text, Figure 4.3 and Figure 4.4).

Table B.6a Effect of mainstream party vote share on Western government for international partnership and military power, 1970–2017.

	(1)	(2)	(3)
	Government support for partnership	Government support for power	Government support for partnership + power
Mainstream party vote share	0.001*	0.001*	0.005**
	(0.000)	(0.000)	(0.002)
Past globalization	0.004*	−0.005*	0.004
	(0.002)	(0.002)	(0.006)
Democracy level	0.013**	−0.015*	−0.001
	(0.004)	(0.008)	(0.021)
Avg. vote share	−0.001	0.005+	0.010
	(0.002)	(0.003)	(0.011)
Voter turnout	−0.000	−0.000	0.000
	(0.001)	(0.003)	(0.008)
Union density	−0.003**	−0.000	−0.012*
	(0.001)	(0.002)	(0.006)
Unemployment rate	0.003	0.003	0.022*
	(0.002)	(0.003)	(0.010)
GDP growth	0.002	−0.003	0.003
	(0.002)	(0.008)	(0.023)
Constant	5.011***	1.301***	0.414
	(0.177)	(0.288)	(0.907)
Decade dummies	Yes	Yes	Yes
Country dummies	Yes	Yes	Yes
R-squared	0.861	0.901	0.856
Observations	1043	1043	1043

(1) DV = Government policy support for international *partnership* (KOF index of globalization policies)

(2) DV = Government policy support for military *power* (military spending, % GDP)

(3) DV = Government policy support for *partnership* + *power* (standardized sum of government policy support for *partnership* and for *power*)

Models are seemingly unrelated regression with OLS coefficients and robust-cluster standard errors (in parentheses) clustered by country. Decade and country fixed effects included but not shown.

*** $p<0.001$, ** $p<0.01$, * $p<0.05$, + $p<0.1$ (two-tailed)

Table B.6b Effect of radical-right party vote share on Western government support for international partnership and military power, 1970–2017.

	(1)	(2)	(3)
	Government support for *partnership*	Government support for *power*	Government support for *partnership* + *power*
Radical-right vote share	−0.002**	−0.004*	−0.015**
	(0.001)	(0.002)	(0.006)
Past globalization	0.004**	−0.004+	0.007
	(0.002)	(0.002)	(0.007)
Democracy level	0.012**	−0.016*	−0.004
	(0.005)	(0.008)	(0.024)
Avg. vote share	−0.000	0.007*	0.015
	(0.002)	(0.003)	(0.010)
Voter turnout	0.000	0.001	0.004
	(0.001)	(0.003)	(0.008)
Union density	−0.003***	−0.001	−0.015*
	(0.001)	(0.002)	(0.006)
Unemployment rate	0.003	0.003	0.021*
	(0.002)	(0.003)	(0.010)
GDP growth	0.002	−0.003	0.002
	(0.002)	(0.008)	(0.022)
Constant	5.016***	0.000	0.473
	(0.162)	(0)	(0.881)
Decade dummies	Yes	Yes	Yes
Country dummies	Yes	Yes	Yes
R-squared	0.866	0.904	0.863
Observations	1043	1043	1043

(1) DV = Government policy support for international *partnership* (KOF index of globalization policies)

(2) DV = Government policy support for military *power* (military spending, % GDP)

(3) DV = Government policy support for *partnership* + *power* (standardized sum of government policy support for *partnership* and for *power*)

Models are seemingly unrelated regression with OLS coefficients and robust-cluster standard errors (in parentheses) clustered by country. Decade and country fixed effects included but not shown.

*** $p<0.001$, ** $p<0.01$, * $p<0.05$, + $p<0.1$ (two-tailed)

Table B.6c Effect of radical-left party vote share on Western government support for international partnership and military power, 1970–2017.

	(1)	(2)	(3)
	Government support for *partnership*	Government support for *power*	Government support for *partnership + power*
Radical-left vote share	0.000	0.005**	−0.013+
	(0.001)	(0.002)	(0.007)
Past globalization	0.004*	−0.005*	0.004
	(0.002)	(0.002)	(0.006)
Democracy level	0.014**	−0.014+	0.005
	(0.004)	(0.007)	(0.021)
Avg. vote share	−0.001	0.005+	0.010
	(0.002)	(0.003)	(0.010)
Voter turnout	−0.000	−0.000	0.000
	(0.001)	(0.002)	(0.008)
Union density	−0.003**	−0.000	−0.012*
	(0.001)	(0.002)	(0.006)
Unemployment rate	0.002	0.003	0.020+
	(0.002)	(0.003)	(0.010)
GDP growth	0.002	−0.002	0.007
	(0.002)	(0.008)	(0.023)
Constant	5.048***	0.000	0.000
	(0.183)	(0)	(0)
Decade dummies	Yes	Yes	Yes
Country dummies	Yes	Yes	Yes
R-squared	0.859	0.904	0.856
Observations	1043	1043	1043

(1) DV = Government policy support for international *partnership* (KOF index of globalization policies)

(2) DV = Government policy support for military *power* (military spending, % GDP)

(3) DV = Government policy support for *partnership + power* (standardized sum of government policy support for *partnership* and for *power*)

Models are seemingly unrelated regression with OLS coefficients and robust-cluster standard errors (in parentheses) clustered by country. Decade and country fixed effects included but not shown.

*** $p<0.001$, ** $p<0.01$, * $p<0.05$, + $p<0.1$ (two-tailed)

Table B.6d Effect of radical party vote share (radical-left plus radical-right parties) on Western government support for international partnership and military power, 1970–2017.

	(1)	(2)	(3)
	Government support for *partnership*	Government support for *power*	Government support for *partnership + power*
All radical vote share	−0.001*	−0.004***	−0.014***
	(0.001)	(0.001)	(0.004)
Past globalization	0.004*	−0.004+	0.006
	(0.001)	(0.002)	(0.006)
Democracy level	0.013**	−0.017*	−0.004
	(0.004)	(0.007)	(0.022)
Avg. vote share	−0.001	0.006*	0.014
	(0.002)	(0.003)	(0.010)
Voter turnout	0.000	0.001	0.004
	(0.001)	(0.002)	(0.008)
Union density	−0.003***	−0.001	−0.015**
	(0.001)	(0.002)	(0.006)
Unemployment rate	0.003	0.003	0.021*
	(0.002)	(0.003)	(0.010)
GDP growth	0.002	−0.003	0.004
	(0.002)	(0.007)	(0.021)
Constant	5.041***	1.339***	0.0001
	(0.164)	(0.283)	(0.001)
Decade dummies	Yes	Yes	Yes
Country dummies	Yes	Yes	Yes
R-squared	0.863	0.907	0.866
Observations	1043	1043	1043

(1) DV = Government policy support for international *partnership* (KOF index of globalization policies)

(2) DV = Government policy support for military *power* (military spending, % GDP)

(3) DV = Government policy support for *partnership + power* (standardized sum of government policy support for *partnership* and for *power*)

Models are seemingly unrelated regression with OLS coefficients and robust-cluster standard errors (in parentheses) clustered by country. Decade and country fixed effects included but not shown.

*** $p<0.001$, ** $p<0.01$, * $p<0.05$, + $p<0.1$ (two-tailed)

Table B.6e Effect of net mainstream vote share (mainstream vote share minus all radical vote share) on Western government support for international partnership and military power, 1970–2017.

	(1)	(2)	(3)
	Government support for *partnership*	Government support for *power*	Government support for *partnership + power*
Net mainstream vote share	0.001*	0.001***	0.005***
	(0.000)	(0.000)	(0.001)
Past globalization	0.004*	−0.005+	0.005
	(0.002)	(0.002)	(0.006)
Democracy level	0.012**	−0.017*	−0.005
	(0.004)	(0.008)	(0.021)
Avg. vote share	−0.001	0.006*	0.011
	(0.002)	(0.003)	(0.011)
Voter turn out	0.000	0.000	0.002
	(0.001)	(0.002)	(0.008)
Union density	−0.003***	−0.001	−0.014*
	(0.001)	(0.002)	(0.006)
Unemployment rate	0.003	0.004	0.023*
	(0.002)	(0.003)	(0.010)
GDP growth	0.002	−0.003	0.002
	(0.002)	(0.008)	(0.022)
Constant	0.000	0.000	0.368
	(0)	(0)	(0.869)
Decade dummies	Yes	Yes	Yes
Country dummies	Yes	Yes	Yes
R-squared	0.862	0.904	0.862
Observations	1043	1043	1043

(1) DV = Government policy support for international *partnership* (KOF index of globalization policies)

(2) DV = Government policy support for military *power* (military spending, % GDP)

(3) DV = Government policy support for *partnership + power* (standardized sum of government policy support for *partnership* and for *power*)

Models are seemingly unrelated regression with OLS coefficients and robust-cluster standard errors (in parentheses) clustered by country. Decade and country fixed effects included but not shown.

*** p<0.001, ** p<0.01, * p<0.05, + p<0.1 (two-tailed)

Table B.7 Party vote share as a function of party platform support for international partnership and military power in Western democracies, 1960–2017 (summarized in the main text, Figure 4.8).

	(1)	(2)	(3)	(4)	(5)	(6)
	Vote share	Vote share	Vote share	Vote share	Vote share	Vote share
Party platform support for *partnership*	−0.06*			−0.086**		
	(0.023)			(0.029)		
Party platform support for *power*		−0.005			0.007	
		(0.023)			(0.032)	
Party platform support for *partnership + power*			−0.034*			−0.048*
			(0.013)			(0.02)
Cold War dummy				−0.254**	−0.159*	−0.209**
				(0.083)	(0.074)	(0.073)
Platform × Cold War				0.058*	−0.021	0.025+
period				(0.031)	(0.024)	(0.018)
Radical-left	−0.078	−0.017	−0.077	−0.077	−0.019	−0.079
	(0.07)	(0.072)	(0.073)	(0.071)	(0.071)	(0.074)
Social Democratic	0.009	−0.016	−0.005	0.008	−0.02	0
	(0.083)	(0.085)	(0.082)	(0.084)	(0.084)	(0.082)
Liberal	0.041	0.001	0.036	0.039	−0.001	0.041
	(0.085)	(0.075)	(0.08)	(0.085)	(0.075)	(0.081)
Christian Democratic	−0.016	−0.055	−0.019	−0.019	−0.059	−0.013
	(0.072)	(0.065)	(0.069)	(0.074)	(0.065)	(0.07)
Conservative	0.212	0.182	0.226	0.211	0.18	0.231
	(0.117)	(0.112)	(0.116)	(0.117)	(0.113)	(0.117)
Radical-right	0.256*	0.332***	0.321**	0.232*	0.324***	0.319**
	(0.095)	(0.086)	(0.094)	(0.098)	(0.085)	(0.096)
Left-right platform	−0.003	−0.002	−0.002	−0.003	−0.002	−0.002
	(0.002)	(0.002)	(0.002)	(0.002)	(0.002)	(0.002)
Lagged vote (t−1)	0.988***	0.988***	0.989***	0.988***	0.988***	0.989***
	(0.002)	(0.003)	(0.002)	(0.002)	(0.003)	(0.002)
Democracy level	−0.027	−0.035	−0.027	−0.023	−0.03	−0.021
	(0.046)	(0.049)	(0.047)	(0.048)	(0.05)	(0.048)

(*continued*)

Table B.7 Continued

	(1)	(2)	(3)	(4)	(5)	(6)
	Vote share	Vote share	Vote share	Vote share	Vote share	Vote share
Past globalization	−0.52	−0.39	−0.48	−0.723	−0.467	−0.652
	(0.541)	(0.543)	(0.565)	(0.515)	(0.552)	(0.554)
Unemployment rate	−0.011	−0.012	−0.012	−0.012	−0.012	−0.012
	(0.008)	(0.008)	(0.009)	(0.008)	(0.008)	(0.008)
Constant	2.744	2.209	2.535	3.767	2.65	3.384
	(2.171)	(2.199)	(2.277)	(2.115)	(2.249)	(2.257)
Country dummies	Yes	Yes	Yes	Yes	Yes	Yes
Decade dummies	Yes	Yes	Yes	Yes	Yes	Yes
R-squared	0.99	0.99	0.99	0.99	0.99	0.99
Observations	5819	5819	5819	5819	5819	5819

DV all models = Party vote share

Models are OLS coefficients and robust-cluster standard errors (in parentheses) clustered by country. Decade and country fixed effects included but not shown.

*** $p<0.001$, ** $p<0.01$, * $p<0.05$

Table B.8 Effect of party platform support for international partnership and for military power on party vote share in Western democracies, moderated by social security transfers and geopolitical threat, 1960–2017 (summarized in the main text, Figure 4.9).

	(1)	(2)	(3)	(4)	(5)	(6)
	Vote share	Vote share	Vote share	Vote share	Vote share	Vote share
Party platform support for *partnership*	−0.155**			−0.055**		
	(0.052)			(0.019)		
Social transfers (% GDP)	0.002	0.006	0.002			
	(0.007)	(0.006)	(0.007)			
Support *partnership* × Social security transfers	0.007+					
	(0.003)					
Party platform support for *power*		−0.115*			−0.011	
		(0.047)			(0.02)	
Support *power* × Social security transfers		0.008*				
		(0.003)				
Party platform support for *partership + power*			−0.119***			−0.034*
			(0.033)			(0.014)
Support *partnership + power* × Social transfers (% GDP)			0.006**			
			(0.002)			
Geopolitical threat				−0.027	0.016	0.022
				(0.08)	(0.071)	(0.075)
Support *partnership* × Geopolitical threat				0.031		
				(0.031)		

(continued)

Table B.8 Continued

	(1)	(2)	(3)	(4)	(5)	(6)
	Vote share	Vote share	Vote share	Vote share	Vote share	Vote share
Support power × Geopolitical threat					-0.019	
					(0.034)	
Support partnership + power × Geopolitical threat						0.004
						(0.023)
Radical-left	-0.091	-0.029	-0.092	-0.059	-0.01	-0.066
	(0.062)	(0.062)	(0.063)	(0.063)	(0.062)	(0.065)
Social Democratic	0.006	-0.031	-0.019	0.12	0.087	0.1
	(0.076)	(0.076)	(0.075)	(0.08)	(0.081)	(0.08)
Liberal	0.042	0	0.035	0.02	-0.021	0.015
	(0.063)	(0.06)	(0.062)	(0.069)	(0.066)	(0.068)
Christian Democratic	-0.012	-0.063	-0.022	-0.026	-0.061	-0.03
	(0.058)	(0.059)	(0.058)	(0.063)	(0.064)	(0.064)
Conservative	0.21*	0.185*	0.23**	0.285**	0.248**	0.287**
	(0.084)	(0.088)	(0.087)	(0.09)	(0.095)	(0.093)
Radical-right	0.261**	0.32***	0.323***	0.264*	0.341**	0.33**
	(0.095)	(0.094)	(0.094)	(0.104)	(0.104)	(0.104)
Left-right platform (adjusted)	-0.003*	-0.002	-0.002	-0.002	-0.001	-0.002
	(0.001)	(0.001)	(0.001)	(0.001)	(0.001)	(0.001)
Lagged vote share	0.988***	0.988***	0.989***	0.987***	0.987***	0.988***
	(0.002)	(0.002)	(0.002)	(0.002)	(0.002)	(0.002)

Democracy level	-0.011	-0.023	-0.011	-0.033	-0.032	-0.024
	(0.038)	(0.038)	(0.038)	(0.04)	(0.039)	(0.04)
Globalization de facto	-0.567	-0.377	-0.512	-0.098	-0.004	-0.05
	(0.346)	(0.343)	(0.348)	(0.38)	(0.384)	(0.389)
Unemployment	-0.021**	-0.021**	-0.023***	-0.008	-0.008	-0.009
	(0.006)	(0.006)	(0.006)	(0.005)	(0.005)	(0.005)
Constant	2.739	1.899	2.484	0.777	0.265	0.447
	(1.42)	(1.42)	(1.436)	(1.55)	(1.586)	(1.59)
Country dummies	Yes	Yes	Yes	Yes	Yes	Yes
Year dummies	Yes	Yes	Yes	Yes	Yes	Yes
R-squared	0.99	0.99	0.99	0.99	0.99	0.99
Observations	5819	5819	5819	4991	4991	4991

DV all models = Party vote share

Models are OLS coefficients and robust-cluster standard errors (in parentheses) clustered by country. Decade and country fixed effects included but not shown.

*** p<0.001, ** p<0.01, * p<0.05, + p<0.10

Table B.9 Effect of party-system fragmentation on de facto globalization (1970–2018) and on voting affinity with Western countries in UN General Assembly (1960–2018) (summarized in the main text, Figure 4.11 and Figure 4.15).

	(1)	(2)	(3)	(4)	(5)	(6)
	KOF de facto globalization all (econ., pol., soc.)	KOF de facto political globalization	Agree with West	Non-West agree with West	Ideal-point similarity with West	Non-West ideal-point similarity with West
Party-system fragmentation	−11.83*	−20.866+	−0.137*	−0.16*	−0.345	−0.431+
	(5.348)	(11.878)	(0.055)	(0.062)	(0.22)	(0.24)
Social transfers (% GDP)	0.334*	−0.161	−0.006*	−0.007*	−0.029**	−0.032**
	(0.119)	(0.236)	(0.002)	(0.002)	(0.01)	(0.011)
Democracy level	0.739***	1.363**	−0.009***	−0.011***	−0.048**	−0.063***
	(0.111)	(0.386)	(0.002)	(0.002)	(0.014)	(0.016)
Union density	−0.055	−0.131+	0.0001	0.0001	−0.001	−0.002
	(0.045)	(0.069)	(0.001)	(0.001)	(0.003)	(0.003)
Unemployment rate	0.373**	0.362	0.003	0.002	0.007	0.006
	(0.1)	(0.208)	(0.002)	(0.003)	(0.01)	(0.011)
GDP growth	−0.112	−0.468	−0.004+	−0.005*	−0.02*	−0.024*
	(0.131)	(0.299)	(0.002)	(0.002)	(0.01)	(0.011)
Voter turnout	−0.073	−0.007	−0.001	−0.001	−0.001	−0.001
	(0.07)	(0.165)	(0.001)	(0.001)	(0.004)	(0.004)
Past trade openness			0.0001*	0.0001*	0.002**	0.002**
			(0.0001)	(0.0001)	(0.001)	(0.001)

Constant	73.45***	103.68***	1.068***	1.1***	−0.015	0.144
	(9.192)	(25.054)	(0.095)	(0.107)	(0.353)	(0.39)
Country dummies	Yes	Yes	Yes	Yes	Yes	Yes
Year dummies	Yes	Yes	Yes	Yes	Yes	Yes
R-squared	0.939	0.871	0.826	0.815	0.841	0.835
Observations	954	954	922	922	922	922

DV models given by column heading. Models are OLS coefficients and robust-cluster standard errors (in parentheses) clustered by country. Decade and country fixed effects included but not shown.

*** $p<0.001$, ** $p<0.01$, * $p<0.05$, + $p<0.10$

Table B.10 (a–c) International organization (IO) authority as a function of party-system fragmentation in Western democracies, 1960–2018 (summarized in the main text, Figure 4.13).

Table B.10a Time series analysis of authority measures in twenty-five IOs with strong Western membership, 1960–2018.

	(1)	(2)	(3)	(4)
	Δ Delegation	Δ Pooling	Δ Dispute-settlement	Δ IO authority
Δ Party-system	−0.137**	−0.174**	−0.064	−0.655**
fragmentation	(0.048)	(0.065)	(0.12)	(0.231)
Constant	0.001	0	0.002	0.005
	(0.001)	(0)	(0.002)	(0.005)
AR(1)	0.724**	0.323	0.611	0.736*
	(0.238)	(0.404)	(0.653)	(0.37)
MA(1)	−0.472	−0.797**	−0.507	−0.584
	(0.27)	(0.256)	(0.661)	(0.395)
Sigma: const.	0.003***	0.003***	0.008***	0.016***
	(0)	(0)	(0)	(0.001)
Log likelihood	240.9	250.9	200.5	251.2
Observations	57	57	57	57

Standard errors are in parentheses
*** $p<0.001$, ** $p<0.01$, * $p<0.05$

Table B.10b Time series analysis of authority measures in thirty-five IOs with little Western membership, 1960–2018.

	(1)	(2)	(3)	(4)
	Δ Delegation	Δ Pooling	Δ Dispute-settlement	Δ IO authority
Δ Party-system	0.001	0.139	−0.32	0.147
fragmentation	(0.125)	(0.15)	(0.353)	(0.743)
Constant	0.002	0	0.004*	0.007
	(0.001)	(0.001)	(0.002)	(0.009)
AR(1)	0.807**	−0.916***	−0.813***	0.849***
	(0.25)	(0.078)	(0.132)	(0.24)
MA(1)	−0.623	1	1	−0.677
	(0.355)	(0)	(104.713)	(0.357)
Sigma: constant	0.005***	0.006***	0.011	0.029***
	(0)	(0)	(0.563)	(0.002)
Log likelihood	200.9	198.9	188.5	179.2
Observations	57	57	57	57

Standard errors are in parentheses
*** $p<0.001$, ** $p<0.01$, * $p<0.05$

Table B.10c Alternative specifications for IO delegation: Time series analysis of delegation for IOs with strong Western membership that underwent change in level of delegated authority.

	(1)	(2)	(3)	(4)
	Δ Delegation	Δ Delegation	Δ Delegation	Δ Delegation
Δ Party-system	−0.113+	−0.133*		
fragmentation	(0.058)	(0.058)		
Δ Effective #			−0.008*	−0.01*
parties			(0.004)	(0.005)
Δ Mainstream vote		−0.0001		−0.0002
		(0.0001)		(0.0002)
Constant	0.001*	0.001*	0.004	0.001*
	(0.001)	(0.001)	(0.156)	(0.001)
AR(1)	0.019	0.036	−0.004	0.019
	(0.238)	(0.161)	(0.156)	(0.147)
Sigma: const.	0.003***	0.003***	0.003***	0.003***
	(0.0002)	(0.0002)	(0.0002)	(0.0003)
Log likelihood	245.4	246.02	245.4	246.2
Observations	57	57	57	57

Standard errors are in parentheses

*** $p<0.001$, ** $p<0.01$, * $p<0.05$, + $p<0.10$

APPENDIX C

List of parties in Western countries by party family.

Radical Left Parties (RL)	
Country	**RL party name**
Austria	Austrian Communist Party
Denmark	Left Socialist Party
Denmark	Danish Communist Party
Denmark	Common Course
Denmark	Red-Green Unity List
Denmark	Socialist People's Party
Finland	Finnish People's Democratic Union
Finland	Democratic Alternative
Finland	Left Wing Alliance
France	Left Front
France	French Communist Party
France	Left Radical Party
France	Indomitable France
Germany	Party of Democratic Socialism
Germany	The Left. Party of Democratic Socialism
Germany	The Left
Greece	Coalition of the Radical Left
Greece	Communist Party of Greece
Greece	Progressive Left Coalition
Greece	Coalition of the Radical Left
Greece	Democratic Left
Greece	Popular Unity
Ireland	United Left Alliance
Ireland	Workers' Party
Ireland	Democratic Left Party
Ireland	Socialist Party
Ireland	People Before Profit Alliance
Ireland	Anti-Austerity Alliance
Ireland	Workers and Unemployment Action
Ireland	We Ourselves
Ireland/UK	We Ourselves
Italy	Civil Revolution
Italy	Proletarian Unity Party
Italy	Proletarian Democracy
Italy	Communist Refoundation Party
Italy	Party of Italian Communists
Italy	Democrats of the Left
Italy	Rose in the Fist
Italy	Left Ecology Freedom
Japan	Japanese Communist Party
Luxembourg	Communist Party of Luxembourg
Luxembourg	The Left

Radical Left Parties (RL)

Country	RL party name
Netherlands	Communist Party of the Netherlands
Netherlands	Socialist Party
Netherlands	Pacifist Socialist Party
Norway	Norwegian Communist Party
Norway	Socialist Left Party
Portugal	Popular Democratic Union
Portugal	Left Bloc
Portugal	Portuguese Communist Party
Portugal	Unified Democratic Coalition
Spain	Popular Unity
Spain	We Can
Spain	United Left
Sweden	Left Party
Switzerland	Swiss Labour Party

Social Democratic Parties (SD)

Country	SD party name
Australia	Australian Labor Party
Australia	Australian Democrats
Australia	Democratic Labor Party
Austria	Austrian Social Democratic Party
Belgium	Socialist Party Different—Spirit
Belgium	Belgian Socialist Party
Belgium	Socialist Party Different
Belgium	Francophone Socialist Party
Belgium	Social, Progressive, International, Democratic and Forward-Looking
Canada	New Democratic Party
Denmark	Social Democratic Party
Finland	Social Democratic League of Workers
Finland	Finnish Social Democrats
France	Socialist Party
Germany	Social Democratic Party of Germany
Greece	Panhellenic Socialist Movement
Greece	Democratic Social Movement
Greece	The River
Ireland	Labour Party
Ireland	Social Democrats
Italy	Pannella-Sgarbi List
Italy	Italian Socialist Party
Italy	Italian Renewal
Italy	Unified Italian Socialist Party-Italy
Italy	Olive Tree
Italy	Italian Democratic Socialist Party
Japan	Social Democratic Party
Japan	Democratic Socialist Party

Social Democratic Parties (SD)	
Country	**SD party name**
Japan	Social Democratic Federation
Luxembourg	Socialist Workers' Party of Luxembourg
Netherlands	Radical Political Party
Netherlands	Labour Party
Netherlands	DENK
New Zealand	New Zealand Labour Party
New Zealand	The Alliance
Norway	Labour Party
Portugal	Popular Democratic Movement
Portugal	Socialist Party
Portugal	Democratic Renewal Party
Portugal	Democratic Intervention
Portugal	Association of Independent Social Democrats
Portugal	Leftwing Union for the Socialist Democracy
Spain	Spanish Socialist Workers' Party
Sweden	Social Democratic Labour Party
Switzerland	Social Democratic Party of Switzerland
Switzerland	Independents' Alliance
United Kingdom	Labour Party
United Kingdom	Social Democratic Party
United Kingdom	Social Democratic and Labour Party
United States	Democratic Party

Liberal parties (L)	
Country	**L party name**
Australia	Palmer United Party
Australia	Nick Xenophon Team
Austria	Liberal Forum
Austria	The New Austria and Liberal Forum
Belgium	Party of Liberty and Progress
Belgium	Open Flemish Liberals and Democrats
Belgium	Liberal Reformation Party
Belgium	Liberal Reformation Party— Francophone Democratic Front
Belgium	Liberal Party
Belgium	Reform Movement
Belgium	List Dedecker
Canada	Liberal Party of Canada
Denmark	Liberal Alliance
Denmark	Danish Social-Liberal Party
Denmark	Liberals
Denmark	Independents' Party
Denmark	Liberal Centre
Finland	Liberal People's Party
Finland	Young Finnish Party

Liberal Parties (L)

Country	L party name
France	Radical Party
France	Republic Onwards!
France	Union of Democrats and Independents
Germany	Free Democratic Party
Greece	Union of Centrists
Ireland	Progressive Democrats
Italy	Italian Republican Party
Italy	Italian Liberal Party
Italy	Daisy—Democracy Is Freedom
Italy	Democratic Party
Italy	Democratic Centre
Italy	Civic Choice
Italy	List Di Pietro—Italy of Values
Japan	Your Party
Japan	Liberal League
Japan	New Party Nippon
Luxembourg	Democratic Party
Netherlands	Democrats '66
Netherlands	People's Party for Freedom and Democracy
New Zealand	ACT New Zealand
New Zealand	United Future New Zealand
New Zealand	Progressive Party
Norway	New People's Party
Norway	Liberal Party
Spain	Citizens
Spain	Union of the Democratic Centre/ Centrist Bloc
Spain	Popular Democratic Party
Spain	Liberal Party
Spain	Union, Progress and Democracy
Sweden	Liberal People's Party
Switzerland	FDP. The Liberals
United Kingdom	Liberal Party
United Kingdom	Liberal Democrats

Christian Democratic Parties (CD)

Country	CD party name
Austria	Austrian People's Party
Belgium	Francophone Christian Social Party
Belgium	Christian Democratic and Flemish
Belgium	Christian Social Party
Denmark	Christian People's Party
Finland	Christian Democrats in Finland
France	Popular Republican Movement
France	Progress and Modern Democracy

Christian Democratic Parties (CD)	
Country	**CD party name**
France	Centre, Democracy and Progress
France	Reformers' Movement
Germany	Christian Democratic Union/Christian Democrats
Germany	Centre Party
Greece	Union of the Democratic Centre
Greece	New Democracy
Greece	Political Spring
Ireland	Family of the Irish
Italy	Italian Popular Party
Italy	Christian Democratic Centre
Italy	White Flower
Italy	Pact for Italy
Italy	Democratic Alliance
Italy	Union of the Center
Japan	New Clean Government Party
Luxembourg	Christian Social People's Party
Netherlands	Christian Democratic Appeal
Netherlands	Catholic People's Party
Netherlands	Anti-Revolutionary Party
Netherlands	Democratic Socialists '70
Netherlands	Christian Historical Union
Netherlands	Christian Union
Netherlands	Reformed Political League
Netherlands	Reformatory Political Federation
Norway	Christian People's Party
Portugal	Social Democratic Center-Popular Party
Spain	Centre Democrats
Sweden	Christian Democrats
Switzerland	Christian Democratic People's Party
Switzerland	Protestant People's Party of Switzerland
Switzerland	Liberal Party of Switzerland
Switzerland	Christian Social Party

Conservative Parties (C)	
Country	**C party name**
Australia	Liberal Party of Australia
Australia	Liberal National Party of Queensland
Australia	Country Liberal Party
Canada	Progressive Conservative Party
Canada	Reform Party of Canada
Canada	Canadian Reform Conservative Alliance
Canada	Conservative Party of Canada
Denmark	Centre Democrats
Denmark	Conservative People's Party
Finland	National Coalition

Conservative Parties (C)	
Country	**C party name**
France	Union for a New Majority—Gaullist
France	Union for a New Majority—Conservatives
France	Union for the Defence of Traders and Artisans
France	Democratic Mouvement
France	Rally for the Republic
France	The Republicans
France	New Centre
France	Centrist Alliance
Germany	German Party
Greece	National Alignment
Ireland	Soldiers of Destiny
Italy	People of Freedom
Italy	Go Italy
Italy	New Italian Socialist Party
Italy	House of Freedom
Italy	Labour and Freedom List
Japan	Japan Restoration Party
Japan	Liberal Democratic Party
Japan	New Liberal Club
Japan	Japan Renewal Party
Japan	New Frontier Party
Japan	Democratic Party of Japan
Japan	Liberal Party
Japan	New Conservative Party
Japan	People's New Party
Japan	Independent's Party
Japan	Japan Innovation Party
New Zealand	New Zealand National Party
New Zealand	New Zealand First Party
Norway	Conservative Party
Portugal	Portugal Ahead
Portugal	Social Democratic Party
Spain	People's Party
Sweden	Moderate Coalition Party
Switzerland	Conservative Democratic Party of Switzerland
United Kingdom	Conservative Party
United Kingdom	Ulster Unionist Party
United States	Republican Party

Radical Right Parties (RR)	
Country	**RR party name**
Australia	Katter's Australian Party

Radical Right Parties (RR)	
Country	**RR party name**
Austria	Austrian Freedom Party
Austria	Alliance for the Future of Austria
Belgium	Flemish Bloc
Belgium	Flemish Interest
Denmark	Danish People's Party
Finland	True Finns
France	National Front
Germany	Alternative for Germany
Greece	Popular Orthodox Rally
Greece	Golden Dawn
Greece	Independent Greeks
Ireland	Republican Party
Italy	Brothers of Italy—National Centre.
Italy	National Alliance
Italy	Northern League
Japan	Party for Future Generations
Netherlands	Livable Netherlands
Netherlands	Centre Party
Netherlands	Centre Democrats
Netherlands	List Pim Fortuyn
Netherlands	Party of Freedom
Netherlands	Forum for Democracy
Norway	Progress Party
Portugal	Popular Monarchist Party
Sweden	Sweden Democrats
Switzerland	Swiss Democrats
Switzerland	Federal Democratic Union
Switzerland	Swiss People's Party
Switzerland	Ticino League
United Kingdom	United Kingdom Independence Party

Categorical measures of government support for liberal internationalism.

Table D.1 Government support for liberal internationalism (*partnership* + *power*, categorical) as a function of social protection and geopolitical threat in Western democracies, 1970–2015 (see discussion of Figures 3.1 and 3.2 in main text).

	(1)	(2)	(3)		
	Liberal Internationalism	Liberal Internationalism	Outcome 1: Isolationism relative to liberal internationalism	Outcome 2: Nationalism relative to liberal internationalism	Outcome 3: Globalism relative to liberal internationalism
Social transfers (% GDP)	0.82***	0.985***	0.312	−0.481**	−0.721*
	(0.146)	(0.171)	(0.399)	(0.176)	(0.347)
Geopolitical threat	−0.324	−1.306	0.437	−2.301	−4.118
	(1.173)	(1.113)	(1.973)	(1.314)	(2.106)
Democracy level	9.539**	13.424***	−1.383	−2.638***	−1.042
	(3.225)	(3.827)	(0.992)	(0.639)	(1.248)
Trade openness	−0.119***	−0.152***	0.195**	0.035	0.193**
	(0.029)	(0.033)	(0.074)	(0.042)	(0.073)
Avg. party vote	−0.415**	−0.501**	−0.295	0.171	−0.303
	(0.16)	(0.155)	(0.21)	(0.112)	(0.244)
Voter turnout	0.215***	0.163*	0.019	0.15	−0.631***
	(0.058)	(0.066)	(0.162)	(0.078)	(0.181)
Union density	−0.172***	−0.185***	−0.075	0.061	0.229*
	(0.048)	(0.042)	(0.097)	(0.053)	(0.095)

(continued)

Table D.1 Continued

	(1)	(2)	(3)		
	Liberal Internationalism	Liberal Internationalism	Outcome 1: Isolationism relative to liberal internationalism	Outcome 2: Nationalism relative to liberal internationalism	Outcome 3: Globalism relative to liberal internationalism
Unemployment rate	−0.3	−0.458**	−0.538	−0.368*	−0.233
	(0.176)	(0.158)	(0.297)	(0.167)	(0.259)
GDP growth	−0.094	−0.213	0.608*	0.226	0.273
	(0.189)	(0.197)	(0.301)	(0.209)	(0.251)
Constant	−98.694**	−136.889***	−45.253	1.865	24.155
	(32.486)	(38.117)	(5154.218)	(8.164)	(1260.921)
Country dummies	Yes	No	Yes	Yes	Yes
Decade dummies	Yes	Yes	Yes	Yes	Yes
Pseudo R^2	.762	.796	.815	.815	.815
Observations	698	496	953	953	953

Models (1) and (2): DV = Government policy support for liberal internationalism (1 = KOF globalization policies>median AND military spending>median; 0 = KOF policies and/or military spending<median)

Model (3): DV = Government policy support for liberal internationalism in categories (1 = lower-than-median KOF policies and lower-than-median military spending; 2 = lower-than-median KOF policies and higher-than-median military spending; 3 = higher-than-median KOF policies and lower-than-median military spending; 4 = higher-than-median KOF policies and higher-than-median military spending)

Model (1) is logistic regression with country and decade dummies (not shown).

Model (2) is multi-level random intercept logistic regression with country as level 2, country-year as level 1, with decade dummies (not shown).

Model (3) is multinomial logit with baseline value being outcome 4 (liberal internationalism = high government support for partnership and high government support for power).

Table D.2 Government support for liberal internationalism (*partnership + power*, categorical) as a function of net mainstream vote share in Western democracies, 1970–2017 (relevant to Figure 4.1).

| | (1) | (2) | (3) | | |
	Liberal internationalism	Liberal internationalism	Outcome 1: Isolationism relative to lib. int'lsm.	Outcome 2: Nationalism relative to lib. int'lsm	Outcome 3: Globalism relative to lib. int'lsm
Net mainstream vote	0.037***	0.045***	−0.024***	−0.029***	−0.019***
	(0.01)	(0.012)	(0.004)	(0.005)	(0.004)
Democracy level	9.454*	9.888**	0.763***	−0.177	0.946***
	(4.149)	(3.218)	(0.159)	(0.093)	(0.162)
Trade openness	−0.143***	−0.154***	0.011***	−0.008*	0.02***
	(0.021)	(0.026)	(0.003)	(0.004)	(0.003)
Avg. party vote	−0.093	−0.105*	0.014	0.064***	−0.03*
	(0.05)	(0.049)	(0.012)	(0.013)	(0.014)
Voter turnout	0.2***	0.146**	−0.014	0.014	−0.02*
	(0.048)	(0.047)	(0.008)	(0.01)	(0.008)
Union density	−0.081*	−0.082**	0.012	0.022**	0.029***
	(0.032)	(0.03)	(0.007)	(0.008)	(0.007)
Unemployment rate	0.073	0.058	0.017	0.029	−0.021
	(0.091)	(0.091)	(0.027)	(0.035)	(0.028)
GDP growth	−0.463***	−0.561***	0.406***	0.056	0.221***
	(0.128)	(0.134)	(0.058)	(0.066)	(0.053)

(continued)

Table D.2 Continued

	(1)	(2)	(3)		
	Liberal internationalism	Liberal internationalism	Outcome 1: Isolationism relative to lib. int'lsm.	Outcome 2: Nationalism relative to lib. int'lsm	Outcome 3: Globalism relative to lib. int'lsm
Constant	−99.742*	−104.023**	−11.263***	−1.854	−10.222***
	(40.933)	(32.851)	(1.722)	(1.112)	(1.694)
Country dummies	Yes	Yes	Yes	Yes	Yes
Decade dummies	Yes	No	Yes	Yes	Yes
Pseudo R²	0.495	0.492	0.313	0.313	0.313
Observations	659	954	1307	1307	1307

Models (1) and (2): DV = Government policy support for liberal internationalism (1 = KOF globalization policies > median AND military spending > median; 0 = KOF policies and/or military spending < median)

Model (3): DV = Government policy support for liberal internationalism in categories (1 = lower-than-median KOF policies AND higher-than-median military spending; 2 = lower-than-median KOF policies AND higher-than-median military spending; 3 = higher-than-median KOF policies AND lower-than-median military spending; 4 = higher-than-median KOF policies AND higher-than-median military spending).

Models (1) is logistic regression with country and decade dummies (not shown).

Models (2) is multi-level random intercept logistic regression with country as level 2, country-year as level 1, with decade dummies (not shown).

Model (3) is multinomial logit with outcome 4 (liberal internationalism) as baseline.

APPENDIX E

Effect of government-voter gap on party politics.

Table E.1 Government-voter gap over international partnership and military power as a function of party vote share and party-system fragmentation in Western democracies, 1970–2018.

	(1) Radical right vote share	(2) Radical left vote share	(3) All radical vote share	(4) Mainstream vote share	(5) Net mainstream vote share	(6) Party-system fragmentation
Government-voter gap: partnership	2.378*	0.523	2.902*	-2.056	-4.957	2.975*
	(0.966)	(1.042)	(1.348)	(2.138)	(3.312)	(1.282)
Government-voter gap: power	-0.859	0.035	-0.824	0.046	0.869	0.027
	(1.018)	(1.177)	(1.723)	(1.387)	(2.922)	(0.836)
Democracy	-0.485	-0.269	-0.754	1.064	1.818*	-0.716*
	(0.327)	(0.283)	(0.442)	(0.53)	(0.847)	(0.27)
Trade openness	-0.027	0.026	-0.001	-0.071	-0.069	0.016
	(0.023)	(0.04)	(0.05)	(0.057)	(0.104)	(0.03)
Average party vote share	0.045	-0.216	-0.171	0.327	0.498	-0.62**
	(0.142)	(0.109)	(0.184)	(0.258)	(0.389)	(0.19)
Voter turnout	-0.093	0.217	0.123	0.19	0.066	0.094
	(0.149)	(0.108)	(0.186)	(0.122)	(0.276)	(0.132)
Union density	0.013	-0.009	0.005	-0.018	-0.023	-0.066
	(0.1)	(0.039)	(0.12)	(0.158)	(0.245)	(0.072)
Unemployment rate	0.062	0.076	0.137	-0.475	-0.613	0.168
	(0.193)	(0.165)	(0.25)	(0.402)	(0.601)	(0.179)
GDP growth	-0.064	-0.123	-0.187	0.419	0.606	-0.058

(continued)

Table E.1 Continued

	(1)	(2)	(3)	(4)	(5)	(6)
	Radical right vote share	Radical left vote share	All radical vote share	Mainstream vote share	Net mainstream vote share	Party-system fragmentation
	(0.318)	(0.2)	(0.408)	(0.571)	(0.921)	(0.155)
Constant	10.971	−6.155	4.816	48.783*	43.967	84.72***
	(13.428)	(9.89)	(14.788)	(17.773)	(28.113)	(11.234)
Country dummies	Yes	Yes	Yes	Yes	Yes	Yes
Decade dummies	Yes	Yes	Yes	Yes	Yes	Yes
R-squared	0.667	0.763	0.708	09.701	0.749	0.87
Observations	954	954	954	954	954	954

Standard errors are in parentheses

*** p<0.001, ** p<0.01, * p<0.05

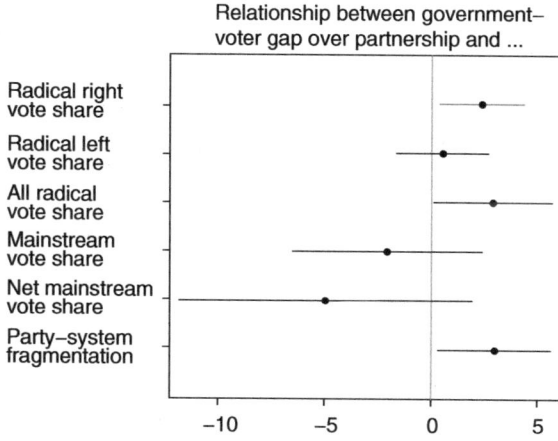

Figure E.1 Effect of government-voter gap over international partnership on party vote shares and party-system fragmentation in Western democracies, 1970–2018

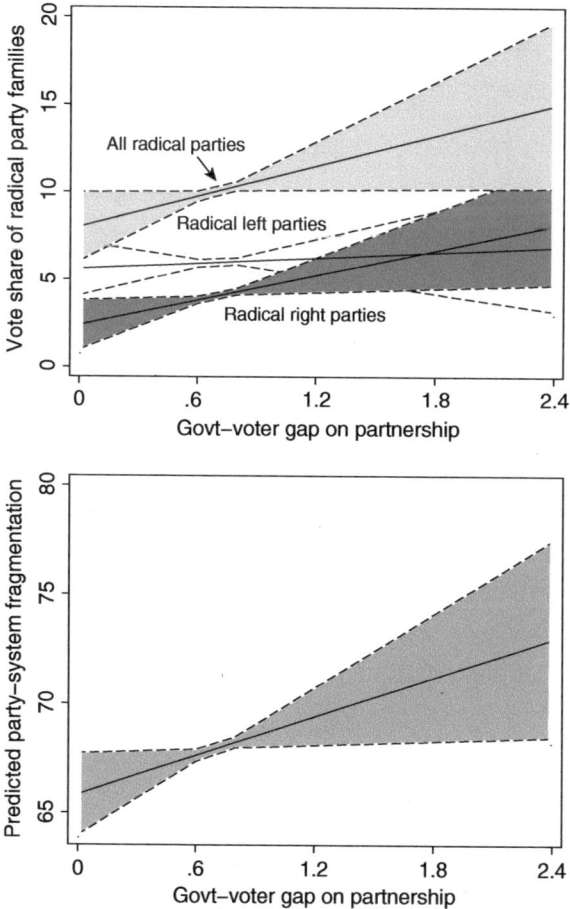

Figure E.2 Predicted radical-party vote share and party-system fragmentation due to government-voter gap over international partnership, 1970–2018

APPENDIX F

Additional figures for selected Western countries.

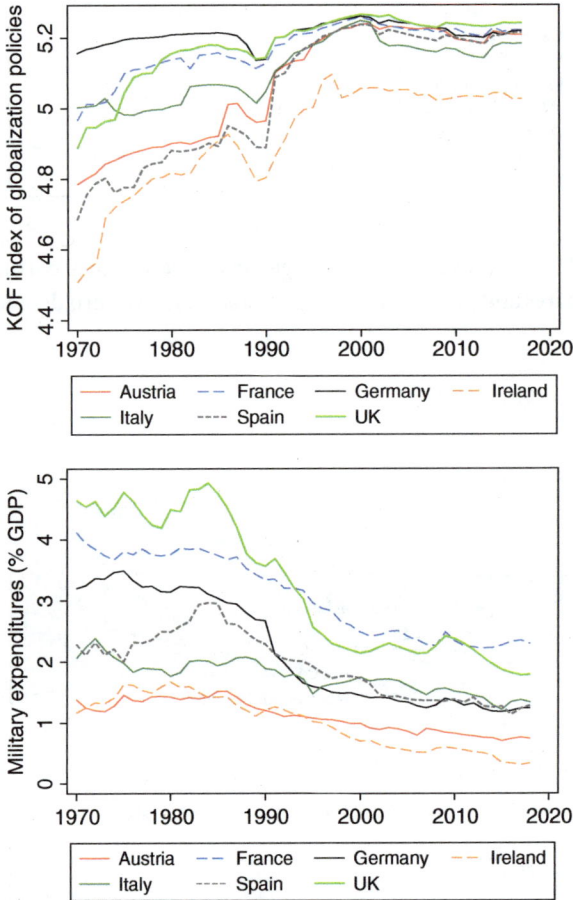

Figure F.1 Convergence of KOF index of globalization policies and military expenditures, selected EU-15 countries, 1970–2017

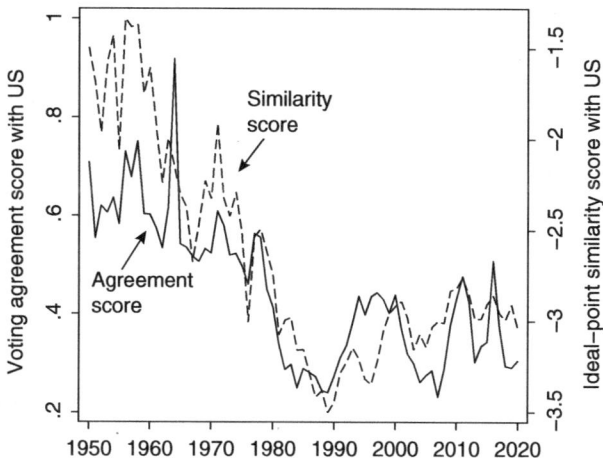

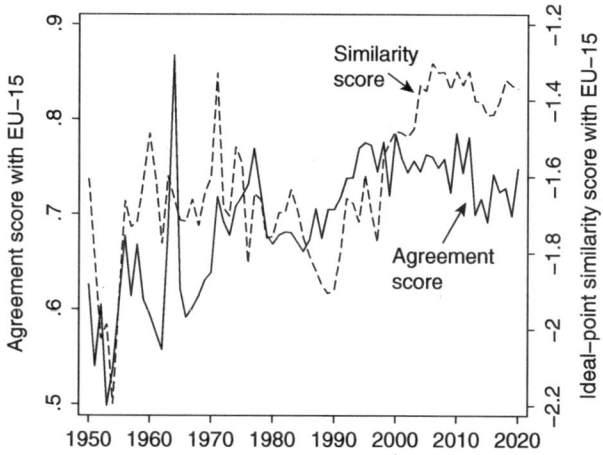

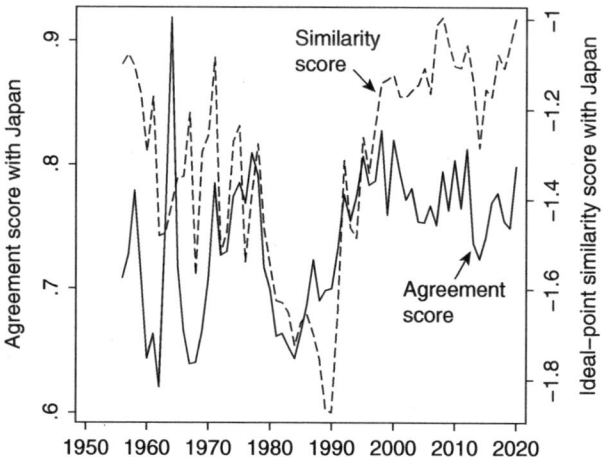

Figure F.2 Voting agreement and ideal-point similarity by EU, Japan, and United States in UN General Assembly, 1950–2020

Notes

Chapter 1

1. Quoted in Sheehan, 2008, 156.
2. In the analysis that follows, the "West" refers to the following twenty-four countries: Australia, Austria, Belgium, Canada, Denmark, Finland, France, Germany, Greece, Iceland, Ireland, Italy, Japan, Luxembourg, the Netherlands, New Zealand, Norway, Portugal, South Korea, Spain, Sweden, Switzerland, the United Kingdom, and the United States. We exclude the Central and Eastern European nations as they joined the West only after the Cold War. However, at several points in the pages that follow, we consider the extent to which our claims about the West also hold up for its newest members.
3. See, for example, Sprout and Sprout, 1968; Olson, 1982; Huntington, 1987; and Kennedy, 1987.
4. Ruggie, 1982.
5. On geopolitical slack and its implications for domestic politics, see Trubowitz, 2011.
6. On the exclusion of states from the liberal order, see Adler-Nissen and Zarakol, 2021. On the exclusion of migration from embedded liberalism, see Goodman and Pepinsky, 2021.
7. On the relationship of military intervention to liberal internationalism, see Cox et al., 2003; Desch, 2007; Mearsheimer, 2018; and Ikenberry, 2020a, chapter 7.
8. Spengler, 1926.
9. Some earlier works that straddle two or three of these fields include: Gilpin, 1975; Kurth, 1979; Tilly, 1985; Levi, 1988; Abdelal and Kirshner, 1999; Mastanduno, 1999; Strange, 1999; Rathbun, 2004; Sil and Katzenstein, 2010; North et al., 2009; and Brooks and Wohlforth, 2016a.
10. States' commitment to military power could also be measured by the use of military force. Since we are principally interested in how much weight governments attach to the international and domestic sides of the national ledger, measuring the use of force is less useful for our purposes. However, national commitment to defense spending is correlated with other military-related indicators, including the use of force. See Trubowitz and Burgoon, 2020.
11. The literature on each of these motivations is substantial. On states' security motivations, see, for example, Waltz, 1979; Walt, 1987; and Mearsheimer, 2001. On the role of economic interests and pressures, see Snyder, 1991. On the impact of disarmament and peace movements, see Ceadel, 1980; Williams, 1998; and Lynch, 1999.
12. The discussion here draws on Trubowitz, 2011, chapter 2.
13. Brodie, 1965.

14. The literature here is extensive. See, for example, Bueno de Mesquita et al., 2003; Narizny, 2003; Trubowitz, 2011; Garfinkel and Skaperdas, 2012; Oatley, 2015; and Obinger et al., 2018.
15. For a discussion of these issues, see Petersen, 2013; and Obinger et al., 2018.
16. See, for example, Cozer, 1956; Mayer, 1969; Skocpol, 1992; Giddens, 1985; and Mann, 1988. For an older but still relevant review of the literature, see Levi, 1988.
17. Obinger and Schmitt, 2011, 250.
18. This is a common strategy in peacetime as well as wartime. See, for example, Blainey, 1973; Mearsheimer, 2001; and Luttwak, 2009.
19. Petersen, 2013, 233.
20. Indeed, scholars have argued that the massive postwar expansion of the welfare state was a byproduct of the Cold War. For a review of the relevant literature, see Obinger and Lee, 2013; and Petersen, 2013. See also the recent histories by Westad, 2018b; and Gerstle, 2022.
21. Obinger and Schmitt, 2011, 252.
22. On the mediating role of political parties in this process, see Trubowitz, 1998 and 2011; Narizny, 2003; Rathbun, 2004; Fordham, 2007; Hoffmann, 2013; Martill, 2019; and Wagner, 2020.
23. The term sovereignty costs is from Moravcsik, 2000. For other work on this issue, see Keohane and Hoffmann, 1991; Moravcsik, 1998; Woods and Narlikar, 2001; Lake, 2007; Rixen and Zangl, 2013; Hafner-Burton et al., 2015; Hooghe and Marks, 2015; Grewal, 2018; and Börzel and Zürn, 2021.
24. Sovereignty costs also vary depending on international institutions' architecture or design. Some, like the Asia-Pacific Economic Cooperation (APEC) forum, involve no delegation or transfer of authority by members to a collective body. In other cases, such as the International Monetary Fund and World Bank, members pool and transfer authority to a collective body that makes binding decisions on its members. These are supranational institutions. For a discussion of the different forms that transfers of national authority to international institutions can take, see Lake, 2007; and Hooghe and Marks, 2015.
25. We are interested here in liberal institutionalized cooperation, but multilateralism can serve illiberal ends too. In the 1930s, Italian and German fascists viewed multilateralism as a means to export their economic models. During the Cold War, the Soviet Union relied on the multilateral Council for Mutual Economic Assistance, or COMECON, to promote economic planning and coordination with its allies in Central and Eastern Europe. On these and other examples, see Helleiner, 2019.
26. On the domestic effects of trade liberalization, see Katzenstein, 1985; Kurzer, 1993; Rodrik, 1998; Trubowitz, 1998; Iversen and Cusack, 2000; Swank, 2002; Scheve and Slaughter, 2004; Finseraas, 2008; Burgoon, 2009; Hays, 2009; Mau and Burkhardt, 2009; Rehm, 2009; Walter, 2010; Autor et al., 2016; Colantone and Stanig, 2018; and Milner, 2019.
27. See Dancygier and Water, 2015; Oesch and Rennwald, 2018; Copelovitch and Pevehouse, 2019; and Konstantinidis et al., 2019.

28. On the role of political parties in this process, see Boix, 1998; Garrett, 1998; Piazza, 2001; Hooghe, 2003; Swank and Betz, 2003; Marks and Steenbergen, 2004; Benoit and Laver, 2006; Kupchan and Trubowitz, 2007; Kriesi et al., 2008; Hobolt, 2009; Hooghe and Marks, 2009; Burgoon, 2012; Ecker-Ehrhardt, 2014; Hutter et al., 2016; Margalit, 2019; Rommel and Walter, 2018; and Zürn, 2019.

29. It is also not hard to imagine foreign policy strategies that straddle two quadrants. As we note below, arguably Wilson's vision of a "community of power" is an example.

30. On globalism, see Rosenboim, 2017; and Slobodian, 2018.

31. These versions of international federation differed principally in terms of the relative weight globalists assigned to international markets versus economic planning at the supranational level. F.A. Hayek was mostly closely identified with the former; Barbara Wootton with the latter. Both were members of the London-based Federal Union that championed international federation as a blueprint for the postwar order. See Rosenboim 2017, especially 130–167.

32. On the connection between the EU and mid-twentieth century globalist thought, see Streeck, 2017, 97–105.

33. This was true too of Hayek and Ludwig Von Mises and others in the Austrian school. See Kjar and Anderson, 2010; and Westley et al., 2011.

34. Quoted in Ikenberry, 2020a, 132.

35. On liberal internationalism's dual commitment to power *and* partnership see Kupchan and Trubowitz, 2007. See also Hoffmann, 1995; Ikenberry, 2009; and Brooks and Wohlforth, 2016a.

36. Wilson as quoted in Ikenberry, 2009.

37. For isolationism and related strategies (e.g., autarky, self-sufficiency), see Borchart, 1990; Nordlinger, 1996; Nichols, 2011; Kupchan, 2020; and Helleiner, 2021.

38. Nichols, 2011.

39. We use the terms radical-right (radical-left), far-right (far-left), and right-wing (left-wing) interchangeably in the text. Chapter 4 describes these party families, and the parties within each of them, in more detail.

40. John Mearsheimer (2011) argues that realism and nationalism are "kissing cousins," and there are certainly similarities. Yet, as Mearsheimer himself notes, realism is a large church with many denominations. Indeed, different strands of realism favor different combinations of power and partnership, putting realists in every quadrant in Figure 1.2 except quadrant 1 (globalism). Some realists (e.g., Brooks and Wohlforth, 2016a) explicitly embrace liberal internationalism. They favor investing in partnership as well as power. Other realists are more drawn to the combination of partnership and power that we have labeled isolationism (e.g., Gholz et al., 1997; Sapolsky et al., 2017; and Thrall and Friedman, 2018). They are not opposed to free trade or investing in military power, but they do not favor large peacetime military establishments or the transfer of sovereignty to "lock in" liberal trade. This variation within the realist school is not surprising. As Robert Gilpin argued, realism, like its counterpart liberalism, is elastic and malleable and better understood as an intellectual tradition rather than a strategy. On realism's elasticity and malleability, see Gilpin, 1987. See also Wohlforth, 2011.

41. On neo-mercantilism, see Hirschmann, 1945; Waltz, 1979; Grieco, 1988; and Drezner, 2010.

42. Henley, 2017.

43. On Trump's foreign policy approach, see Mead, 2017; Schweller, 2018; and Mastanduno, 2020.

44. See Dahl, 1965, 19.

45. In 2018, *Front National* changed its name to *Rassemblement National*. We use *Front National* throughout when referring to the party.

46. See Mair, 2013, 1.

47. Supporting material and links to data used in this book can be found at the authors' webpages.

48. Our measures of international threat rely on Dreyer and Thompson, 2011; Gibler et al., 2016; Goertz et al., 2016; Hensel et al., 2008; Kim, 2018; Markowitz and Fariss, 2018; and Palmer et al., 2021. All of our measures of social protection rely on OECD data on social transfers and expenditures (see Chapter 3 for details).

49. The strengths and limits of this particular measurement instrument have been widely debated. See Budge et al., 2001; Klingemann et al., 2006; and Benoit et al., 2009.

50. The coding unit in the Manifesto database is the number of sentences or sentence fragments in party platforms that take a position (for or against) on a particular foreign (or domestic policy) issue. Here we focus on foreign policy issues that concern international partnership (e.g., open markets, international cooperation) and military power (e.g., military spending and military preparedness). These are described in Chapter 2.

51. There are few systematic cross-national studies on public support for foreign policy, and even fewer studies tracking public support for foreign policy spanning time-frames as long as the one here. Most studies focus on a single nation, usually the United States. Moreover, these cross-national studies tend to focus on specific events or issues (e.g., the 2003 Iraq War; nuclear weapons) and thus, do not permit broad comparisons of support for different types of foreign policy strategies (e.g., liberal internationalism, isolationism) over time. For a recent effort to address some of these limitations, see Gravelle et al., 2017.

52. For discussion of approaches to gauging voter support for policy issues based on voter support for parties with systematically measured policy positions, see Kim and Fording, 1998, 2003; and De Neve, 2011. For a discussion of the limits of this approach, see Warwick and Zakharova, 2013. Perhaps the greatest concern is that voters do not usually vote for a party based solely on that party's stated position on a single issue. We address this concern in various ways, including estimating the effects of a party's platform position on a single issue (e.g., support for defense spending) only after controlling for the party's platform positions on other salient issues.

53. Voter support estimates are based on the country-year means of party platform support for international partnership and military power for any given political party, weighted by that party's actual electoral vote share won partly on its manifesto positions on partnership and power. For a discussion of this and related approachs, see Kim and Fording, 1998; De Neve, 2011; and Lindvall and Rueda, 2018. See

Chapter 2 for a description of the items in the Manifesto database used to create party measures of partnership and power.

54. Previous research indicates that indirect voter-weighted manifesto measures like the ones used here correlate significantly with direct measures of public opinion (e.g., Kim and Fording, 1998; McGregor, 2013; and Caughey et al., 2019). More related to the specific focus of our study, Burgoon et al. (2019) find that manifesto positions on the EU and trade tend to correlate with direct questions on these issues in European Social Survey data.

55. See, for example, Acharya, 2014; Allison, 2018; Barma et al., 2007; Nye, 2019; and Adler-Nissen and Zarakol, 2021.

56. See, for example, Mearsheimer, 2019; Cooley and Nexon, 2020; Ikenberry, 2020a; Lake et al., 2021; Krastev and Holmes, 2020; Kornprobst and Paul, 2021; and Katzenstein and Kirshner, 2022. Some scholars take issue with how "liberal" and "coherent" the Western international order was, but not with the idea that Western democracies are experiencing domestic blowback from their foreign policies. See, for example, Porter, 2020; and Barnett, 2021.

57. See Fukuyama, 1989; and Krauthammer, 1990.

58. See, for example, Posen, 2014; Mearsheimer, 2018; Porter, 2020; and Walt, 2018.

59. See, for example, Kriesi et al., 2008; Burgoon, 2009; Guiso et al., 2017; Colantone and Stanig, 2018; Hooghe and Marks, 2018; Rommel and Walter, 2018; Dippel et al., 2015; Pástor and Veronesi, 2018; Autor et al., 2020; Rodrik, 2021; and Caselli et al., 2021.

60. As Charles Tilly's well-known phrase in describing the rise of states in Europe, "War made the state and the state made war," reminds us, it is also hardly new. Tilly, 1975, 42.

Chapter 2

1. Kagan, 2003, 3–4.

2. See, for example, Lindberg, 2005; Anderson et al., 2008; Dorman and Kaufman, 2011; and Lake, 2018.

3. On the various visions for the postwar era, see Rosenboim, 2017.

4. Lundestad, 1986; and Forsberg, 2000.

5. Young, 1996.

6. Kane, 2016.

7. McCormick, 1995.

8. McCormick, 1995, 89.

9. Known as the "San Francisco system," the Asian regional alliance network rested on a series of treaties between the United States and Japan (1951), Australia and New Zealand (1951), the Philippines (1951), South Korea (1953), and Thailand (1954), as part of the Southeast Asian Treaty Organization (Cha, 2000). San Francisco was the site of the conference that led to the signing of the 1951 US-Japan Treaty of Mutual Cooperation and Security. See Hemmer and Katzenstein, 2002.

10. In the 1960s, America's allies in Asia invested 2.7 percent of GDP in defense on average, though notably Japan spent only 0.8 percent of GDP on defense (Chai, 1997; Sandler and George, 2016). In Europe, defense spending as a share of GDP averaged just under 4 percent during the same period, with Britain, France, and Germany each investing more in the common defense than the West European average (Nikolaidou, 2008).

11. Ruggie, 1982.

12. On class and industrial sector support of liberal internationalism in the United States, see Block, 1977; Ferguson, 1984; Frieden, 1988; and Trubowitz, 1998. For the European states, see Cameron, 1978; Katzenstein, 1978, 1985; and Eichengreen, 1996, 2007.

13. Deporte, 1979, 197.

14. Beckley et al., 2018.

15. Authors' calculations using OECD *Country Statistical Profiles* (OECD, 2020).

16. Following the initial GATT round in 1947, there were five rounds between 1949 and 1967: the Annecy Round (1949); Torquay Round (1951); Geneva Round (1956); Dillon Round (1960–1961); and the Kennedy Round (1964–1967). The Tokyo Round began in 1973, but was not completed until 1979.

17. By 1973, multinational corporations had invested $200 billion dollars globally, with three quarters of it going into the advanced industrial countries. Frieden, 2006, 293.

18. Again, we include the following twenty-four countries under the heading of the "West": Australia, Austria, Belgium, Canada, Denmark, Finland, France, West Germany, Greece, Iceland, Ireland, Italy, Japan, Luxembourg, Netherlands, New Zealand, Norway, Portugal, South Korea, Spain, Sweden, Switzerland, the United Kingdom, and the United States.

19. Military spending as a share of GDP figures prominently in national election campaigns and public debate about "burden-sharing." We treat this as a proxy for military preparedness and resource commitments. This measure does not provide explicit information about actual military missions, deployments, and use of force. But scholars and policy analysts regularly focus on this indicator to compare national investments in military power (e.g., Sandler and George, 2016). In our inferential analyses in Chapters 3 and 4, we also consider alternative specifications, particularly spending per capita, yielding patterns that corroborate our baseline focus on share of GDP.

20. KOF's widely used and cited database includes a range of policy and flow measures of globalization for more than 200 countries and territories over the period 1970 to 2016. Here we use only those measures representing national government *policies* that enable or constrain economic and political globalization—measures that the current version of the dataset refers to as "de jure" as opposed to "de facto" measures that represent actual cross-border flows and actions. See Dreher, 2006; Gygli et al., 2019.

21. Our indices exclude the dataset's economic data on actual flows of trade, foreign direct investment and migration, and also measures of sociocultural globalization.

22. The KOF treaty party diversity measure refers to the degree to which a country's investment treaties are multilateral in nature.

23. Our partnership measure is a weighted index of these two KOF indices from 1970 through 2017, the most recent available year. There are many ways of aggregating, normalizing, and weighting the various components. Our baseline simply adds these two KOF indices, providing an intuitive composite measure of global engagement and international cooperation and the pooling (sacrificing) of national sovereignty.

24. To provide reference points, we set the axes in Figure 2.1 using the worldwide (193 countries) sample medians for all 9,408 observations on each dimension for the full time-period (1970–2017). These median values yield rough approximations of the four quadrants in Figures 1.1 and 1.2 in Chapter 1. We use logged values because log transformation improves the visibility of the relative positions of the countries. Our analysis is the same whether we use raw or logged values.

25. Greece, Portugal, and Spain did not transition to democracy until the mid-1970s.

26. One limitation of the KOF data is that few countries that were members of the former Communist bloc appear in the data set before the 1990s. We are thus unable to plot the Soviet Union and most other members of the Communist bloc in Figures 2.1 and 2.2. Two exceptions are China (CHN) and Hungary (HUN), which are both located in the nationalist quadrant (quadrant 4) in Figure 2.1. After the Cold War, China and Hungary, like many other countries, move northward on the vertical axis in support of greater economic integration and institutionalized cooperation. See Figure 2.3 below.

27. Frieden, 2006, 363.

28. Crozier, Huntington, and Watanuki, 1975.

29. Frieden, 2006, 173–194.

30. Burnham, 1978; Scharpf, 1991; and Reid-Henry, 2019, 78–95.

31. O'Connor, 1973.

32. SIPRI, 2018. Calculations by authors.

33. In 1975, Chile imposed economic liberalization, privatization of state-owned companies, and fighting inflation anticipated many of the policies. Its economic policies were a precursor to many of the steps that Reagan, Thatcher, and other Western leaders took.

34. Gilpin, 2002, 99–103.

35. Slobodian, 2018, 257.

36. Slobodian, 2018.

37. Reid-Henry, 2019, 743.

38. Frieden, 2006, 383.

39. For accounts of this shift in Western governments' foreign economic policies, see Frieden, 2006; Rodrik, 2011; and Reid-Henry, 2019.

40. See, Ikenberry, 2009; Slobodian, 2018; Börzel and Zürn, 2021.

41. Reid-Henry, 2019, 312–313.

42. Britain, Denmark, and Sweden remained outside the new euro zone.

43. Irwin, 2022.

44. Simmons et al., 2008, 3.

45. Bloodgood, 2016; Börzel and Zürn, 2021.

46. Krastev and Homes, 2019.

47. Reid-Henry, 2019, 315–326.

48. Frieden, 2006, 431–432.

49. Mann, 1999.

50. Frieden, 2006, 425.

51. Ikenberry, 2019.

52. Johnston, 2019, 107.

53. Indeed, some international relations scholars have argued that these efforts to reshape the Western security architecture, especially by allowing in states from Russia's Near Abroad fueled Moscow's mistrust and expansion (e.g., Mearsheimer, 2019).

54. Liff, 2015, 81; Heginbotham and Samuels, 2018, 136–137.

55. Glanville, 2014.

56. Lind and Wohlforth, 2019.

57. Lindsay, 2000; Eichenberg and Stoll, 2003.

58. Sandler and George, 2016, 182.

59. The rise in globalization in this period (1997–2017) covers roughly 18 percent of the full sample variation, while the drop in military spending during the same time span covers 19 percent of the sample variation.

60. Marquand, 2004; Frum, 2005.

61. Tooze, 2018, 159.

62. IMF, 2009.

63. Hufbauer and Jung, 2016.

64. The actual effect of these measures on global trade also proved to be relatively modest. See Wolfe, 2012; Drezner, 2014, 132, 135–136.

65. Di Bella and Grigoli, 2019.

66. Aggregate economic growth numbers tell a similar story. In 2009, global economic output dropped. 0.59 percent. However, growth quickly returned. For the next two years, average global output growth was comparable to the growth rate recorded for the decade preceding the financial crisis. Drezner, 2014, 131.

67. Woods, 2010; Frieden, 2012; Kahler, 2013; Drezner, 2014.

68. The membership of the G20 includes nineteen major industrialized and developing economies plus the European Union.

69. Some of the slippage was also made up by increased enthusiasm for regional and bilateral FTAs. In the four years before the 2008 crash, 51 FTAs were reported to the WTO; in the four years following the crisis, 58 FTAs were registered with the international body. Drezner, 2014, 146.

70. Kahler, 2013, 64.

71. The EU-15 includes Austria, Belgium, Denmark, Finland, France, (West) Germany, Greece, Ireland, Italy, Luxembourg, Netherlands, Portugal, Spain, Sweden, and the United Kingdom. For visual clarity, we display even years only, except for 2001 in the U.S. case.

72. Calculations by authors. SIPRI, 2018.

73. Historically, FTAs were considered closed-door measures. However, in the 1990s they came to be seen as complements to WTO efforts to promote trade liberalization. See Urata, 2009.

74. Liff, 2015, 81–82.

75. In Figure F.1 in Appendix F, we show that the same pattern holds when the EU-15 is disaggregated by individual countries: Austria, France, Germany, Ireland, Italy, Spain, and the United Kingdom.

76. Quoted in Slobodian, 2018, 275.

77. Stephens, Huber, and Ray, 1999, 179.

78. Flynn and Rattinger, 1985, 384.

79. See Almond, 1960; and Lindberg and Scheingold, 1970, 41–42.

80. See Domke et al., 1987, 404.

81. See Chapter 1 for a description of the Manifesto Project Database. The Manifesto coding unit is sentences or quasi-sentences (single statements) in party platforms that take a pro- and an anti-position on issues relevant to a given issue. This allows the analyst to gauge the level of support for, or opposition to, a given position (e.g., for or against more open trade) by individual parties (cf. Burgoon, 2009; Lowe et al., 2011; Milner and Judkins, 2004).

82. Our Manifesto measure of international partnership refers to the (logged) percentage of total sentences or quasi-sentences (single statements) expressing support for general internationalism, free trade (low trade protectionism) and the European Union minus the (logged) percentage of (quasi-) sentences expressing opposition to each. This net measure includes every reference to open markets, international cooperation, and global governance in the Manifesto database (per107 + per108 + per407 + .5) and (per109 + per110 + per406 +.5). Our Manifesto measure of "military power" refers to the (logged) percentage of total sentences or quasi-sentences in favor of military spending, preparedness, security, and defense generally minus the (logged) percentage of statements expressing doubt and criticism of defense spending, military conscription, and the use of military power to solve conflict. Following Lowe et al. (2011), we take the natural log of each component, to ensure a more normal distribution of the measures, and add .5 to avoid zeros in the calculations.

83. To compare such voter support between countries, we weight the results for a given policy position by the average vote share in a party system (since countries with only two choices will have higher vote shares on average than countries with many party choices).

84. The full-sample median benchmarks are based on all countries and years for which the Manifesto project provides data since 1950. These median values yield rough approximations of the four quadrants in Figure 2.6, comparable to quadrants in Figures 2.1 through 2.4. When using voting support measures, it is also possible to set the benchmark at a score of zero on each axis. This is because the zero-line demarcates net voter support from net voter opposition on each dimension. For example, on the vertical axis, scores greater than zero indicate voter-support levels for platforms that are more positive than negative about international partnership. Conversely, scores lower than zero indicate voter support for platforms that are more negative than positive about partnership. The equivalent holds for the measures of voter-support for military power displayed on the horizontal axis. We considered both benchmarks— the zero-lines as well as the sample-medians—in interpreting the data. For the sake of consistency with our measures of government and party positions elsewhere in the analysis, we use the full-sample median here.

85. This finding is broadly consistent with recent public opinion research on rising anti-globalist sentiment towards trade liberalization and institutionalized cooperation. See Bearce and Jolliff Scott, 2019; Copelovitch, et al., 2020; and De Vries, et al., 2020.

86. Western political elites were more willing to live with the threat of nuclear war than their publics were. On this point, see Domke et al., 1987, 405.

87. Corman et al., 2015.

88. Schilde et al., 2019, 155.

89. Madison, 2019.

90. Clinton, 1997.

Chapter 3

1. Strange, 1997, 365, 369.

2. Our baseline models throughout the chapter focus on our sample of twenty-four OECD countries. However, the results broadly hold for wider samples that include Central and East European countries.

3. Greider, 2018; and Walt, 2019.

4. Polanyi, 1944.

5. John Ruggie was the first to recognize this connection. See Ruggie, 1982.

6. The nature of liberal internationalism's social supports in Western welfare states varied considerably. They ranged from the extensive social insurance and social investments characteristic of Europe's Scandinavian and small Continental states (e.g., Belgium, the Netherlands), and the conservative, status-preserving social protection model dominant in West Germany, France, and Italy, to the more market-oriented, minimalist model in the United States and other Anglo countries, to the more informal and firm-based social insurance model found in East Asia. These variations in social provision reflected national differences in public-private ownership, government investment, and corporate governance, as well as in the character and strength of unions. The classic account of these models of welfare capitalism is Esping-Andersen, 1990. For important revisions and extensions, see Korpi and Palme, 1998 and 2003; Éstevez-Abe et al., 2001; Arts and Gelissen, 2002; Iversen, 2005; Aspalter, 2006; Pontusson, 2005; Éstevez-Abe, 2008; Lim and Burgoon, 2020.

7. DeLong, 1997; Bordo et al., 2007; and Hays, 2019.

8. On these many proposals, see Rosenboim, 2017.

9. These protections also varied considerably across the West, both in terms of the benefits provided and levels of spending. Some welfare-state systems relied on means-tested provisions while others offered broader entitlements. Some countries offered social transfers and insurance (e.g., income supplements), while others included social services (e.g., training or health services). Countries also differed in how broadly they defined social protection—many, but not all, included child care, health care, and old-age provisions. Despite these differences, Western governments shared a commitment to manage the market risks arising from international openness.

10. To measure Western government support for *partnership, power,* and the two combined (*partnership + power*), we use the same measures we introduced in Chapter 2: KOF's globalization policy measures to gauge support for international partnership, and defense spending as a percentage of GDP to measure investment in military power. *Partnership + Power* is the sum of the standardized measures of *partnership* and *power*. This provides a rough approximation of liberal internationalism (*partnership + power*), though it smooths over which of the two components— partnership or power—accounts for year-to-year or cross-country difference. We explored other measurement approaches, such as categorizing values of *partnership* and *power* into the four categories or quadrants introduced in Figure 1.1 in Chapter 1, including the category liberal internationalism, where partnership and power are higher than the sample medians. These specifications, which are summarized in Appendix D, yield results similar to the baseline results in Figures 3.1 and 3.2.

11. *Social protection,* our explanatory variable here, is based on social security transfers as a percentage of GDP, a widely used measure of social protection in the comparative political economy literature. This is a particularly useful measure for our purposes. Among the available measures of social protection, social security transfers have a large economic impact and are thus politically salient. This measure has the added advantage of providing the most complete coverage for all of the OECD countries in our sample from 1960 to 2017. We use country-year data from OECD, 2019. The results reported here are also broadly supported using other measures such as social welfare generosity (1970–2011) and OECD social expenditures (transfers and services) (1980–2017).

12. The descriptive patterns are not as strong for *power,* and stronger for *partnership,* but the positive correlation holds for both.

13. For full results, see Table B.1 in Appendix B. Controls for the country-level analyses (where the unit of analysis is country-year) include democratic representativeness, unemployment rate, union density, voter turnout, past trade openness, and GDP growth. All of these control variables are lagged five-year moving averages to take into account the time it often takes for these factors to register in government policy. In addition to these substantive controls, the models include "dummies" (or indicator variables) for each sample country and decade to control for "fixed effects" of country-level or general conditions that do not vary over the time period.

14. This is consistent with other research that has focused more narrowly on the relationship between social safety net compensation and government support for trade liberalization, capital mobility, and so on. See, for example, Burgoon et al., 2012; and Ha and Tsebelis, 2010. Of course, there is also a large literature that explores globalization's effects on social compensation: cf. Cameron, 1978; Katzenstein, 1985; Rodrik, 1998; and Adsera and Boix, 2002.

15. The explanatory variables capturing social protection, and geopolitical threat, as well as the control variables, are lagged values of five-year moving averages. We use five-year lagged moving averages to account for the time it takes political and economic conditions to fully affect party or voter position-taking.

16. We calculate the party's left-right orientation using Manifesto's "RILE" (Right-Left) parameter, excluding platform positions we use to generate our party platform measures of *partnership* and *power*. The "RILE" measure is a composite variable made up of platform positions (for or against) on issues highly related to "left versus right" ideological orientation, such as government regulation, social welfare, market efficiency, and economic inequality.

17. For presentational purposes, we restrict the analysis by individual party families to *partnership + power*. See Table B.2 in Appendix B for the full regression results.

18. Burgoon, 2009 and 2012; and Burgoon and Schakel, 2022.

19. See, for example, Inglot, 2008; Mishra, 1993; Obinger and Schmitt, 2011; and Obinger and Lee, 2013. For a review of the literature, see Petersen, 2013.

20. Shantz, 2008, 798.

21. Hobsbawm, 1990, 21, cited in Obinger and Schmitt, 2011, 247.

22. Full regression results are shown in Table B.3 of Appendix B. Figure 3.4 is based on the results in models (1) to (3). These show that the results for *partnership + power*, which captures the broadest, most inclusive specification, are statistically significant.

23. In estimating these vote-weighted scores, controlling for other platform positions in a party's manifesto (including the party's adjusted left-right composite of platform positions) is important. Otherwise, one cannot be sure that the associations between social protection, geopolitical threat (below), and other explanatory variables with vote-weighted manifesto scores (as outcome variables) reflect the influence of a party's position on other platform issues. Supplemental analyses (available upon request) consider other non-foreign policy aspects of a party's platform positioning (e.g., welfare state provisions, environmental safety, democracy, traditional moral values, etc.).

24. We estimate voter support by weighting a party's platform support for international partnership and military power by the portion of that party's actual electoral vote share that can be attributed to its manifesto positions on partnership and power. These estimates are based on linear interpolation between election years for a given party's vote-weighted platform. See Chapter 2 for a description of the items in the Manifesto Project Database used to create voter support estimates of *partnership* and *power*.

25. See the discussion in Chapter 1.

26. In addition to the standard country and decade dummy variables, controls for these models include: democratic representativeness, international openness, country's average vote share, unemployment rate, GDP growth, party family and party's left-right orientation. Controlling for party platform orientation helps zero in on how social protection, geopolitical threat (below), and other explanatory variables correlate with vote-weighted manifesto scores on *partnership* and *power* (our outcome variables), as distinct from other party platform issues. In supplemental analyses, we consider the "effects" of party platform positions on issues such as welfare state provision, environmental safety, democracy, and moral values. These are available upon request.

27. Studies that are especially relevant to the argument here include Swank and Betz, 2003; Walter, 2010; Kersbergen and Vis, 2013; Halikiopoulou and Vlandas, 2016; Dal Bó et al., 2018; Fetzer, 2019; Foster and Frieden, 2019; and Gingrich, 2019.

28. Scharpf, 2000; Prasad, 2006; and Thelen, 2014.

29. Rodrik, 2011; and Subramanian and Kessler, 2013.

30. Betz, 1994; Jackman and Volpert, 1996; Lubbers and Scheepers, 2000; Golder, 2003; Swank and Betz, 2003; Jesuit and Mahler, 2004; Kessler and Freeman, 2005.

31. Knigge, 1998; Lubbers et al., 2002; Van der Brug et al., 2005; and Arzheimer and Carter, 2006.

32. Hays et al., 2005; and Scheve and Slaughter, 2006.

33. This adjustment is important to make because when unemployment rises, more people file for unemployment insurance benefits or fall into the income brackets that make them eligible for means-tested benefits, or both. Since we are interested in measuring public commitment to social protection or welfare effort, it is necessary to normalize spending by the unemployment rate so that unemployment-induced increases in social spending (that do not involve changes in policy) are not mischaracterized as increases in welfare effort.

34. This process began during the later stages of the Cold War, but it accelerated in the post–Cold War era. See Karns and Mingst, 2010.

35. Mathews, 1997.

36. Featherstone, 1994. In France, a referendum on the Maastricht treaty narrowly passed. In Denmark, the treaty was initially rejected in a close vote. It passed in a second referendum.

37. On the history of political opposition to multilateral institutions in the United States, see Patrick, 2017.

38. See Chapter 2, Figure 2.7.

39. Lefkofridi and Michel, 2017; Roth, et al., 2018; and Michel, 2019.

40. Heinisch, 2003; and Höbelt, 2003, 99.

41. Hainsworth, 2004, 106.

42. Swank and Betz, 2003; and Hernández and Kriesi, 2016.

43. Farage also connected EU membership to the issue of immigration, arguing that the best way to limit immigration was to leave the supranational institution.

44. Miller, 2016; Semuels, 2016.

45. Autor et al., 2020.

46. Ironically, many on the left also now saw multilateral institutions as a means to help achieve this goal. By regulating social-welfare and labor standards across national borders, international institutions could help protect vulnerable workers, businesses, and communities from market-induced regional and global "races to the bottom." Following the signing of the Maastricht treaty in 1992, the call for a new "social Europe" that would harmonize welfare and labor costs across Europe united most West European parties on the left. Instead of using the European Union to shield international business from domestic politics, they argued "federal Europe" should be repurposed to defend working families from the vicissitudes of global market forces. See Sassoon, 2014, 721.

47. In West Germany, Italy, and elsewhere, ruling Christian Democrats also exploited public fears about communism to shore up political support for their foreign and domestic policies (Mazower, 1999, 292–293; and Corduwener, 2016). Similar tactics were employed by political elites in the United States to silence progressive "one worlders" on the political left and to keep isolationist and nationalist opposition to American international leadership on the far right in check (Doenecke, 1979; and Dudziak, 2012). In Japan, conservatives used various means, including legislation (e.g., Subversive Activities Prevention Bill), to attack and marginalize socialists and communists (Hayes, 2009, 88).
48. Gaddis, 2005.
49. Sassoon, 1992, 215.
50. Sassoon, 1992, 168–169.
51. Midford, 2011.
52. Rosenbluth and Thies, 2010, 60.
53. Midford, 2011, 57.
54. Samuels, 2007, 32; and Pyle, 2018, 360–361.
55. Hughes, 2017, 82.
56. Eichenberg, 1989; and Holsti, 1992.
57. Domke et al., 1987
58. Ikenberry, 2020a.
59. Talbott, 2008, 329–330, as cited in Ikenberry, 2020a, 263.
60. Ikenberry, 2020a, 259.
61. De Spiegeleire et al., 2017, v, figure 1.2; and Henke and Maher, 2021.
62. Alonso and da Fonseca, 2012; Halikiopoulou et al., 2012; and Burgoon and Schakel, 2022.
63. Autor et al., 2020.
64. Midford, 2011, 15–16; Hughes, 2017, 79; and Madison, 2019.
65. The country-year measures included in our baseline model are: Hensel et al.'s (2008) ICOW-based territorial rivalries index; Dreyer and Thompson's (2011) strategic rivalries index; Palmer et al.'s (2021) and Gibler et al.'s (2016) binary Militarized International Disputes (MIDs) measure; Goertz, et al.'s (2016) interstate peace scale with neighbors; Kim's (2018) categorical measure of hostile relations with neighbors; and Markowitz and Fariss's (2018) spatial lag measure of geopolitical competition. The resulting scale is the standardized and equally weighted sum of the seven measures. In constructing the scale, we used casewise deletion where a country-year observation lacked any of the seven components, with a Cornbach's alpha of .78 as a threshold for internal consistency. In addition to our baseline model, we developed a supplementary measure that also includes system-wide variation in the risk of nuclear war based on the Bulletin of Atomic Scientists' annual updating of its "Doomsday Clock."
66. The measures differ in how they define threats (military as opposed to economic and political), the extent to which threats involve territorial claims, and whether the threat entails actual hostilities.

67. Given that our concern is with geopolitical challenges broadly defined, aggregating these indicators into a composite index allows us to capture the different ways international threats manifest and, importantly, to offset the substantive and methodological limitations inherent in any particular measure.

68. Vine, 2021.

69. The analyses here start in 1960 because many of the control variables are only available from that year.

70. The regression analyses underlying these three figures, while focused on how geopolitical threat is associated with *partnership* and *power*, follow the same respective specifications discussed above with respect to the effects of social transfers: Figure 3.8 focuses on the country-level (specification summarized in discussion of Figures 3.2 above); Figure 3.9 focuses on the party level (specification discussed for Figure 3.3 above); and Figure 3.10 focuses on the voter level (specification summarized in discussion of Figure 3.4).

71. For the full results underlying Figure 3.8, see Table B.1 in Appendix B. For the full results underlying Figure 3.9, see Table B.4 in Appendix B.

72. See Table B.3 in Appendix B, for the full results.

73. Voters may feel better placed to pass judgment on issues like international trade that directly impact their pocketbooks, than on "high politics" issues such as military balances, modernization, and deployments. See McCormick et al., 1992; and Holsti, 1978.

74. Trubowitz, 2011.

75. Nuti et al., 2015; Tompkins, 2016; Conze et al., 2017.

76. Others have recognized this too. See Broz et al., 2021.

77. See, for example, Katz and Mair, 1995; Kirshner, 2014; Hopkin and Blyth, 2019; Tooze, 2018; and Blyth, 2021.

78. See, for example, Featherstone, 1994; De Vries and McNamara, 2018; and Börzel and Zürn, 2021.

79. Colgan and Keohane, 2017.

80. Mair, 2013, 109; Slobodian, 2018.

81. See Scheve and Slaughter, 2001; Scheve and Slaughter, 2006; and Boix, 2019.

82. Przeworski, 2019, 111.

83. KOF's *de facto economic globalization* index includes trade in goods and in services, trade partner diversity, FDI, portfolio investment, international debt, international reserves, and international income payments. The KOF *de facto political globalization* index comprises number of embassies, UN peacekeeping missions, and international non-governmental organizations operating in country. Our *de facto all globalization* index includes these *de facto* economic and political indices, plus KOF's *de facto* socio-cultural measures (international voice traffic, international tourism, international students, internet bandwidth, IKEA and McDonald's stores, international trademarks). For details, see Gygli et al., 2019.

84. Right-party government (percentage of cabinet posts) comes from Armingeon et al., 2020. All explanatory variables are five-year lagged moving averages, to address the

lag in effects and also to help isolate the direction of association—to assess our causal inferences about statistically significant predictors. For each of our measures of de facto globalization, we consider two specifications: without any controls; and with substantive controls and country fixed effects. See Table B.5 in Appendix B.

85. We created a country-year *government-voter gap* index measuring the degree to which OECD government and public support for liberalized trade and institutionalized cooperation were different (similar). We rely on the KOF globalization policy indices to measure government *policy* support for partnership. Voter support estimates are based on our country-level vote-weighted indices measuring the voting public's support of partnership. The *government-voter gap* measure for partnership is the adjusted value of the difference between standardized government support for partnership and the standardized vote-weighted party support for partnership.

86. For our baseline, we recode negative government-voter gaps—i.e., situations where the voting public wants more trade liberalization and institutionalized cooperation than their government currently supports—as 0. We make this adjustment because there is no reason to assume that the voting public prefers government policies that are more supportive of international partnership than government policy, or less so. It is the magnitude of the overreach that we are interested in.

87. See Table B.5 in Appendix B for the full results. We considered a wide range of alternative specifications, including adding further measures of partnership in party platforms and *de jure* globalization (indices that go into our outcome measure).

88. The results in Figure 3.11 are based on the specification with the fullest battery of controls. See columns 2, 4, and 6 in Table B.5, Appendix B.

89. We obtain similar results using narrower measures of economic globalization, such as financial flows or capital openness.

90. Since these de facto measures might be affected by past *de jure* measures that inform our measures of *government-voter gap* we also considered models that include our measures of government support for globalization (KOF index of *de jure* political and economic globalization) and average vote-weighted party support for partnership. The results also show a significant effect of de facto *all globalization*.

91. For a review of these debates, see Mastanduno, 1999.

Chapter 4

1. Computations by authors based on data from the Manifesto Project Database.
2. Trubowitz, 1998, 178–183.
3. Kupchan and Trubowitz, 2007.
4. Young, 1996.
5. Hanrieder, 1989, 337–354; and Sassoon, 2014, 220–221.
6. Bogdanor, 2020, 14–16; and Sassoon, 2014, 184–185.
7. Samuels, 2007; and Pyle, 2018, 224.
8. Rosenbluth and Thies, 2010.

9. Doenecke, 1979; Griffith, 1979; and McCormick, 1995.

10. Sassoon, 1996, 167–185.

11. Sassoon, 1996, 183.

12. Pyle, 2018, 182.

13. Rosenbluth and Thies, 2010, 59.

14. McCormick, 1995, 89.

15. Mochizuki, 1983, 153–154.

16. See Chapter 1 for a description of the Manifesto Project data and Chapter 2 for how we have categorized parties.

17. See Chapter 2 for a description of our Manifesto measures of international partnership and military power.

18. Following many other analysts (Huber and Inglehardt, 1995; Mair, 1997; March and Mudde, 2005; and Rooduijn et al., 2018), we classify parties as mainstream, radical-left, and radical-right, depending on their ideology. Mainstream parties refer to our four center-left and center-right party families: Social Democrats, Liberals, Christian Democrats, and Conservatives. Radical-left parties include political parties usually associated with communist or, in the post-Cold War period, post-communist ideologies (e.g., Spain's Podemos; Germany's The Left; Finland's Left Alliance). On the radical right are parties associated with nationalist and/or populist appeals to nativism, traditionalism, and statism (e.g., France's *Front National* (FN); Austria's Freedom Party (FPÖ); the Danish People's Party (DPP)). See Appendix C for mainstream, radical-left and radical-right party coding by core Western countries.

19. The number of parties each dot represents thus varies. In the case of mainstream parties, each dot can represent multiple mainstream parties, as it was not uncommon for European democracies to have more than one center-left and center-right and multiple parties on the left or right in any given year.

20. The reference lines in Figure 4.1 demarcating foreign policy strategic orientations could also be set at the zero-points, since here, too, each dimension is measuring *net* partnership and *net* power—that is, the relative share of platforms devoted to supporting partnership (power) minus the share of platforms opposing partnership (power). As noted in Chapter 2, for consistency we use sample-medians as the benchmark here and in Figures 4.2, 4.6, and 4.7.

21. See Sassoon, 1992, 209–240.

22. Sassoon, 2014, 463.

23. The FPÖ's coordinate position in Figure 4.2 is 1.4 on the horizontal axis and 2.3 on the vertical axis, putting it quite solidly in the upper-right quadrant for this later Cold War period. See also Dolezal, 2008, 111.

24. The FN's coordinate position in Figure 4.2 is 2.1 on the horizontal axis and −.45 on the vertical axis, putting it in the lower-right quadrant.

25. See Appendix B Table B.6a–B.6e for full results of the regression analyses.

26. This is important since government decisions to invest in military power (e.g., defense spending) can be made simultaneously with decisions to join international organizations and other forms of international partnership. To address this, we use regression estimators to model the outcomes of interest (*partnership, power,* and *partnership +*

power) for a given set of explanatory conditions. In doing so, we take into account how those explanatory conditions affect each outcome in ways related to their effects for other outcomes. In statistical terms, seemingly unrelated regression models factor in such dependence, treating the error terms of the respective models as linked. For a discussion, see Zellner, 1962; and Greene, 2012. The model coefficients are ordinary least squares (OLS) with robust cluster standard errors (clustered by country), including controls for level of democracy, unemployment rate, real GDP growth, average party vote share, past openness, voting turnout, union density, along with fixed effects for the twenty-four Western countries and decade dummies. To reduce endogeneity and address delays in outcomes, we use lagged moving averages (five-year) for the explanatory variables.

27. Again, *partnership + power* is the sum of the standardized measure of our KOF globalization index (partnership) and the standardized measure of defense spending as a share of GDP (power). This provides a rough approximation of liberal internationalism though it smooths over which of the two components—partnership or power—account for year-to-year differences. We also considered alternative approaches to standardize and combine our measures of partnership and power (e.g., creating categories for different combinations of partnership and power; developing scales using principal component analysis). These yielded similar patterns to those reported using our baseline measures.

28. See Appendix A for the summary statistics on these and all country-year and party-year variables explored in this chapter.

29. Since the horizontal axes capture the full sample variation for our twenty-four OECD countries, we can compare the substantive size of effects across party families and government policy.

30. The results reported here are corroborated using other approaches to combining of partnership and power. See, for example, the categorical specifications in Table D.2 of Appendix D.

31. Mainstream parties benefited too from the fact that parties on the far left and far right disagreed sharply over defense spending and military preparedness. Nuclear disarmament also made it difficult for them to find common ground on an alternative foreign policy strategy.

32. Lipset and Rokkan, 1967. For a recent discussion of the Lipset and Rokkan cleavage model, see Ford and Jennings, 2020.

33. Clark, 2019; and Voce and Clarke, 2021. On the decline of mainstream party vote share more generally, see Katz and Mair, 2018, chapter 7.

34. Golosov, 2010; Best, 2013; Pildes, 2021.

35. Computations by authors based on data from Swank, 2018.

36. Mettler and Leavitt, 2019, cited in Pildes, 2021, 146.

37. See, for example, Kitschelt, 1997; Mudde, 2007; Kriesi et al., 2008; Bolleyer and Bytzek, 2013; Inglehart and Norris, 2017; Burgoon et al., 2019; De Vries et al., 2021; and Mutz, 2018.

38. Przeworski and Sprague, 1986; Kitschelt, 1994; Clark and Lipset, 2001; Gingrich and Häusermann, 2015; Boix, 2019; Hall, 2020; and Rennwald and Pontussen, 2021.

39. At the same time, Social Democratic parties pushed to reform social insurance systems and labor market regulations in ways that often disadvantaged traditional blue-collar workers, while extending coverage to previously excluded groups, such as female service-sector workers. See Häusermann, 2010.

40. Häusermann, 2017, cited in Boix, 2019, 9.

41. Denmark and the UK agreed to the treaty's commitment to allow goods and people to move freely across national borders, but not to the European Union's common currency.

42. Sassoon, 2014, 739. Center-left and center-right parties in Western Europe were less enthusiastic about extending membership to the fledgling democracies of post-Communist Central and Eastern European countries (CEEC). The prevailing view was incorporating CEEC nations into NATO should take priority over EU membership. Offering NATO membership was easier and less costly, politically as well as economically. Already, radical-right parties like France's FN had reversed course on the issues of economic and political integration and were attacking the idea of EU citizenship and a single currency (Mudde, 2007). EU enlargement would come, but for mainstream parties, it was double-edged, politically. While the vast majority of Western European elites supported it, mass support was considerably less enthusiastic. In 2005, public support for the European Union among EU citizens was only about 50 percent. Significantly, opposition was strongest among those without degrees and workers. See McLaren, 2005, cited in Eatwell and Goodwin, 2018, 102.

43. Trubowitz, 2011.

44. Clinton understood that moving in this direction would anger liberal constituencies within the party and, to some extent, sought to soften the blow by imposing unilateral sanctions against European and Japanese exporters accused of dumping goods in the US market and using the Commerce Department to actively promote US manufactured exports. See Trubowitz, 2011, 122.

45. Shoch, 2001, 228–230.

46. Scheve and Slaughter, 2001; Shoch, 2001; and Hiscox, 2020.

47. Pempel, 1998; Schoppa, 2011.

48. Rosenbluth and Thies, 2010, 155, 118; Schoppa, 2011, 36–38.

49. Koizumi's agenda was enormously popular with urban voters, but rural members of the party attacked and sometimes defeated his policy proposals. In an effort to blunt the political impact of those criticisms, Koizumi made annual high-profile symbolic visits to the controversial Yasukuni Shrine that had "deep and special meaning for rural voters" (Rosenbluth and Thies, 2010, 167). While these annual visits were roundly criticized by Beijing and Seoul for being insensitive and nationalistic, the gestures allowed Koizumi to solidify his exposed flank with conservative, rural voters.

50. Under Koizumi, Japan launched its first big surge in Economic Partnership Agreements (FTAs) with other countries in the Pacific region. See Urata, 2009. Historically, FTAs were considered closed-door measures. However, in the 1990s they came to be seen as complements to WTO efforts to promote "open regionalism." See Drezner, 2014, 146.

51. Reid-Henry, 2019, 559–565.

52. Abe served briefly as prime minister in 2006–2007.

53. Davis, 2019.

54. Government policy and mainstream party platforms also diverge over defense spending, albeit in the reverse direction. After the Cold War Western governments sharply reduced defense spending as a share of GDP after the Cold War. However, as Figure 4.7 makes clear, mainstream party leaders, overall, continued to run on platforms calling for a strong national defense. This divergence likely reflects mainstream party leaders' lingering concerns about appearing weak on national defense, especially given increased voter support for military spending (see Figure 2.7 in Chapter 2).

55. And in their willingness to enter into governing coalitions with Social Democratic and socialist parties. See Tarrow, 2005; Rooduijn et al., 2017; and Hooghe et al., 2019b.

56. Burgoon, 2009; Hooghe et al., 2019b.

57. Kaldor, 2000.

58. On radical-left (and radical-right) parties' stance on trade liberalization, see Rone, 2020; and Waal and de Koster, 2018.

59. See Jamitzky, 2015; Shaw, 2016; and Davis, 2019.

60. Burgoon, 2009; Rooduijn et al., 2017.

61. In some cases (e.g., Britain's UKIP; the Netherland's Party for Freedom) Euroskepticism was initially the principal line of foreign policy attack against the center. On Euroskepticism, see Judt, 2005, 742–745; Chryssogelos, 2010; Braun et al., 2019; and Hooghe et al., 2019b.

62. FN's position on partnership and power averaged −1.8 and 2.2, respectively, while DPP averaged −2.4 and 1.3, respectively—both clearly in Figure 4.6's lower-right nationalist quadrant.

63. In the full post–Cold War period captured by Figure 4.6, UKIP, which formed in 1993, averaged −2.1 and 1.03 on partnership and power, respectively, putting it squarely in the nationalist quadrant. AfD, which formed in 2013, is located in the nationalist quadrant, averaging −1.3 and 1.2 on partnership and power, respectively.

64. See Mudde, 2007, 187–188; Hernández and Kriesi, 2016; Bale, 2018; Eatwell and Goodwin, 2018, 284; Boix, 2019; and Szöcsik and Polyakova, 2019.

65. See Swank and Betz, 2003; Kriesi et al., 2008; Autor, et al., 2016; Colantone and Stanig, 2018; Burgoon et al., 2019; Broz et al., 2021; and De Vries et al., 2021.

66. Henley, 2017.

67. As with the party-level and voter-level analyses in Chapter 3, we rely here on the Manifesto Project's right-to-left scale for each party year. In our baseline models, we use this scale to control for party families and general party platform left-right orientations, lagged party vote, country and decade fixed effects, along with country-year levels of democracy, globalization, and unemployment. See Appendix B, Table B.7, for full specification and results.

68. That effect of the Cold War is apparent in models 4–6 in Appendix B, Table B.7. It shows that the interaction term between party support for partnership and the Cold War period dummy variable is positive and significant. This means that the negative

association between a party's support for partnership and its subsequent electoral share was less negative, or even positive, during the Cold War.

69. Social protection is based on social security transfers as a percentage of GDP. See Chapter 3 for a discussion.

70. See Appendix B, Table B.7, for the full results. The reported panels in Figure 4.8 correspond to models 2–3 in Table B.7.

71. Studies that are especially relevant to the argument here include Swank and Betz, 2003; Walter, 2010; Kersbergen and Vis, 2013; Halikiopoulou and Vlandas, 2016; Dal Bó et al., 2018; Fetzer, 2019; Foster and Frieden, 2019; and Gingrich, 2019.

72. The patterns hold when controlling for other economic and political conditions (i.e., GDP per capita, economic inequality, government debt, inflation, party system, measures of corruption). They also hold up to changes in sample size: for instance, including the CEEC countries and other countries like Turkey and Brazil in the models. The results also hold up to different estimators (e.g., multi-level random intercept models) and alternative ways of calculating standard errors (e.g., simple robust standard errors).

73. See Appendix E for these results.

74. Well-known works in this genre include Keohane and Nye, 1971; Kindleberger, 1973; Gilpin, 1975; Keohane, 1984; Mearsheimer, 1990; and Ikenberry, 2001.

75. Fearon, 1994; Schultz, 2001.

76. Cha, 2000; Mastanduno, 1997; and Ikenberry 2020a, 200–202.

77. Acheson, 1969, 97.

78. Simmons et al. (2008), cited in Ikenberry, 2020a, 265.

79. For a description of the KOF *de facto* globalization index, see Chapter 3.

80. See also Voeten, 2013; and Bailey et al., 2017.

81. Rae's index is a straightforward measure of party fragmentation, ranging between 1 (maximal fractionalization) and 0 (minimal fractionalization). The index data comes from Armingeon et al.'s (2020) CPDS database.org (variable *rae_leg*). The results hold up to related measures such as the effective number of parties in party systems (Laakso and Taagepera, 1979), as well as different methods of calculating fragmentation in party systems.

82. Table B.9 in Appendix B provides the full regression results. Model 1 shows the result that is the basis for Figure 4.11.

83. These include the Bank for International Settlements (BIS), Benelux Union, Central Commission for Navigation on the Rhine (CCNR), European Organization for Nuclear Research (CERN), Council of Europe (COE), European Economic Area (EEA), European Free Trade Association (EFTA), European Space Agency (ESA), European Union (EU), International Bank for Reconstruction and Development (IBRD), International Civil Aviation Organization (ICAO), International Labor Organization (ILO), International Monetary Fund (IMF), International Maritime Organization (IMO), International Criminal Police Organization (INTERPOL), International Telecommunication Union (ITU), International Whaling Commission (IWC), North American Free Trade Agreement (NAFTA), North Atlantic Treaty Organization (NATO), Organization for Economic Cooperation and Development

(OECD), Organization for Security and Co-operation in Europe (OSCE), United Nations (UN), UN World Tourism Organization (UNWTO), World Health Organization (WHO), and the World Trade Organization (WTO). We exclude international governmental organizations that have less to do with the West: e.g., the African Union (AU), ASEAN, OPEC, and Gulf Cooperation Council (GCC). We also consider specifications for only those IOs that underwent some change in delegation. For the full list of international governmental organizations in the dataset, see https://besirceka.com/wp-content/uploads/2017/02/Appendix-I-IOs_03.17.pdf.

84. The concepts and data are discussed and explored in general terms in Hooghe et al., 2017. While the components should be analyzed separately since they are conceptually and empirically distinct, we also consider the results of measures that combine them (Cornbach's alpha = .71). That is worth doing to see if the results for the individual components offset one another and wash away the general pattern suggested by the individual components.

85. Our linking of IO data to party-system fragmentation has no panel or cross-international authority variation. This is because our measures of average electoral fragmentation do not vary across a given international body, but instead, only for a given grouping of countries varying over time. We use ARIMAX models because they take into account non-stationarity, autocorrelation, and time-wise heteroskedasticity in both the international authority and party-system fragmentation time-series data. Dickey-Fuller tests revealed strong evidence of unit-root in all the international authority measures and party-system fragmentation summarized in Figure 4.13. The best fit specifications of the time-series analyses include first-differencing of the outcome and explanatory variables of interest (to address non-stationarity), one lagged dependent variable AR-1 term of the dependent variable.

86. The full models and results are summarized in Table B.10, panel 10a in Appendix B.

87. See model 4 in Table B.10, panel 10a, Appendix B. By contrast, the effects of party-system fragmentation are considerably weaker for international organizations that have historically had little to do with the West (see Table B.10, panel 10b, in Appendix B). Panel 10c focuses on those IOs of particular importance to the advanced industrialized West that underwent change in the level of delegated authority. For these IOs, party-fragmentation tends to diminish the delegation level along the lines of our baseline specification displayed in Figure 4.13.

88. We draw here on distinctions made by Voeten et al., 2009; and Bailey et al., 2017.

89. This number is based on the average share for the twenty-four OECD countries in our sample. We calculate the share of all votes cast by each OECD country in a given year that are in agreement with the votes of all other countries (except for the other twenty-three OECD countries).

90. We report the results separately for the United States, EU-15, and Japan in Appendix F, Figure F.2. While the lack of voting with the United States is notably lower than for the EU-15 and Japan, since the turn of the millennium non-Western agreement with all three has leveled off.

91. For full regression results, see models 3–6 of Table B.9 in Appendix B. The specification is summarized above in the discussion introducing Figure 4.11.

92. Hence, the regression analyses include lagged moving-averages not only of our fragmentation measure, but also the same battery of controls described above (see Figure 4.11).

93. Lincoln was referring to anti-war Democrats in the North who threatened the Union cause against the Confederacy.

94. See, for example, Fukuyama, 1989; and Krauthammer, 1990.

Chapter 5

1. Lippmann, 1943, 9–10.

2. The phrase is Huntington's. See Huntington, 1988.

3. Kahl and Wright, 2021; Tooze, 2021; Wondreys and Mudde, 2022.

4. See, for example, Posen, 2014; Mearsheimer, 2018; Walt, 2018; and Porter, 2020.

5. In sharp contrast to declining voter support for parties favoring partnership, support for parties advocating greater military spending and preparedness has increased since the 1990s. Voter support fell during the Iraq War, but it rebounded after the 2008 global crash, and has been rising ever since. See Trubowitz and Burgoon, 2020.

6. See, for example, Kriesi et al., 2008; Burgoon, 2009; Colantone and Stanig, 2018; Hooghe and Marks, 2018; Rommel and Walter, 2018; Autor et al., 2020; and Rodrik, 2021.

7. Obinger and Schmitt, 2011, 252.

8. Some stress the rise of new post-material social values and generational change that have led political elites and voters to polarize over issues such as immigration, race, and gender. Others emphasize the effects of rising income inequality and the loss of high-paying jobs due to globalization and automation as reasons radical parties on the left and right have increased their share of the national vote in one country after another. Economic and social anxiety have made voters apprehensive about free trade, European integration, and immigration, especially in hard-pressed manufacturing regions.

9. De Vries and Hobolt, 2019.

10. See, for example, Gholtz et al., 1997; Layne, 1997; Bacevitch, 2002; Preble, 2009; Morefield, 2014; Posen, 2014; Mearsheimer, 2018; Thrall and Friedman, 2018; Walt, 2018; Immerwahr, 2020; and Porter, 2020. There is no comparable school of strategic thought in Europe or Asia today. The closest approximation are the calls for greater "strategic autonomy" from the United States. In Europe, the case for greater autonomy, and a stronger national defense, is especially popular among nationalist parties such as France's *Front National* and Germany's AfD. In Japan, these arguments, which harken back to the early Cold War period when conservative "Gaullist" factions in the LDP made the case for remilitarization and greater autonomy from the United States, have resurfaced on the far right. On the EU, see Grajewski, 2021. On Japan, see Hughes, 2017.

11. On the restraint school's diverse strands, see Deudney and Ikenberry, 2021.

12. See, for example, Mearsheimer, 2014.

13. Some advocates of strategic restraint do not favor offshore balancing. See, for example, Gholtz et al., 1997; and Posen, 2014.

14. On the limitations of strategic restraint as an American strategy, see Brooks and Wohlforth, 2016a; and Deudney and Ikenberry, 2021.

15. Sartori, 1976.

16. Trubowitz, 1998.

17. Brands, 2021; Lind, 2018; Brooks, 2019; and Beckley, 2022.

18. Galston, 2022.

19. Simmel, 1955; and Coser, 1956. For a recent statement and application to great power politics, see Lascurettes, 2020.

20. On this point, see Westad, 2018a; Leffler, 2019; Tooze, 2020; and Christensen, 2021.

21. Westad, 2018b, 220–221; and Gerstle, 2022, 10–11.

22. Leffler, 2019.

23. Trubowitz and Seo, 2012.

24. See Silver et al., 2021, 12.

25. See, for example, Leali, 2021; and Oltermann, 2021.

26. See, for example, Colgan and Keohane, 2017; Snyder, 2019; Ikenberry, 2020a; Katzenstein and Kirshner, 2022. Recommendations for re-embedding liberalism range from broad welfare state interventions, including social security transfers, to more active labor market provisions. On the latter, see Autor, Mindell, and Reynolds, 2020; and Rodrik and Sabel, 2021.

27. Trubowitz and Harris, 2019; and Kupchan and Trubowitz, 2021.

28. See Kurth, 1979; Gourevitch, 1986; and Trubowitz, 1998.

References

Abdelal, Rawi, and Jonathan Kirshner (1999). "Strategy, Economic Relations, and the Definition of National Interests." *Security Studies* 9, no. 1–2: 119–156.

Acharya, Amitav (2014). "Global International Relations (IR) and Regional Worlds: A New Agenda for International Studies." *International Studies Quarterly* 58, no. 4: 647–659.

Acheson, Dean (1969). *Present at the Creation: My Years at the State Department*. New York: W.W. Norton.

Adler-Nissen, Rebecca, and Ayşe Zarakol (2021). "Struggles for Recognition: The Liberal International Order and the Merger of Its Discontents." *International Organization* 75, no. 2: 611–634.

Adsera, Alicia, and Carles Boix (2002). "Trade, Democracy, and the Size of the Public Sector: The Political Underpinnings of Openness." *International Organization* 56, no. 2: 229–262.

Allison, Graham (2018). "The Myth of the Liberal Order: From Historical Accident to Conventional Wisdom." *Foreign Affairs* 97, no. 4: 124–133.

Alonso, Sonia, and Sara Claro da Fonseca (2012). "Immigration, Left and Right." *Party Politics* 18, no. 6: 865–884.

Anderson, Jeffrey, G., John Ikenberry, and Thomas Risse, eds. (2008). *The End of the West? Crisis and Change in the Atlantic Order*. Ithaca: Cornell University Press.

Anderson, Nicholas D. (2017). "Anarchic Threats and Hegemonic Assurances: Japan's Security Production in the Postwar Era." *International Relations of the Asia-Pacific* 17, no. 1: 101–135.

Archibugi, Daniele, and David Held (1995). *Cosmopolitan Democracy: An Agenda for a New World Order*. Cambridge: Polity Press.

Archibugi, Daniele, and David Held (2011). "Cosmopolitan Democracy: Paths and Agents." *Ethics & International Affairs* 25, no. 4: 433–461.

Arias, Eric, James R. Hollyer, and B. Peter Rosendorff (2018). "Cooperative Autocracies: Leader Survival, Creditworthiness, and Bilateral Investment Treaties." *American Journal of Political Science* 62, no. 4: 905–921.

Armingeon, Klaus, Sarah Engler, and Lucas Leemann (2020). *Comparative Political Data Set 1960–2018*. Zurich: Institute of Political Science, University of Zurich.

Arts, Wil, and John Gelissen (2002). "Three Worlds of Welfare Capitalism or More? A State-of-the-Art Report." *Journal of European Social Policy* 12, no. 2: 137–158.

Arzheimer, Kai, and Elisabeth Carter (2006). "Political Opportunity Structures and Right-wing Extremist Party Success." *European Journal of Political Research* 45, no. 3: 419–443.

Aspalter, Christian (2006). "The East Asian Welfare Model." *International Journal of Social Welfare* 15, no. 4: 290–301.

Autor, David, David Dorn, Gordon Hanson, and Kaveh Majlesi (2020). "Importing Political Polarization? The Electoral Consequences of Rising Trade Exposure." *American Economic Review* 110, no. 10: 3139–3183.

Autor, David H., David Dorn, and Gordon H. Hanson (2016). "The China Shock: Learning from Labor-Market Adjustment to Large Changes in Trade." *Annual Review of Economics* 8: 205–240.

Autor, David, David Mindell, and Elisabeth Reynolds (2020). "The Work of the Future: Building Better Jobs in an Age of Intelligent Machines." *MIT Task Force on the Work of the Future.* https://workofthefuture.mit.edu/research-post/the-work-of-the-future-building-better-jobs-in-an-age-of-intelligent-machines/.

Bacevitch, Andrew (2002). *American Empire: The Realities and Consequences of U.S. Diplomacy.* Cambridge, MA: Harvard University Press.

Bafumi, Joseph, and Joseph M. Parent (2012). "International Polarity and America's Polarization." *International Politics* 49, no. 1: 1–35.

Bailey, Michael A., Anton Strezhnev, and Erik Voeten (2017). "Estimating Dynamic State Preferences from United Nations Voting Data." *Journal of Conflict Resolution* 61, no. 2: 430–456.

Bailey, Thomas A. (1943). "Review of *U. S. Foreign Policy: Shield of the Republic*, by Walter Lippmann." *Political Science Quarterly* 58, no. 3: 429–431.

Baldwin, Richard E., and Philippe Martin (1999). "Two Waves of Globalisation: Superficial Similarities, Fundamental Differences." *NBER Working Paper* w6904: 1–30.

Bale, Tim (2018). "Who Leads and Who Follows? The Symbiotic Relationship between UKIP and the Conservatives—and Populism and Euroscepticism." *Politics* 38, no. 3: 263–277.

Barma, Naazneen, Ely Ratner, and Steven Weber (2007). "A World Without the West." *National Interest*, no. 90: 23–30.

Barnett, Michael (2021). "International Progress, International Order, and the Liberal International Order." *Chinese Journal of International Politics* 14, no. 1: 1–22.

Bearce, David H., and Brandy J. Jolliff Scott (2019). "Popular Non-support for International Organizations: How Extensive and What Does This Represent?" *The Review of International Organizations* 14, no. 2: 1–30.

Beckley, Michael (2022). "Enemies of My Enemy: How Fear of China is Forging a New World Order." *Foreign Affairs* 101, no. 2: 68–85.

Beckley, Michael, Yusaku Horiuchi, and Jennifer M. Miller (2018). "America's Role in the Making of Japan's Economic Miracle." *Journal of East Asian Studies* 18, no. 1: 1–21.

Benoit, Kenneth, and Michael Laver (2006). *Party Policy in Modern Democracies.* London: Routledge.

Benson, Brett V., Adam Meirowitz, and Kristopher W. Ramsay (2014). "Inducing Deterrence through Moral Hazard in Alliance Contracts." *Journal of Conflict Resolution* 58, no. 2: 307–335.

Beramendi, Pablo, Silja Häusermann, Herbert Kitschelt, and Hanspeter Kriesi, eds. (2015). *The Politics of Advanced Capitalism.* New York: Cambridge University Press.

Best, Robin E. (2013). "How Party System Fragmentation Has Altered Political Opposition in Established Democracies." *Government and Opposition* 48, no. 3: 314–342.

Betz, Hans-Georg (1994). *Radical Right-wing Populism in Western Europe.* New York: St. Martin's Press, 1994.

Blainey, Geoffrey (1974). *The Causes of War.* London: Macmillan.

Block, Fred L. (1977). *The Origins of International Economic Disorder: A Study of United States International Monetary Policy from World War II to the Present.* Berkeley: University of California Press.

Bloodgood, Elizabeth (2016). "The Yearbook of International Organizations and Quantitative Non-State Actor Research." In *The Ashgate Research Companion to Non-State Actors*, edited by Bob Reinalda, 31–46. London: Routledge.

Blyth, Mark (2021). "The End of Social Purpose? Great Transformations of American Order." In *The Downfall of the American Order: Liberalism's End*, edited by Peter Katzenstein and Jonathan Kirshner, 35–53. Ithaca: Cornell University Press.

Bogdanor, Vernon (2020). *Britain and Europe in a Troubled World*. New Haven: Yale University Press.

Boix, Carles (1998). *Political Parties, Growth and Equality: Conservative and Social Democratic Economic Strategies in the World Economy*. Cambridge: Cambridge University Press.

Boix, Carles (2019). *Democratic Capitalism at the Crossroads: Technological Change and the Future of Politics*. Princeton: Princeton University Press.

Bolleyer, Nicole, and Evelyn Bytzek (2013). "Origins of Party Formation and New Party Success in Advanced Democracies." *European Journal of Political Research* 52, no. 6: 773–796.

Bomberg, E. (2002). "The Europeanisation of Green Parties: Exploring the EU's Impact." *West European Politics* 25, no. 3: 29–50.

Bordo, Michael D., Alan M. Taylor, and Jeffrey G. Williamson, eds. (2007). *Globalization in Historical Perspective*. Chicago: University of Chicago Press.

Börzel, Tanja A., and Michael Zürn (2021). "Contestations of the Liberal International Order: From Liberal Multilateralism to Postnational Liberalism." *International Organization* 75, no. 2: 282–305.

Brady, David, and Hang Young Lee (2014). "The Rise and Fall of Government Spending in Affluent Democracies, 1971–2008." *Journal of European Social Policy* 24, no. 1: 56–79.

Brands, Hal (2021). "Why Containment Can Stop the China Threat." *The National Interest* April 23. https://nationalinterest.org/feature/why-containment-can-stop-china-threat-183423.

Braun, Daniela, Sebastian Adrian Popa, and Hermann Schmitt (2019). "Responding to the Crisis: Eurosceptic Parties of the Left and Right and Their Changing Position towards the European Union." *European Journal of Political Research* 58, no. 3: 797–819.

Brodie, Bernard (1965). *Strategy in the Missile Age*. Princeton: Princeton University Press.

Brooks, David (2019). "How China Brings Us Together: An Existential Threat for the 21st Century." *New York Times*, 14 February. https://www.nytimes.com/2019/02/14/opinion/china-economy.html.

Brooks, Stephen G., and William C. Wohlforth (2016a). *America Abroad: The United States' Global Role in the 21st Century*. New York: Oxford University Press.

Brooks, Stephen G., and William C. Wohlforth (2016b). "The Rise and Fall of the Great Powers in the Twenty-First Century: China's Rise and the Fate of America's Global Position." *International Security* 40, no. 3: 7–53.

Brown, Garrett W., and David Held (2010). *The Cosmopolitanism Reader*. Cambridge: Polity.

Broz, J. Lawrence, Jeffry Frieden, and Stephen Weymouth (2021). "Populism in Place: The Economic Geography of the Globalization Backlash." *International Organization* 75, no. 2: 464–494.

Brummer, Klaus, and Kai Oppermann (2016). "Germany's Foreign Policy after the End of the Cold War: 'Becoming Normal?'" *Oxford Handbooks Online: Political Science*, April: 1–30.

Budge, Ian, and Michael Laver (1992). *Party Policy and Government Coalitions*. London: St. Martin's Press.

Burgoon, Brian (2001). "Globalization and Welfare Compensation: Disentangling the Ties That Bind." *International Organization* 55, no. 3: 509–551.

Burgoon, Brian (2009). "Globalization and Backlash: Polanyi's Revenge?" *Review of International Political Economy* 16, no. 2: 145–177.

Burgoon, Brian (2012). "Inequality and Anti-Globalization Backlash by Political Parties." *European Union Politics* 14, no. 3: 408–435.

Burgoon, Brian, Panicos Demetriades, and Geoffrey Underhill (2012). "Sources and Legitimacy of Financial Liberalization." *European Journal of Political Economy* 28, no. 2: 147–161.

Burgoon, Brian, Sam van Noort, Matthijs Rooduijn, and Geoffrey Underhill (2019). "Positional Deprivation and Support for Radical Right and Radical Left Parties." *Economic Policy* 34, no. 97: 49–93.

Burgoon, Brian, and Wouter Schakel (2022). "Embedded Liberalism or Embedded Nationalism? How Welfare States Affect Anti-Globalisation Nationalism in Party Platforms." *West European Politics* 45, no. 1: 50–76.

Burnham, Walter Dean (1978). "Thoughts on the 'Governability Crisis' in the West." *Washington Quarterly* 1, no. 3: 46–57.

Cameron, David R. (1978). "The Expansion of the Public Economy: A Comparative Analysis." *American Political Science Review* 72, no. 4: 1243–1261.

Cantillon, Bea (2020). "Poverty and Inequality." In *Handbook on Society and Social Policy*, edited by Nicholas Ellison and Tina Haux, 23–34. Northhampton: Edward Elgar Publishing.

Caselli, Mauro, Andrea Fracasso, and Silvio Traverso (2021). "Globalization, Robotization, and Electoral Outcomes: Evidence from Spatial Regressions for Italy." *Journal of Regional Science* 61, no. 1: 86–111.

Caughey, Devin, Tom O'Grady, and Christopher Warshaw (2019). "Policy Ideology in European Mass Publics, 1981–2016." *American Political Science Review* 113, no. 3: 674–693.

Ceadel, Martin (1980). *Pacifism in Britain, 1914–1945*. Oxford: Clarendon Press.

Centeno, Miguel, and Joseph Nathan Cohen (2012). "The Arc of Neoliberalism." *Annual Review of Sociology* 38: 317–340.

Cha, Victor D. (2000). "Abandonment, Entrapment, and Neoclassical Realism in Asia: The United States, Japan, and Korea." *International Studies Quarterly* 44, no. 2: 261–291.

Chai, Sun-Ki (1997). "Entrenching the Yoshida Defense Doctrine: Three Techniques for Institutionalization." *International Organization* 51, no. 3: 389–412.

Chryssogelos, Angelos-Stylianos (2010). "Undermining the West from Within: European Populists, the US and Russia." *European View* 9, no. 2: 267–277.

Clark, D. (2019). "Share of Votes for CDU and SPD in German Elections 1953–2017." September 23, 2019. https://www.statista.com/statistics/1037985/cdu-and-spd-vote-share-by-election/.

Clark, Terry Nichols, and Seymour Martin Lipset (2001). *The Breakdown of Class Politics: A Debate on Post-Industrial Stratification*. Baltimore: Johns Hopkins University Press.

Clifford, Bob (2012). *The Global Right Wing and the Clash of World Politics*. New York: Cambridge University Press.

Clinton, William Jefferson (1997). "Address by President Bill Clinton to the UN General Assembly." September 22. https://2009-2017.state.gov/p/io/potusunga/207553.htm.

Colantone, Italo, and Piero Stanig (2018). "Global Competition and Brexit." *American Political Science Review* 112, no. 2: 201–218.

Colgan, Jeff D., and Robert O. Keohane (2017). "The Liberal Order Is Rigged: Fix It Now or Watch It Wither." *Foreign Affairs* 96, no. 3: 36–44.

Conze, Eckart, Martin Klimke, and Jeremy Varon, eds. (2017). *Nuclear Threats, Nuclear Fear, and the Cold War of the 1980s.* Cambridge: Cambridge University Press.

Cooley, Alexander, and Daniel H. Nexon (2020). *Exit From Hegemony: The Unraveling of the American Global Order.* New York: Oxford University Press.

Cooper, Robert (2000). "The Post-Modern State and the World Order." London: Demos.

Copelovitch, Mark, Sara B. Hobolt, and Stefanie Walter (2020). "Challenges to the Contemporary Global Order: Cause for Pessimism or Optimism?" *Journal of European Public Policy* 27, no. 7: 1114–1125.

Copelovitch, Mark, and Jon C.W. Pevehouse (2019). "International Organizations in a New Era of Populist Nationalism." *Review of International Organizations* 14, no. 2: 169–1286.

Corduwener, Pepijn (2016). "Democracy as a Contested Concept in Post-War Western Europe: A Comparative Study of Political Debates in France, West Germany, and Italy." *Historical Journal* 59, no. 1: 197–220.

Corman, Juliane, Kim Harris, David Levin, Jeffrey Schulte, and Brittany Shanks. (2015). "Support for Defense and Military Spending." *Public Opinion Quarterly* 79, no. 1: 166–180.

Coser, Lewis A. (1956). *The Functions of Social Conflict.* Glencoe, IL: Free Press.

Cox, Michael, John Ikenberry, and Takashi Inoguchi (2000). *American Democracy Promotion: Impulses, Strategies, and Impacts.* Oxford: Oxford University Press.

Crozier, Michel J., Samuel P. Huntington, and Joji Watanuki (1975). "The Crisis of Democracy: Report on the Government of Democracies to the Trilateral Commission." New York: New York University Press.

Dahl, Robert A. (1965). "Reflections on Opposition in Western Democracies." *Government and Opposition* 1, no. 1: 7–24.

Dal Bó, Ernesto, Frederico Finan, Olle Folke, Torsten Persson, and Johanna Rickne (2018). "Economic Losers and Political Winners: Sweden's Radical Right." Unpublished manuscript.

Dancygier, Rafaela, and Stefanie Walter (2015). "Globalization, Labor Market Risks, and Class Cleavages." In *The Politics of Advanced Capitalism*, edited by Hanspeter Kriesi, Herbert Kitschelt, Pablo Beramendi, and Silja Häusermann, 133–156. Cambridge: Cambridge University Press.

Davis, Christina L. (2019). "Japan: Interest Group Politics, Foreign Policy Linkages, and the TPP." In *Megaregulation Contested: Global Economic Ordering After TPP*, edited by Benedict Kingsbury, David M. Malone, Paul Mertenskötter, Richard B. Stewart, Thomas Streinz, and Atsushi Sunami, 573–591. Oxford: Oxford University Press.

De Mesquita, Bruce Bueno, Alastair Smith, Randolph M. Siverson, and James D. Morrow (2003). *The Logic of Political Survival.* Cambridge: MIT Press.

De Neve, Jan-Emmanuel (2011). "The Median Voter Data Set: Voter Preferences Across 50 Democracies." *Electoral Studies* 30, no. 4: 865–871.

De Spiegeleire, Stephan, Clarissa Skinner, and Tim Sweijs (2017). "The Rise of Populist Sovereignism: What it is, Where it Comes from, and What it Means for International Security and Defense." Hague Centre for Strategic Studies.

De Vries, Catherine E., and Sara Hobolt (2019). *Political Entrepreneurs: The Rise of Challenger Parties in Europe.* Princeton, NJ: Princeton University Press.

De Vries, Catherine E., Sara Hobolt, and Stefanie Walter (2021). "Politicizing International Cooperation: The Mass Public, Political Entrepreneurs, and Political Opportunity Structures." *International Organization* 75, no. 2: 306–332.

De Vries, Catherine E., and Kathleen R. McNamara (2018). "How Choice Can Save Europe: The EU Needs Less Technocracy and More Democracy." *Foreign Affairs.* https://www.foreignaffairs.com/articles/europe/2018-05-14/how-choice-can-save-europe.

DeLong, J. Bradford (1997). "America's Peacetime Inflation: The 1970s." In *Reducing Inflation: Motivation and Strategy,* edited by Christina D. Romer and David H. Romer, 247–280. Chicago: University of Chicago Press.

Deporte, Anton William (1979). *Europe between the Superpowers: The Enduring Balance.* New Haven: Yale University Press.

Desch, Michael C. (2007). "America's Liberal Illiberalism: The Ideological Origins of Overreaction in U.S. Foreign Policy." *International Security* 32, no. 3: 7–43.

Deudney, Daniel, and G. John Ikenberry (2021). "Misplaced Restraint: The Quincy Coalition versus Liberal Internationalism." *Survival* 63, no. 4: 7–32.

Di Bella, Gabriel, and Francesco Grigoli (2019). "Optimism, Pessimism, and Short-term Fluctuations." *Journal of Macroeconomics* 60: 79–96.

Dippel, Christian, Robert Gold, and Stephan Heblich (2015). "Globalization and Its (Dis-)Content: Trade Shocks and Voting Behavior." NBER Working Paper. Cambridge, MA: National Bureau of Economic Research. https://econpapers.repec.org/paper/nbrnberwo/21812.htm.

Doenecke, Justus D. (1979). *Not to the Swift: The Old Isolationists in the Cold War Era.* Lewisburg: Bucknell University Press.

Dolezal, Martin (2008). "Austria: Transformation Driven by an Established Party." In *West European Politics in the Age of Globalization,* edited by Hanspeter Kriesi, Edgar Grande, Romain Lachat, Martin Dolezal, Simon Bornschier, and Timotheos Frey, 105–129. Cambridge: Cambridge University Press.

Domke, William K., Richard C. Eichenberg, and Catherine M. Kelleher (1987). "Consensus Lost?: Domestic Politics and the 'Crisis' in NATO." *World Politics* 39, no. 3: 382–407.

Dorman, Andrew M., and Joyce P. Kaufman, eds. (2011). *The Future of Transatlantic Relations: Perceptions, Policy, and Practice.* Stanford: Stanford University Press.

Dreher, Axel (2006). "Does Globalization Affect Growth? Evidence from a New Index of Globalization." *Applied Economics* 38, no. 10: 1091–1110.

Dreyer, David, and William R. Thompson (2011). *Handbook of International Rivalries.* 1st ed. Washington, DC: CQ Press.

Drezner, Daniel W. (2010). "Mercantilist and Realist Perspectives on the Global Political Economy." *Oxford Research Encyclopedias: International Studies.* https://oxfordre.com/internationalstudies/display/10.1093/acrefore/9780190846626.001.0001/acrefore-9780190846626-e-260.

Drezner, Daniel W. (2014). "The System Worked: Global Economic Governance during the Great Recession." *World Politics* 66, no. 1: 123–164.

Dudziak, Mary L. (2012). *War Time: An Idea, Its History, Its Consequences.* New York: Oxford University Press.

Dupuy, Kendra, James Ron, and Aseem Prakash (2016). "Hands Off My Regime! Governments' Restrictions on Foreign Aid to Non-Governmental Organizations in Poor and Middle-Income Countries." *World Development* 84: 299–311.

Eatwell, Roger, and Matthew Goodwin (2018). *National Populism: The Revolt Against Liberal Democracy.* London: Pelican.

Ecker-Ehrhardt, Matthias (2014). "Why Parties Politicise International Institutions: On Globalisation Backlash and Authority Contestation." *Review of International Political Economy* 21, no. 6: 1275–1312.

Edelstein, David M., and Joshua R. Itzkowitz Shifrinson (2018). "It's a Trap!: Security Commitments and the Risks of Entrapment." In *US Grand Strategy in the 21st Century: The Case for Restraint*, edited by A. Trevor Thrall and Benjamin H. Friedman, 19–41. London: Routledge.

Eichenberg, Richard C. (1989). *Public Opinion and National Security in Western Europe: Consensus Lost?* New York: Macmillan.

Eichenberg, Richard C., and Richard Stoll (2003). "Representing Defense: Democratic Control of the Defense Budget in the United States and Western Europe." *Journal of Conflict Resolution* 47, no. 4: 399–422.

Eichengreen, Barry J. (1996). *Globalizing Capital: A History of the International Monetary System*. Princeton: Princeton University Press.

Eichengreen, Barry J. (2007). *The European Economy since 1945: Coordinated Capitalism and Beyond*. Princeton, NJ: Princeton University Press.

Esping-Andersen, Gösta (1990). *The Three Worlds of Welfare Capitalism*. Princeton: Princeton University Press.

Esping-Andersen, Gösta (2002). *Why We Need a New Welfare State*. New York: Oxford University Press.

Estevez-Abe, Margarita (2008). *Welfare and Capitalism in Postwar Japan*. New York: Cambridge University Press.

Estevez-Abe, Margarita, Torben Iversen, and David Soskice (2001). "Social Protection and the Formation of Skills: A Reinterpretation of the Welfare State." In *Varieties of Capitalism*, edited by Peter Hall and David Soskice, 145–183. Oxford: Oxford University Press.

Evans, Gareth (2008). *The Responsibility to Protect: Ending Mass Atrocity Crimes Once and For All*. Washington, DC: Brookings Institution Press.

Falk, Richard (1998). "Global Civil Society: Perspectives, Initiatives, Movements." *Oxford Development Studies* 26, no. 1: 99–110.

Falk, Richard A. (1987). *The Promise of World Order: Essays in Normative International Relations*. Brighton: Wheatsheaf.

Fearon, James D. (1994). "Domestic Political Audiences and the Escalation of International Disputes." *American Political Science Review* 88, no. 3: 577–592.

Featherstone, Kevin (1994). "Jean Monnet and the 'Democratic Deficit' in the European Union." *JCMS: Journal of Common Market Studies* 32, no. 2: 149–170.

Ferguson, Thomas (1984). "From Normalcy to New Deal: Industrial Structure, Party Competition, and American Public Policy in the Great Depression." *International Organization* 38, no. 1: 41–94.

Ferrera, Maurizio (2008). "The European Welfare State: Golden Achievements, Silver Prospects." *West European Politics* 31, no. 1–2: 82–107.

Ferrera, Maurizio, and Martin Rhodes (2000). "Recasting European Welfare States: An Introduction." *West European Politics* 23, no. 2: 1–10.

Fettweis, Christopher, J. (2010). *Dangerous Times? The International Politics of Great Power Peace*. Washington, DC: Georgetown University Press.

Fetzer, Thiemo (2019). "Did Austerity Cause Brexit?" *American Economic Review* 109, no. 11: 3849–3886.

Finseraas, Henning (2008). "Immigration and Preferences for Redistribution: An Empirical Analysis of European Survey Data." *Comparative European Politics* 6, no. 4: 407–431.

Flynn, Gregory, and Hans Rattinger, eds. (1985). *The Public and Atlantic Defense.* New York: Routledge.

Ford, Robert, and Will Jennings (2020). "The Changing Cleavage Politics of Western Europe." *Annual Review of Political Science* 23: 295–314.

Fordham, Benjamin O. (1998). "Economic Interests, Party, and Ideology in Early Cold War Era U.S. Foreign Policy." *International Organization* 52, no. 2: 359–396.

Fordham, Benjamin O. (2007). "The Evolution of Republican and Democratic Positions on Cold War Military Spending: A Historical Puzzle." *Social Science History* 31, no. 4: 603–636.

Forsberg, Aaron (2000). *America and the Japanese Miracle: The Cold War Context of Japan's Postwar Economic Revival, 1950–1960.* Chapel Hill: University of North Carolina Press.

Foster, Chase, and Jeffry Frieden (2019). "Compensation, Austerity, and Populism: Social Spending and Voting in 17 Western European Countries." Working Paper (December). https://www.hks.harvard.edu/centers/mrcbg/programs/growthpolicy/compensation-austerity-and-populism.

Frieden, Jeffry (1988). "Sectoral Conflict and Foreign Economic Policy, 1914–1940." *International Organization* 42, no. 1: 59–90.

Frieden, Jeffry A. (2006). *Global Capitalism: Its Fall and Rise in the Twentieth Century.* New York: W. W. Norton.

Frieden, Jeffry (2012). "Global Economic Governance After the Crisis." *Perspektiven Der Wirtschaftspolitik* 13 (Special Issue): 1–12.

Frum, David (2005). "The End of the Transatlantic Affair." Financial Times, 30 January. https://www.ft.com/content/e78283f2-72f4-11d9-86a0-00000e2511c8.

Fukuyama, Francis (1989). "The End of History?" *National Interest*, no. 16: 3–18.

Gaddis, John Lewis (2005). *Strategies of Containment: A Critical Appraisal of American National Security Policy during the Cold War.* Rev. and expanded ed. New York: Oxford University Press.

Galston, William A. (2022). "The New Axis of Autocracy." *Wall Street Journal*, February 8, 2022. https://www.wsj.com/articles/axis-autocracy-russia-putin-ukraine-china-france-germany-commit-defense-invasion-scholz-biden-macron-11644336548.

Garfinkel, Michelle R., and Stergios Skaperdas, eds. (2012). *The Oxford Handbook of the Economics of Peace and Conflict.* Oxford: Oxford University Press.

Garrett, Geoffrey (1998). *Partisan Politics in the Global Economy.* Cambridge: Cambridge University Press.

Garten, Jeffrey E. (1992). *A Cold Peace: America, Japan, Germany, and the Struggle for Supremacy.* New York: Times Books.

Gerstle, Gary (2022). *The Rise and Fall of the Neoliberal Order: America and the World in the Free Market Era.* New York: Oxford University Press.

Gholz, Eugene, Daryl G. Press, and Harvey M. Sapolsky (1997). "Come Home, America: The Strategy of Restraint in the Face of Temptation." *International Security* 21, no. 4: 5–48.

Gibler, Douglas, Steven Miller, and Erin Little (2016). "An Analysis of the Militarized Interstate Dispute (MID) Dataset, 1816–2001." *International Studies Quarterly* 60, no. 4: 719–730.

Giddens, Anthony (1985). *The Nation-State and Violence.* Chichester: Polity Press.

Gidron, Noam, and Daniel Ziblatt (2019). "Center-Right Political Parties in Advanced Democracies." *Annual Review of Political Science* 22, no. 1: 17–35.

Gilens, Martin (2014). *Affluence and Influence: Economic Inequality and Political Power in America*. Princeton: Princeton University Press.

Gilmore, Jonathan (2015). *The Cosmopolitan Military: Armed Forces and Human Security in the 21st Century*. New Security Challenges Series. London: Palgrave Macmillan.

Gilpin, Robert (1975). *U.S. Power and the Multinational Corporation: The Political Economy of Foreign Direct Investment*. New York: Basic Books.

Gilpin, Robert (1987). *The Political Economy of International Relations*. Princeton: Princeton University Press.

Gilpin, Robert (2002). *The Challenge of Global Capitalism: The World Economy in the 21st Century*. Princeton: Princeton University Press.

Gingrich, Jane (2019). "Did State Responses to Automation Matter for Voters?" *Research & Politics* 6, no. 1: 1–9.

Gingrich, Jane, and Silja Häusermann (2015). "The Decline of the Working-Class Vote, the Reconfiguration of the Welfare Support Coalition and Consequences for the Welfare State." *Journal of European Social Policy* 25, no. 1: 50–75.

Glanville, Luke (2014). *Sovereignty and the Responsibility to Protect: A New History*. Chicago: University of Chicago Press.

Goertz, Gary, Paul F. Diehl, and Alexandru Balas (2016). *The Puzzle of Peace: The Evolution of Peace in the International System*. Oxford: Oxford University Press.

Golder, Matt (2003). "Explaining Variation in the Success of Extreme Right Parties in Western Europe." *Comparative Political Studies* 36, no. 4: 432–466.

Golosov, Grigorii (2010). "The Effective Number of Parties: A New Approach." *Party Politics* 16, no. 2: 171–192.

Goodman, Sara Wallace, and Thomas B. Pepinsky (2021). "The Exclusionary Foundations of Embedded Liberalism." *International Organization* 75, no. 2: 411–439.

Gourevitch, Peter (1986). *Politics in Hard Times: Comparative Responses to International Economic Crises*. Ithaca: Cornell University Press.

Gourevitch, Peter Alexis (1977). "International Trade, Domestic Coalitions, and Liberty: Comparative Responses to the Crisis of 1873–1896." *Journal of Interdisciplinary History* 8, no. 2: 281–313.

Grajewski, Marcin (2021). "The EU Strategic Autonomy Debate [What Think Tanks Are Thinking]." *European Parliament*, March 30, 2021.

Gravelle, Timothy B., Jason Reifler, and Thomas J. Scotto (2017). "The Structure of Foreign Policy Attitudes in Transatlantic Perspective: Comparing the United States, United Kingdom, France and Germany." *European Journal of Political Research* 56, no. 4: 757–776.

Greene, William E. (2012). *Econometric Analysis*. 7th ed. Upper Saddle River: Prentice Hall.

Greider, William (2018). "American Hubris, or, How Globalization Brought Us Donald Trump." *Nation*, April 19. https://www.thenation.com/article/archive/american-hub ris-or-how-globalization-brought-us-donald-trump/

Grewal, David S. (2018). "Three Theses on the Current Crisis of International Liberalism." *Indiana Journal of Global Legal Studies* 25, no. 2: 595–621.

Grieco, Joseph M. (1988). "Anarchy and the Limits of Cooperation: A Realist Critique of the Newest Liberal Institutionalism." *International Organization* 42, no. 3: 485–507.

Griffith, Robert (1979). "Old Progressives and the Cold War." *Journal of American History* 66, no. 2: 334–347.

Guiso, Luigi, Helios Herrera, Massimo Morelli, and Tommaso Sonno (2017). "Demand and Supply of Populism." *EIEF Working Papers Series*. Einaudi Institute for Economics and Finance (EIEF). https://ideas.repec.org/p/eie/wpaper/1703.html.

Gygli, Savina, Florian Haelg, Niklas Potrafke, and Jan-Egbert Sturm (2019). "The KOF Globalisation Index—Revisited." *Review of International Organizations* 14, no. 3: 543–574.

Ha, Eunyoung, and George Tsebelis (2010). "Globalization and Welfare: Which Causes Which?" *APSA Meeting Paper*. https://ssrn.com/abstract=1657519.

Hafner-Burton, Emilie M., Edward D. Mansfield, and Jon C. W. Pevehouse (2015). "Human Rights Institutions, Sovereignty Costs and Democratization." *British Journal of Political Science* 45, no. 1: 1–27.

Hainsworth, Paul (2004). "The Extreme Right in France: The Rise and Rise of Jean-Marie Le Pen's Front National." *Representation* 40, no. 2: 101–114.

Halikiopoulou, Daphne, Kyriaki Nanou, and Sofia Vasilopoulou (2012). "The Paradox of Nationalism: The Common Denominator of Radical Right and Radical Left Euroscepticism." *European Journal of Political Research* 51, no. 4: 504–539.

Halikiopoulou, Daphne, and Tim Vlandas (2016). "Risks, Costs and Labour Markets: Explaining Cross-National Patterns of Far Right Party Success in European Parliament Elections." *Journal of Common Market Studies* 54, no. 3: 636–655.

Hall, Peter A. (2018). "How Growth Strategies Evolve in the Developed Democracies." In *Growth and Welfare in Advanced Capitalist Economies*, edited by Anke Hassel and Bruno Palier, 57–97. Oxford: Oxford University Press.

Hall, Peter A. (2020). "The Electoral Politics of Growth Regimes." *Perspectives on Politics* 18, no. 1: 185–199.

Hall, Peter A., and David Soskice (2001). *Varieties of Capitalism: The Institutional Foundations of Comparative Advantage*. Oxford: Oxford University Press.

Halliday, Fred (1983). "The New Cold War." *Bulletin of Peace Proposals* 14, no. 2: 125–129.

Hanrieder, Wolfram F. (1989). *Germany, America, and Europe: Forty Years of German Foreign Policy*. New Haven: Yale University Press.

Harteveld, Eelco (2016). "Winning the 'Losers' but Losing the 'Winners'? The Electoral Consequences of the Radical Right Moving to the Economic Left." *Electoral Studies* 44: 225–234.

Hass, Ryan (2021). "Playing the China Card." *Noēma Magazine*. May 20. https://www.noemamag.com/playing-the-china-card/.

Häusermann, Silja (2010). *Politics of Welfare State Reform in Continental Europe: Modernization in Hard Times*. New York: Cambridge University Press.

Hayes, Louis D. (2009). *Introduction to Japanese Politics*. Armonk, NY: M.E. Sharpe.

Hays, Jude (2009). *Globalization and the New Politics of Embedded Liberalism*. New York: Oxford University Press.

Hays, Jude C., Sean D. Ehrlich, and Clint Peinhardt (2005). "Government Spending and Public Support for Trade in the OECD: An Empirical Test of the Embedded Liberalism Thesis." *International Organization* 59, no. 2: 473–494.

Heginbotham, Eric, and Richard J. Samuels (2018). "Active Denial: Redesigning Japan's Response to China's Military Challenge." *International Security* 42, no. 4: 128–169.

Heinisch, Reinhard (2003). "Success in Opposition – Failure in Government: Explaining the Performance of Right-wing Populist Parties in Public Office." *West European Politics* 26, no. 3: 91–130.

Helleiner, Eric. (2021). "The Diversity of Economic Nationalism." *New Political Economy* 26, no. 2: 229–238.

Held, David (1995). *Democracy and the Global Order: From the Modern State to Cosmopolitan Governance.* Stanford: Stanford University Press.

Hemerijck, Anton (2012). *Changing Welfare States.* Oxford: Oxford University Press.

Hemerijck, Anton, ed. (2017). *The Uses of Social Investment.* Oxford: Oxford University Press.

Hemmer, Christopher, and Peter J. Katzenstein (2002). "Why Is There No NATO in Asia? Collective Identity, Regionalism, and the Origins of Multilateralism." *International Organization* 56, no. 3: 575–607.

Henke, Marina, and Richard Maher (2021). "The Populist Challenge to European Defense." *Journal of European Public Policy* 28, no. 3: 389–406.

Henley, Jon (2017). "Marine Le Pen Promises Liberation from the EU with France-First Policies." *Guardian,* February 5. https://www.theguardian.com/world/2017/feb/05/marine-le-pen-promises-liberation-from-the-eu-with-france-first-policies.

Hensel, Paul R., Sara McLaughlin Mitchell, Thomas E. Sowers, and Clayton L. Thyne (2008). "Bones of Contention: Comparing Territorial, Maritime, and River Issues." *Journal of Conflict Resolution* 52, no. 1: 117–143.

Hernández, Enrique, and Hanspeter Kriesi (2016). "The Electoral Consequences of the Financial and Economic Crisis in Europe." *European Journal of Political Research* 55, no. 2: 203–224.

Hirschman, Albert O. (1945). *National Power and the Structure of Foreign Trade.* Berkeley: University of California Press.

Hiscox, Michael J. (2020). *International Trade and Political Conflict.* Princeton: Princeton University Press.

Höbelt, Lothar (2003). *Defiant Populist Jörg Haider and the Politics of Austria.* Indiana: Purdue University Press.

Hix, Simon (1999). *The Political System of the European Union.* European Union Series. Palgrave Macmillan.

Hobolt, Sara Binzer (2009). *Europe in Question: Referendums on European Integration. Europe in Question.* Oxford: Oxford University Press.

Hobsbawm, Eric J. (1990). "Goodbye to All That." *Marxism Today,* October: 18–23.

Hoffmann, Stanley (1995). "The Crisis of Liberal Internationalism." *Foreign Policy, no.* 98: 159–77.

Hoffmann, Stephanie, C. (2013). *European Security in NATO's Shadow: Party Ideologies and Institution Building.* Cambridge: Cambridge University Press.

Holmes, Michael, and Simon Lightfoot (2007). "The Europeanisation of Left Political Parties: Limits to Adaptation and Consensus." *Capital & Class* 31, no. 3: 141–158.

Holsti, Kal J. (1978). "A New International Politics? Diplomacy in Complex Interdependence." *International Organization* 32, no. 2: 513–530.

Holsti, O.R. (1992). "Public Opinion and Foreign Policy: Challenges to the Almond-Lippmann Consensus." *International Studies Quarterly* 36, no. 4: 439–466.

Holsti, Ole R., and James N. Rosenau (1996). "Liberals, Populists, Libertarians, and Conservatives: The Link between Domestic and International Affairs." *International Political Science Review* 17, no. 1: 29–54.

Hooghe, Liesbet (2003). "Europe Divided?: Elites vs. Public Opinion on European Integration." *European Union Politics* 4, no. 3: 281–304.

Hooghe, Liesbet, Tobias Lenz, and Gary Marks (2019a). *A Theory of International Organization*. Oxford: Oxford University Press.

Hooghe, Liesbet, Tobias Lenz, and Gary Marks (2019b). "Contested World Order: The Delegitimation of International Governance." *Review of International Organizations* 14, no. 4: 731–743.

Hooghe, Liesbet, and Gary Marks (2009). "A Postfunctionalist Theory of European Integration: From Permissive Consensus to Constraining Dissensus." *British Journal of Political Science* 39, no. 1: 1–23.

Hooghe, Liesbet, and Gary Marks (2015). "Delegation and Pooling in International Organizations." *Review of International Organizations* 10, no. 3: 305–328.

Hooghe, Liesbet, and Gary Marks (2018). "Cleavage Theory Meets Europe's Crises: Lipset, Rokkan, and the Transnational Cleavage." *Journal of European Public Policy* 25, no. 1: 109–135.

Hooghe, Liesbet, Gary Marks, and Carole J. Wilson (2002). "Does Left/Right Structure Party Positions on European Integration?" *Comparative Political Studies* 35, no. 8: 965–989.

Hooghe, Liesbet, Gary Marks, Tobias Lenz, Jeanine Bezuijen, Besir Ceka, Svet Derderyan (2017). *Measuring International Authority*. Oxford: Oxford University Press.

Hopkin, Jonathan (2020). *Anti-System Politics: The Crisis of Market Liberalism in Rich Democracies*. Oxford: Oxford University Press.

Hopkin, Jonathan, and Mark Blyth (2019). "The Global Economics of European Populism: Growth Regimes and Party System Change in Europe." *Government and Opposition* 54, no. 2: 193–225.

Huber, John, and Ronald Inglehart (1995). "Expert Interpretations of Party Space and Party Locations in 42 Societies." *Party Politics* 1, no. 1: 73–111.

Hufbauer, Gary Clyde, and Euijin Jung (2016). "Why Has Trade Stopped Growing? Not Much Liberalization and Lots of Micro-Protection." *Peterson Institute for International Economics*, March 23, 2016. https://www.piie.com/blogs/trade-investment-policy-watch/why-has-trade-stopped-growing-not-much-liberalization-and-lots.

Hughes, Christopher W. (2017). "Japan's Grand Strategic Shift: From the Yoshida Doctrine to an Abe Doctrine?" In *Strategic Asia 2017–18: Power, Ideas, and Military Strategy in the Asia-Pacific*, edited by Ashley J. Tellis, Alison Szalwinski, and Michael Wills, 73–105. Washington, DC: National Bureau of Asian Research.

Huntington, Samuel P. (1987/1988). "Coping with the Lippmann Gap." *Foreign Affairs* 66, no. 3: 453–477.

Huntington, Samuel P. (1988). "The U.S.: Decline or Renewal?" *Foreign Affairs* 67, no. 2: 76–96.

Huntington, Samuel P. (1993). "The Clash of Civilizations?" *Foreign Affairs* 72, no. 3: 22–49.

Hutter, Swen, Edgar Grande, and Hanspeter Kriesi, eds. (2016). *Politicising Europe: Integration and Mass Politics*. Cambridge: Cambridge University Press.

Ikenberry, G. John (2001). *After Victory: Institutions, Strategic Restraint, and the Rebuilding of Order after Major Wars*. Princeton: Princeton University Press.

Ikenberry, G. John (2009). "Liberal Internationalism 3.0: America and the Dilemmas of Liberal World Order." *Perspectives on Politics* 7, no. 1: 71–87.

Ikenberry, G. John (2019). "Reflections on After Victory." *British Journal of Politics and International Relations* 21, no. 1: 5–19.

Ikenberry, G. John (2020a). *A World Safe for Democracy: Liberal Internationalism and the Crises of Global Order*. New Haven: Yale University Press.

Ikenberry, G. John (2020b). "The Light That Failed: Why the West Is Losing the Fight for Democracy." *Foreign Affairs* 14, no. 1: 133–136.

Ikenberry, G. John (2020c). "The Next Liberal Order: The Age of Contagion Demands More Internationalism, Not Less." *Foreign Affairs* 99, no. 4:133–142.

Immerwahr, Daniel (2020). *How to Hide an Empire: A History of the Greater United States*. New York: Vintage.

Inglehart, Ronald, and Pippa Norris (2017). "Trump and the Populist Authoritarian Parties: The *Silent Revolution* in Reverse." *Perspectives on Politics* 15, no. 2: 443–454.

Inglot, Tomasz (2008). *Welfare States in East Central Europe, 1919–2004*. Cambridge: Cambridge University Press.

International Monetary Fund (IMF) (2009). "World Economic Outlook: Crisis and Recovery." World Economic and Financial Surveys. https://www.imf.org/en/Publicati ons/WEO/Issues/2016/12/31/Crisis-and-Recovery.

Irwin, Douglas A. (1993). "Multilateral and bilateral trade policies in the world trading system: an historical perspective." *New Dimensions in Regional Integration* 90: 90–119.

Iversen, Torben (2005). *Capitalism, Democracy, and Welfare*. New York: Cambridge University Press.

Iversen, Torben, and Thomas R. Cusack (2000). "The Causes of Welfare State Expansion: Deindustrialization or Globalization?" *World Politics* 52, no. 3: 313–349.

Jackman, Robert W., and Karin Volpert (1996). "Conditions Favoring Parties of the Extreme Right in Western Europe." *British Journal of Political Science* 26, no. 4: 501–521.

Jacobs, Lawrence R., and Benjamin I. Page (2005). "Who Influences U.S. Foreign Policy?" *American Political Science Review* 99, no. 1: 107–123.

Jamitzky, Ulli (2015). "Diffusion of Japanese Preferential Trade Agreements: Why Is No Evaluation Underway?" *Japanese Economy* 41, no. 1–2: 1–13.

Jenson, Jane (2010). "Diffusing Ideas for After Neoliberalism: The Social Investment Perspective in Europe and Latin America." *Global Social Policy* 10, no. 1: 59–84.

Jesuit, David, and Vincent Mahler (2004). "Electoral Support for Extreme Right-Wing Parties: A Subnational Analysis of Western European Elections in the 1990s." LIS Working Paper Series, no. 391. Luxembourg Income Study (LIS), Luxembourg.

Johnston, Alastair Iain (2019). "The Failures of the 'Failure of Engagement' with China." *Washington Quarterly* 42, no. 2: 99–114.

Judt, Tony (2005). *Postwar: A History of Europe since 1945*. London: Vintage.

Kafura, Craig, and Dina Smeltz (2021). "Republicans and Democrats Split on China Policy." *The Chicago Council on Global Affairs*. December 10. https://www.thechicago council.org/research/public-opinion-survey/republicans-and-democrats-split-china-policy.

Kagan, Robert (2003). *Paradise and Power: America and Europe in the New World Order*. New York: Alfred A. Knopf.

Kahl, Colin, and Thomas Wright (2021). *Aftershocks: Pandemic Politics and the End of the Old International Order*. New York: St. Martin's Press.

Kahler, Miles (2013). "Economic Crisis and Global Governance: The Stability of a Globalized World." *Procedia—Social and Behavioral Sciences* 77: 55–64.

Kaldor, Mary (2000). "Civilising Globalisation? The Implications of the 'Battle in Seattle.'" *Millennium* 29, no. 1: 105–114.

Kaldor, Mary (2003). "American Power: From 'Compellance' to Cosmopolitanism?" *International Affairs* 79, no. 1: 1–22.

Kaldor, Mary H. (1999). "The Idea of 1989: The Origins of the Concept of Global Civil Society." *Transnational Law & Contemporary Problems* 9, no. 2: 475–488.

Kane, Tim (2016). "The Decline of American Engagement: Patterns in U.S. Troop Deployments." Economics Working Paper 16101. https://www.hoover.org/research/decline-american-engagement-patterns-us-troop-deployments.

Karns, Margaret P., and Karen A. Mingst (2010). *International Organizations: The Politics and Process.* New York: Lynne Rienner.

Katz, Richard S., and Peter Mair (1995). "Changing Models of Party Organization and Party Democracy: The Emergence of the Cartel Party." *Party Politics* 1, no. 1: 5–28.

Katz, Richard S., and Peter Mair (2018). *Democracy and the Cartelization of Political Parties.* Oxford: Oxford University Press.

Katzenstein, Peter J., ed. (1978). *Between Power and Plenty: Foreign Economic Policies of Advanced Industrial States.* Madison: University of Wisconsin Press.

Katzenstein, Peter J. (1985). *Small States in World Markets: Industrial Policy in Europe.* Ithaca: Cornell University Press.

Katzenstein, Peter J., and Jonathan Kirshner, eds. (2022). *The Downfall of the American Order: Liberalism's End?* Ithaca: Cornell University Press.

Kennedy, Paul (1987). *The Rise and Fall of the Great Powers.* New York: Random House.

Kenneth, Benoit, Michael Laver, and Slava Mikhaylov (2009). "Treating Words as Data with Error: Uncertainty in Text Statements of Policy Positions." *American Journal of Political Science* 53, no. 2: 495–513.

Keohane, Robert O. (1984). *After Hegemony: Cooperation and Discord in the World Political Economy.* Princeton, NJ: Princeton University Press.

Keohane, Robert O., and Stanley Hoffmann, eds. (1991). *The New European Community: Decisionmaking and Institutional Change.* Boulder: Westview Press.

Keohane, Robert O., and Joseph S. Nye (1971). *Power and Interdependence.* Glenview: Scott, Foresman.

Kersbergen, Kees van, and Barbara Vis (2013). *Comparative Welfare State Politics: Development, Opportunities, and Reform.* Cambridge: Cambridge University Press.

Kertzer, Joshua D. (2013). "Making Sense of Isolationism: Foreign Policy Mood as a Multilevel Phenomenon." *Journal of Politics* 75, no. 1: 225–240.

Kessler, Alan E. and Gary P. Freeman (2005). "Public Opinion in the EU on Immigration from Outside the Community." *Journal of Common Market Studies* 43, no. 4: 825–850.

Kim, Nam Kyu (2018). "International Conflict, International Security Environment, and Military Coups." *International Interactions* 44, no. 5: 936–952.

Kim, Heemin, and Richard C. Fording (1998). "Voter Ideology in Western Democracies, 1946–1989." *European Journal of Political Research* 33, no. 1: 73–97.

Kindleberger, Charles P. (1973). *The World in Depression, 1929–1939.* Berkeley: University of California Press.

Kirshner, Jonathan (2014). *American Power after the Financial Crisis.* Ithaca: Cornell University Press.

Kitschelt, Herbert (1994). *The Transformation of European Social Democracy.* Cambridge: Cambridge University Press.

Kitschelt, Herbert (1997). *The Radical Right in Western Europe: A Comparative Analysis.* Ann Arbor, MI: University of Michigan Press.

Kjar, Scott A., and William L. Anderson (2010). "War and the Austrian School: Applying the Economics of the Founders." *Economics of Peace and Security Journal* 5, no. 1: 6–11.

Klingemann, Hans-Dieter, and Andrea Volkens, Ian Budge, Judith Bara, and Michael D. McDonald (2006). *Mapping Policy Preferences II: Estimates for Parties, Electors, and Governments in Eastern Europe, European Union and OECD 1990–2003*. Oxford: Oxford University Press.

Knigge, Pia (1998). "The Ecological Correlates of Right-wing Extremism in Western Europe." *European Journal of Political Research* 34, no. 2: 249–279.

Konstantinidis, Nikitas, Matakos Konstantinos, and Mutlu-Eren Hande (2019). "'Take Back Control'? The Effects of Supranational Integration on Party-System Polarization." *Review of International Organizations* 14, no. 2: 297–333.

Koopmans, Ruud, and Michael Zürn (2019). "Cosmopolitanism and Communitarianism—How Globalization Is Reshaping Politics in the Twenty-First Century." In *The Struggle Over Borders: Cosmopolitanism and Communitarianism*, edited by Michael Zürn, Oliver Strijbis, Pieter de Wilde, Ruud Koopmans, and Wolfgang Merkel, 1–34. Cambridge: Cambridge University Press.

Kornprobst, Markus, and T.V. Paul (2021). "Globalization, Deglobalization and the Liberal International Order." *International Affairs (London)* 97, no. 5: 1305–1316.

Korpi, Walter, and Joakim Palme (1998). "The Paradox of Redistribution and Strategies of Equality: Welfare State Institutions, Inequality, and Poverty in the Western Countries." *American Sociological Review* 63, no. 5: 661–687.

Korpi, Walter, and Joakim Palme (2003). "New Politics and Class Politics in the Context of Austerity and Globalization: Welfare State Regress in 18 Countries, 1975–95." *American Political Science Review* 97, no. 3: 425–446.

Krastev, Ivan, and Stephen Holmes (2019). "How Liberalism Became 'the God That Failed' in Eastern Europe." *Guardian*, October 24, sec. World news. https://www.theguardian.com/world/2019/oct/24/western-liberalism-failed-post-communist-eastern-europe.

Krastev, Ivan, and Stephen Holmes (2020). *The Light That Failed: A Reckoning*. London: Penguin Books.

Krauthammer, Charles (1990). "The Unipolar Moment." *Foreign Affairs* 70, no. 1: 23–33.

Kriesi, Hanspeter, Edgar Grande, Romain Lachat, Martin Dolezal, Simon Bornschier, and Timotheos Frey (2008). *West European Politics in the Age of Globalization*. Cambridge: Cambridge University Press.

Kupchan, Charles A. (2020). *Isolationism: A History of America's Efforts to Shield Itself from the World*. New York: Oxford University Press.

Kupchan, Charles A., and Peter L. Trubowitz (2007). "Dead Center: The Demise of Liberal Internationalism in the United States." *International Security* 32, no. 2: 7–44.

Kupchan, Charles A., and Peter L. Trubowitz (2021). "The Home Front: Why an Internationalist Foreign Policy Needs a Stronger Domestic Foundation." *Foreign Affairs* 100, no. 3: 92–101.

Kurth, James R. (1979). "The Political Consequences of the Product Cycle: Industrial History and Political Outcomes." *International Organization* 33, no. 1: 1–34.

Kurzer, Paulette (1993). *Business and Banking: Political Change and Economic Integration in Western Europe*. Ithaca: Cornell University Press.

Laakso, Markku, and Rein Taagepera (1979). "'Effective' Number of Parties: A Measure with Application to West Europe." *Comparative Political Studies* 12, no. 1: 3–27.

Lake, David A. (2007). "Delegating Divisible Sovereignty: Sweeping a Conceptual Minefield." *Review of International Organizations* 2, no. 3: 219–237.

Lake, David A. (2018). "International Legitimacy Lost? Rule and Resistance When America Is First." *Perspectives on Politics* 16, no. 1: 6–21.

Lake, David A., Lisa L. Martin, and Thomas Risse (2021). "Challenges to the Liberal Order: Reflections on International Organization." *International Organization* 75, no. 2: 225–257.

Lascurettes, Kyle M. (2020). *Orders of Exclusion: Great Powers and the Strategic Sources of Foundational Rules in International Relations.* New York: Oxford University Press.

Layne, Christopher (1993). "The Unipolar Illusion: Why New Great Powers Will Rise." *International Security* 17, no. 4: 5–51.

Layne, Christopher (1997). "From Preponderance to Offshore Balancing: America's Future Grand Strategy." *International Security* 22, no. 1: 86–124.

Leali, Giorgio (2021). "EU-China Deal Spells Trouble for Macron at Home." *Politico.* March 18. *https://www.politico.eu/article/eu-china-deal-spells-trouble-for-macron-at-home/*

Leffler, Melvyn P. (2019). "China Isn't the Soviet Union: Confusing the Two Is Dangerous." *The Atlantic,* December 2. https://www.theatlantic.com/ideas/archive/2019/12/cold-war-china-purely-optional/601969/.

Lefkofridi, Zoe, and Elie Michel (2017). "The Electoral Politics of Solidarity: The Welfare Agendas of Radical Right Parties." In *The Strains of Commitment: The Political Sources of Solidarity in Diverse Societies,* edited by Keith Banting and Will Kymlicka, 233–267. Oxford: Oxford University Press.

Levi, Margaret (1988). *Of Rule and Revenue.* Berkeley: University of California Press.

Liff, Adam P. (2015). "Japan's Defense Policy: Abe the Evolutionary." *Washington Quarterly* 38, no. 2: 79–99.

Lim, Sijeong, and Brian Burgoon (2020). "Globalization and Support for Unemployment Spending in Asia: Do Asian Citizens Want to Embed Liberalism?" *Socio-Economic Review* 18, no. 2: 519–553.

Lind, Jennifer M. (2004). "Pacifism or Passing the Buck? Testing Theories of Japanese Security Policy." *International Security* 29, no. 1: 92–121.

Lind, Jennifer M., and William C. Wohlforth (2019). "The Future of the Liberal Order Is Conservative: A Strategy to Save the System." *Foreign Affairs* 98, no. 2: 70–80.

Lind, Michael (2018). "U.S. & China Relations: Cold War II." *National Review,* May 10. https://www.nationalreview.com/magazine/2018/05/28/us-china-relations-cold-war-ii/.

Lindberg, Leon N., and Stuart A. Scheingold (1970). *Europe's Would-Be Polity: Patterns of Change in the European Community.* Englewood Cliffs: Prentice Hall.

Lindberg, Tod, ed. (2005). *Beyond Paradise and Power: Europe, America, and the Future of a Troubled Partnership.* New York: Routledge.

Lindert, Peter H. (2004). *Growing Public: Social Spending and Economic Growth since the Eighteenth Century: Volume 1: The Story.* Cambridge: Cambridge University Press.

Lindsay, James M. (2000). "The New Apathy: How an Uninterested Public Is Reshaping Foreign Policy." *Foreign Affairs* 79, no. 5: 2–8.

Lindvall, Johannes, and David Rueda (2018). "Public Opinion, Party Politics, and the Welfare State." In *Welfare Democracies and Party Politics: Explaining Electoral Dynamics in Times of Changing Welfare Capitalism,* edited by Philip Manow, Bruno Palier, and Hanna Schwander, 89–118. Oxford: Oxford University Press.

Lippmann, Walter (1943). *U.S. Foreign Policy: Shield of the Republic.* Boston: Little, Brown.

Lipset, Seymour M., and Stein Rokkan (1967). *Party Systems and Voter Alignments: Cross-National Perspectives.* New York: Free Press.

Lowe, Will, Kenneth Benoit, Slava Mikhaylov, and Michael Laver (2011). "Scaling Policy Preferences from Coded Political Texts." *Legislative Studies Quarterly* 36, no. 1: 123–155.

Lubbers, Marcel, Mérove Gijsberts, and Peer Scheepers (2002). "Extreme Right-wing Voting in Western Europe." *European Journal of Political Research* 41, no. 3: 345–378.

Lubbers, Marcel, and Peer Scheepers (2000). "Individual and Contextual Characteristics of the German Extreme Right-Wing Vote in the 1990s. A Test of Complementary Theories." *European Journal of Political Research* 38, no. 1: 63–94.

Lundestad, Geir (1986). "Empire by Invitation? The United States and Western Europe, 1945–1952." *Journal of Peace Research* 23, no. 3: 263–277.

Luttwak, Edward (2009). *The Grand Strategy of the Byzantine Empire.* Cambridge, MA: Harvard University Press.

Lynch, Cecilia, M. (1999). *Beyond Appeasement: Interpreting Interwar Peace Movements in World Politics.* Ithaca: Cornell University Press.

Madison, Cory (2019). "Tracking Public Support for Japan's Remilitarization Policies: An Examination of Elitist and Pluralist Governance." *Asian Journal of Comparative Politics* 4, no. 2: 123–140.

Mair, Peter (1997). *Party System Change: Approaches and Interpretations.* Oxford: Clarendon Press.

Mair, Peter (2013). *Ruling the Void: The Hollowing of Western Democracy.* London: Verso.

Mann, Jim (1999). *About Face: A History of America's Curious Relationship with China from Nixon to Clinton.* New York: Alfred Knopf.

Mann, Michael (1988). *States, War and Capitalism: Studies in Political Sociology.* Oxford: Basil Blackwell.

March, Luke, and Cas Mudde (2005). "What's Left of the Radical Left? The European Radical Left After 1989: Decline and Mutation." *Comparative European Politics* 3, no. 1: 23–49.

Margalit, Yotam (2019). "Economic Insecurity and the Causes of Populism, Reconsidered." *Journal of Economic Perspectives* 33, no. 4: 152–170.

Markowitz, Jonathan N., and Christopher J. Fariss (2018). "Power, Proximity, and Democracy: Geopolitical Competition in the International System." *Journal of Peace Research* 55, no. 1: 78–93.

Marks, Gary, Tobias Lenz, Besir Ceka, and Brian Burgoon (2014). "Discovering Cooperation: A Contractual Approach to Institutional Change in Regional International Organizations." *EUI Working Paper*, 65, Robert Schuman Centre for Advanced Studies, Global Governance Program.

Marks, Gary, and Marco R. Steenbergen, eds. (2004). *European Integration and Political Conflict.* Themes in European Governance. Cambridge: Cambridge University Press.

Marquand, David (2004). *Decline of the Public: The Hollowing Out of Citizenship.* Malden: Polity Press.

Martill, Benjamin (2019). "Center of Gravity: Domestic Institutions and the Victory of Liberal Strategy in Cold War Europe." *Security Studies* 28, no. 1: 116–158.

Mastanduno, Michael (1997). "Preserving the Unipolar Moment: Realist Theories and U.S. Grand Strategy after the Cold War." *International Security* 21, no. 4: 49–80.

Mastanduno, Michael (1999). "A Realist View: Three Images of the Coming International Order." In *International Order and the Future of World Politics*, edited by Paul T. V. and Hall John A., 19–40. London: Cambridge University Press.

Mastanduno, Michael (2020). "Trump's Trade Revolution." *The Forum* 17, no. 4: 523–548.

Mathews, Jessica T. (1997). "Power Shift." *Foreign Affairs* 76, no. 1: 50–66.

Mau, Steffen, and Christoph Burkhardt (2009). "Migration and Welfare State Solidarity in Western Europe." *Journal of European Social Policy* 19, no. 3: 213–229.

Mayer, Arno J. (1969). "Internal Causes and Purposes of War in Europe, 1870–1956: A Research Assignment." *Journal of Modern History* 41, no. 3: 292–303.

Mazower, Mark (1999). *Dark Continent: Europe's Twentieth Century.* London: Penguin Books.

McCormick, James M., and Eugene R. Wittkopf (1992). "At the Water's Edge: The Effects of Party, Ideology, and Issues on Congressional Foreign Policy Voting, 1947 to 1988." *American Politics Quarterly* 20, no. 1: 26–53.

McGregor, R. Michael (2013). "Measuring 'Correct Voting' Using Comparative Manifestos Project Data." *Journal of Elections, Public Opinion and Parties* 23, no. 1: 1–26.

McLaren, Lauren (2005). *Identity, Interests and Attitudes to European Integration.* Palgrave Studies in European Union Politics. Basingstoke: Palgrave Macmillan.

Mead, Walter Russell (2017). "The Jacksonian Revolt: American Populism and the Liberal Order." *Foreign Affairs* 96, no. 2: 2–7.

Mearsheimer, John J. (1990). "Back to the Future: Instability in Europe after the Cold War." *International Security* 15, no. 1: 5–56.

Mearsheimer, John J. (2001). *The Tragedy of Great Power Politics.* New York: Norton.

Mearsheimer, John J. (2011). "Kissing Cousins: Nationalism and Realism." Unpublished manuscript. http://www.sneps.net/t/images/Articles/11Mearsheimer_national ism%20and%20realism.PDF.

Mearsheimer, John J. (2014). "Why the Ukraine Crisis Is the West's Fault: The Liberal Delusions That Provoked Putin." *Foreign Affairs* 93, no. 5: 1–12.

Mearsheimer, John J. (2018). *Great Delusion: Liberal Dreams and International Realities.* New Haven: Yale University Press.

Mearsheimer, John J. (2019). "Bound to Fail: The Rise and Fall of the Liberal International Order." *International Security* 43, no. 4: 7–50.

Mettler, Suzanne, and Claire Leavitt (2019). "Public Policy and Political Dysfunction," in *Can America Govern Itself?* edited by Frances E. Lee and Nolan McCarty, 239–71. Cambridge: Cambridge University Press.

Michel, Elie (2019). "The Strategic Adaption of the Populist Radical Right in Western Europe: Shifting the Party Message," in *The Oxford Handbook of Electoral Persuasion,* edited by Elizabeth Suhay, Bernard Grofman, and Alexander H. Trechsel, 838–862. New York: Oxford University Press.

Midford, Paul (2011). *Rethinking Japanese Public Opinion and Security: From Pacifism to Realism?* Stanford: Stanford University Press.

Miller, S.A. (2016). "Donald Trump Vows to Cancel Trans-Pacific Partnership as President, Puts NAFTA on Notice." *Washington Times,* June 28. https://m.washingtonti mes.com/news/2016/jun/28/donald-trump-vows-to-cancel-trans-pacific-partners/

Milner, Helen V. (2019). "Globalisation, Populism and the Decline of the Welfare State." *Survival* 61, no. 2: 91–96.

Milner, Helen V., and Benjamin Judkins (2004). "Partisanship, Trade Policy, and Globalization: Is There a Left-Right Divide on Trade Policy?" *International Studies Quarterly* 48, no. 1: 95–119.

Mishra, Ramesh (1993). "Social Policy in the Postmodern World." In *New Perspectives on the Welfare State in Europe,* edited by Catherine Jones, 18–42. London: Routledge.

Mochizuki, Mike M. (1983). "Japan's Search for Strategy." *International Security* 8, no. 3: 152.

Moravcsik, Andrew (1998). *The Choice for Europe: Social Purpose and State Power from Messina to Maastricht*. Ithaca: Cornell University Press.

Moravcsik, Andrew (2000). "The Origins of Human Rights Regimes: Democratic Delegation in Postwar Europe." *International Organization* 54, no. 2: 217–252.

Morefield, Jeanne (2014). *Empire Without Imperialism: Anglo-American Decline and Politics of Deflection*. Oxford: Oxford University Press.

Mudde, Cas (2007). *Populist Radical Right Parties in Europe*. Cambridge: Cambridge University Press.

Mueller, John (1994). "The Catastrophe Quota: Trouble after the Cold War." *Journal of Conflict Resolution* 38, no. 3: 355–375.

Mutz, Diana C. (2018). "Status Threat, Not Economic Hardship, Explains the 2016 Presidential Vote." *Proceedings of the National Academy of Sciences* 115, no. 19: 4330–4339.

Narizny, Kevin (2003). "Both Guns and Butter, or Neither: Class Interests in the Political Economy of Rearmament." *American Political Science Review* 97, no. 2: 203–220.

Nichols, Christopher McKnight (2011). *Promise and Peril: America at the Dawn of a Global Age*. Cambridge, MA: Harvard University Press.

Nikolaidou, Eftychia (2008). "The Demand for Military Expenditure: Evidence from the EU15 (1961–2005)." *Defence and Peace Economics* 19, no. 4: 273–292.

Nordlinger, Eric (1996). *Isolationism Reconfigured: American Foreign Policy for a New Century*. Princeton: Princeton University Press.

Norris, Pippa (2000). "Global Governance and Cosmopolitan Citizens." *Governance in a Globalizing World* 155: 173–175.

North, Douglass C., John Joseph Wallis, and Barry R. Weingast (2009). *Violence and Social Orders: A Conceptual Framework for Interpreting Recorded Human History*. Cambridge: Cambridge University Press.

Nuti, Leopoldo, Frédéric Bozo, Marie-Pierre Rey, and Bernd Rother (2015). *The Euromissile Crisis and the End of the Cold War*. Washington, DC: Woodrow Wilson Center Press.

Nye, Joseph S. (1995). "East Asian Security: The Case for Deep Engagement." *Foreign Affairs* 74, no. 4: 90–102.

Nye, Joseph S. (2019). "The Rise and Fall of American Hegemony from Wilson to Trump." *International Affairs* 95, no. 1: 63–80.

Oatley, Thomas (2015). *A Political Economy of American Hegemony: Buildups, Booms, and Busts*. New York: Cambridge University Press.

Obinger, Herbert, and Shinyong Lee (2013). "The Cold War and the Welfare State in Divided Korea and Germany." *Journal of International and Comparative Social Policy* 29, no. 3: 258–275.

Obinger, Herbert, and Klaus Petersen (2015). "Review Article: Mass Warfare and the Welfare State—Causal Mechanisms and Effects." *British Journal of Political Science* 47, no. 1: 203–227.

Obinger, Herbert, and Carina Schmitt (2011). "Guns and Butter? Regime Competition and the Welfare State during the Cold War." *World Politics* 63, no. 2: 246–270.

Obinger, Herbert, Klaus Petersen, and Peter Starke, eds. (2018). *Warfare and Welfare: Military Conflict and Welfare State Development in Western Countries*. Oxford: Oxford University Press.

O'Connor, James (1973). *The Fiscal Crisis of the State*. New York: St. Martin's Press.

Oesch, Daniel, and Line Rennwald (2018). "Electoral Competition in Europe's New Tripolar Political Space: Class Voting for the Left, Centre-Right and Radical Right." *European Journal of Political Research* 57, no. 4: 783–807.

Olson, Mancur (1982). *The Rise and Decline of Nations: Economic Growth, Stagflation, and Social Rigidities*. New Haven: Yale University Press.

Oltermann, Philip (2021). "Stand up to China and Putin? Foreign policy at heart of Germany vote." *Guardian*. May 2. https://www.theguardian.com/world/2021/may/02/stand-up-to-china-and-putin-foreign-policy-at-heart-of-germany-vote.

Orbie, Jan, and Olufemi Babarinde (2008). "The Social Dimension of Globalization and EU Development Policy: Promoting Core Labour Standards and Corporate Social Responsibility." *Journal of European Integration* 30, no. 3: 459–477.

Organization of Economic Cooperation and Development (OECD) (2019). *OECD National Accounts Statistics (database)*. https://doi.org/10.1787/na-data-en.

Organization of Economic Cooperation and Development (OECD) (2020). *Country Statistical Profiles: Key Tables from OECD (electronic resource)*. English ed. https://doi.org/10.1787/20752288.

Palmer, Glenn, Michael R. Kenwick, Mikaela Karstens, Chase Bloch, Nick Dietrich, Kayla Kahn, and Kellan Ritter (2021). "The MID5 Dataset, 2011–2014: Procedures, Coding Rules, and Description." *Conflict Management and Peace Science* 39, no. 4: 470–482.

Pástor, Lubos, and Pietro Veronesi (2018). "Inequality Aversion, Populism, and the Backlash Against Globalization." NBER Working Paper. National Bureau of Economic Research. https://www.nber.org/papers/w24900.

Patrick, Stewart (2017). *The Sovereignty Wars: Reconciling America with the World*. Washington, DC: Brookings Institution Press.

Pempel, T. J. (1998). *Regime Shift: Comparative Dynamics of the Japanese Political Economy*. Ithaca, NY: Cornell University Press.

Petersen, Klaus (2013). "The Early Cold War and the Western Welfare State." *Journal of International and Comparative Social Policy* 29, no. 3: 226–240.

Piazza, James (2001). "De-Linking Labor: Labor Unions and Social Democratic Parties under Globalization." *Party Politics* 7, no. 4: 413–435.

Pieterse, Jan Nederveen (2006). "Emancipatory Cosmopolitanism: Towards an Agenda." *Development and Change* 37, no. 6: 1247–57.

Pildes, Richard H. (2021). "The Age of Political Fragmentation." *Journal of Democracy* 32, no. 4: 146–159.

Plehwe, Dieter, Quinn Slobodian, and Philip Mirowski, eds. (2020). *Nine Lives of Neoliberalism*. London: Verso.

Polanyi, Karl (1944). *The Great Transformation: The Political and Economic Origins of Our Time*. New York: Farrar & Rinehart.

Pontusson, Jonas (2005). *Inequality and Prosperity: Social Europe vs. Liberal America*. Ithaca: Cornell University Press.

Porter, Patrick (2020). *The False Promise of Liberal Order: Nostalgia, Delusion and the Rise of Trump*. Cambridge: Polity Press.

Posen, Barry (2014). *Restraint: A New Foundation for U.S. Grand Strategy*. Ithaca: Cornell University Press.

Prasad, Monica (2006). *The Politics of Free Markets: The Rise of Neoliberal Economic Policies in Britain, France, Germany, and the United States*. Chicago: University of Chicago Press.

Pring, Hayley (2021). "Does Populism Affect Trade? How Audience Costs Affect the Design of Preferential Trade Agreements." PEIO Draft. https://www.peio.me/wp-cont ent/uploads/2021/papers/PEIOo21_paper_86.pdf.

Przeworski, Adam (2019). *Crises of Democracy*. New York: Cambridge University Press.

Przeworski, Adam, and John Sprague (1986). *Paper Stones: A History of Electoral Socialism*. Chicago: University of Chicago Press.

Pyle, Kenneth B. (2018). *Japan in the American Century*. Cambridge, MA: Harvard University Press.

Rathbun, Brian C. (2004). *Partisan Interventions: European Party Politics and Peace Enforcement in the Balkans*. Ithaca: Cornell University Press.

Rehm, Philipp (2009). "Risks and Redistribution: An Individual-Level Analysis." *Comparative Political Studies* 42, no. 7: 855–881.

Reid-Henry, Simon (2019). *Empire of Democracy: The Remaking of the West Since the Cold War, 1971–2017*. New York: Simon & Schuster.

Rennwald, Line, and Jonas Pontusson (2021). "*Paper Stones* Revisited: Class Voting, Unionization and the Electoral Decline of the Mainstream Left." *Perspectives on Politics* 9, no. 1: 36–54.

Rixen, Thomas, and Bernhard Zangl (2013). "The Politicization of International Economic Institutions in US Public Debates." *Review of International Organizations* 8, no. 3: 363–387.

Rodrik, Dani (1998). "Has Globalization Gone Too Far?" *Challenge* 41, no. 2: 81–94.

Rodrik, Dani (2011). *The Globalization Paradox: Why Global Markets, States, and Democracy Can't Coexist*. Oxford: Oxford University Press USA—OSO.

Rodrik, Dani (2021). "Why Does Globalization Fuel Populism? Economics, Culture, and the Rise of Right-Wing Populism." *Annual Review of Economics* 13: 133–170.

Rodrik, Dani, and Charles F. Sabel (2022). "Building a Good Jobs Economy." In *A Political Economy of Justice*, edited by Danielle Allen, Yochai Benkler, Leah Downey, Rebecca Henderson, and Josh Simmons, 61–95. Chicago: University of Chicago Press.

Rommel, Tobias, and Stefanie Walter (2018). "The Electoral Consequences of Offshoring: How the Globalization of Production Shapes Party Preferences." *Comparative Political Studies* 51, no. 5: 621–658.

Rone, Julia (2020). *Contesting Austerity and Free Trade in the EU: Protest Diffusion in Complex Media and Political Arenas*. New York: Routledge.

Rooduijn, Matthijs (2018). "What Unites the Voter Bases of Populist Parties? Comparing the Electorates of 15 Populist Parties." *European Political Science Review* 10, no. 3: 351–368.

Rooduijn, Matthijs, Brian Burgoon, Erika J. van Elsas, and Herman G. van de Werfhorst (2017). "Radical Distinction: Support for Radical Left and Radical Right Parties in Europe." *European Union Politics* 18, no. 4: 536–559.

Rooduijn, Matthijs, Stijn Van Kessel, Caterina Froio, Andrea Pirro, Sarah De Lange, Daphne Halikiopoulou, Paul Lewis, Cas Mudde, and Paul Taggart (2019). "The PopuList: An Overview of Populist, Far Right, Far Left and Eurosceptic Parties in Europe." www.popu-list.org.

Rosenbluth, Frances McCall (2012). "Japan in 2011: Cataclysmic Crisis and Chronic Deflation." *Asian Survey* 52, no. 1: 15–27.

Rosenbluth, Frances McCall, and Michael F. Thies (2010). *Japan Transformed: Political Change and Economic Restructuring*. Princeton: Princeton University Press.

Rosenboim, Or (2017). *The Emergence of Globalism: Visions of World Order in Britain and the United States, 1939–1950*. Princeton: Princeton University Press.

Röth, Leonce, Alexandre Afonso, and Dennis C. Spies (2018). "The Impact of Populist Radical Right Parties on Socio-Economic Policies." *European Political Science Review* 10, no. 3: 325–350.

Ruggie, John Gerard (1982). "International Regimes, Transactions, and Change: Embedded Liberalism in the Postwar Economic Order." *International Organization* 36, no. 2: 379–415.

Ruggie, John Gerard (2002). "At Home Abroad, Abroad at Home: International Liberalization and Domestic Stability in the New World Economy." In *The Globalization of Liberalism*, edited by Eivind Hovden and Edward Keene, 99–122. London: Palgrave Macmillan.

Rydgren, Jens (2005). "Is Extreme Right-Wing Populism Contagious? Explaining the Emergence of a New Party Family." *European Journal of Political Research* 44, no. 3: 413–437.

Samuels, Richard J. (2007). *Securing Japan: Tokyo's Grand Strategy and the Future of East Asia* Ithaca, NY: Cornell University Press.

Sandler, Todd, and Justin George (2016). "Military Expenditure Trends for 1960–2014 and What They Reveal." *Global Policy* 7, no. 2: 174–184.

Sapolsky, Harvey M., Benjamin H. Friedman, Eugene Gholz, and Daryl G. Press (2009). "Restraining Order: For Strategic Modesty." *World Affairs* 172, no. 2: 84–94.

Sartori, Giovanni (1976). *Parties and Party Systems: A Framework for Analysis*. Cambridge: Cambridge University Press.

Sassoon, Donald (1992). "The Rise and Fall of West European Communism 1939–48." *Contemporary European History* 1, no. 2: 139–169.

Sassoon, Donald (1996). *Social Democracy at the Heart of Europe*. London: Institute for Public Policy Research.

Sassoon, Donald (2014). *One Hundred Years of Socialism: The West European Left in the Twentieth Century*. London: I.B. Tauris.

Scharpf, Fritz W. (1991). *Crisis and Choice in European Social Democracy*. Ithaca: Cornell University Press.

Scharpf, Fritz W. (2000). "Economic Changes, Vulnerabilities, and Institutional Capabilities." In *Welfare and Work in the Open Economy Volume I: From Vulnerability to Competitiveness in Comparative Perspective*, edited by Fritz W. Scharpf and Vivien A. Schmidt, 21–121 Oxford: Oxford University Press.

Scheve, Kenneth F., and Matthew J. Slaughter (2001). "Labor Market Competition and Individual Preferences over Immigration Policy." *Review of Economics and Statistics* 83, no. 1: 133–145.

Scheve, Kenneth, and Matthew J. Slaughter (2004). "Economic Insecurity and the Globalization of Production." *American Journal of Political Science* 48, no. 4: 662–674.

Scheve, Kenneth, and Matthew J. Slaughter (2006). "Public Opinion, International Economic Integration, and the Welfare State." In *Globalization and Egalitarian Redistribution*, edited by Pranab Bardhan, Samuels Bowles, and Michael Wallerstein, 217–60. Princeton: Princeton University Press.

Schilde, Kaija E., Stephanie B. Anderson, and Andrew D. Garnerb (2019). "A More Martial Europe? Public Opinion, Permissive Consensus, and EU Defence Policy." *European Security* 28, no. 2: 153–172.

Schlesinger, Arthur M. (1949). *The Vital Center: The Politics of Freedom*. Boston: Houghton Mifflin Company.

Schonhardt-Bailey, Cheryl (1998). "Parties and Interests in the 'Marriage of Iron and Rye.'" *British Journal of Political Science* 28, no. 2: 291–332.

Schoppa, Leonard J. (2011). *The Evolution of Japan's Party System: Politics and Policy in an Era of Institutional Change*. Toronto: University of Toronto Press.

Schultz, Kenneth A. (2001). *Democracy and Coercive Diplomacy*. Cambridge; New York: Cambridge University Press.

Schweller, Randall (2018). "Opposite but Compatible Nationalisms: A Neoclassical Realist Approach to the Future of US–China Relations." *Chinese Journal of International Politics* 11, no. 1: 23–48.

Semuels, Alana (2016). "TPP's Death Won't Help the American Middle Class." *Atlantic*, November 15. https://www.theatlantic.com/business/archive/2016/11/tpps-death-wont-help-the-american-middle-class/507683/.

Shantz, Jeff (2008). "Social Policy." In Ruud van Dijk, ed., *Encyclopedia of the Cold War*, vol. 2, 797–799. New York: Routledge.

Shaw, Timothy M. (2016). *Comparative Regionalisms for Development in the 21st Century: Insights from the Global South*. New York: Routledge.

Sheehan, James J. (2008). *Where Have All the Soldiers Gone? The Transformation of Modern Europe*. Boston: Houghton Mifflin Harcourt.

Sheingate, Adam D. (2001). *The Rise of the Agricultural Welfare State: Institutions and Interest Group Power in the United States, France and Japan*. Princeton: Princeton University Press.

Shoch, James (2001). *Trading Blows: Party Competition and U.S. Trade Policy in a Globalizing Era*. Chapel Hill: University of North Carolina Press.

Sil, Rudra, and Peter J. Katzenstein (2010). "Analytic Eclecticism in the Study of World Politics: Reconfiguring Problems and Mechanisms across Research Traditions." *Perspectives on Politics* 8, no. 2: 411–431.

Silver, Laura, Kat Devlin, and Christine Huang (2021). "Most Americans Support Tough Stance Toward China on Human Rights, Economic Issues." Pew Research Center, 4 March. https://www.pewresearch.org/global/2021/03/04/most-americans-support-tough-stance-toward-china-on-human-rights-economic-issues/.

Silver, Laura, Christine Huang, and Laura Clancy (2022). "Negative Views of China Tied to Critical Views of Its Policies on Human Rights." *Pew Research Center*, July 29. https://www.pewresearch.org/global/2022/06/29/negative-views-of-china-tied-to-critical-views-of-its-policies-on-human-rights/.

Simmel, Georg (1955). *Conflict and the Web of Group-Affiliations*. New York: Free Press.

Simmons, Beth A., Frank Dobbin, and Geoffrey Garrett (2008). "Introduction: The Diffusion of Liberalization." In *The Global Diffusion of Markets and Democracy*, edited by Beth A. Simmons, Frank Dobbin, and Geoffrey Garrett, 1–63. Cambridge: Cambridge University Press.

Skocpol, Theda (1992). *Protecting Soldiers and Mothers: The Political Origins of Social Policy in the United States*. Cambridge, MA: Harvard University Press.

Slobodian, Quinn (2018). *Globalists: The End of Empire and the Birth of Neoliberalism*. Cambridge, MA: Harvard University Press.

Snyder, Jack (2019). "The Broken Bargain: How Nationalism Came Back." *Foreign Affairs* 98, no. 2: 54–60.

Snyder, Jack, Robert Y. Shapiro, and Yaeli Bloch-Elkon (2009). "Free Hand Abroad, Divide and Rule at Home." *World Politics* 61, no. 1: 155–187.

Spengler, Oswald (1926). *The Decline of the West, Vol.1: Form and Actuality.* Translated by C. F. Atkinson. London: George Allen and Unwin.

Sprout, Harold, and Margaret Sprout (1968). "The Dilemma of Rising Demands and Insufficient Resources." *World Politics* 20, no. 4: 660–693.

Stephens, John D., Evelyne Huber, and Leonard Ray (1999). "The Welfare State in Hard Time." In *Continuity and Change in Contemporary Capitalism,* edited by Herbert Kitschelt, Peter Lange, Gary Marks, and John D. Stephens, 164–193. Cambridge: Cambridge University Press.

Stockholm International Peace Research Institute, (SIPRI), and Stockholm International Peace Research Institute (2018). "Military Expenditures Database." https://www.sipri.org/databases/milex.

Strange, Susan (1997). "The Erosion of the State." *Current History* 96, no. 613: 365–369.

Strange, Susan (1999). "The Westfailure System." *Review of International Studies* 25, no. 3: 345–354.

Streeck, Wolfgang (2017). *Buying Time: The Delayed Crisis of Democratic Capitalism.* Revised second edition. London: Verso.

Subramanian, Arvind, and Martin Kessler (2013). "The Hyperglobalization of Trade and its Future." Peterson Institute for International Economics Working Paper No. 13–6.

Swank, Duane (2002). *Global Capital, Political Institutions, and Policy Change in Developed Welfare States.* New York: Cambridge University Press.

Swank, Duane (2018). "Comparative Political Parties Dataset: Electoral, Legislative, and Government Strength of Political Parties by Ideological Group in 21 Capitalist Democracies, 1950–2015." Electronic Database. Department of Political Science, Marquette University. https://datafinder.qog.gu.se/dataset/sw.

Swank, Duane, and Hans-Georg Betz (2003). "Globalization, the Welfare State and Right-Wing Populism in Western Europe." *Socio-Economic Review* 1, no. 2: 215–245.

Szöcsik, Edina, and Alina Polyakova (2019). "Euroscepticism and the Electoral Success of the Far Right: The Role of the Strategic Interaction between Center and Far Right." *European Political Science* 18, no. 3: 400–420.

Talbott, Strobe (2008). *The Great Experiment: The Story of Ancient Empires, Modern States, and the Quest for a Global Nation.* New York: Simon and Schuster.

Tarrow, Sidney (2005). *The New Transnational Activism.* Cambridge: Cambridge University Press.

Thelen, Kathleen (2014). *Varieties of Liberalization and the New Politics of Social Solidarity.* Cambridge: Cambridge University Press.

Thrall, A. Trevor, and Benjamin H. Friedman (2018). *US Grand Strategy in the 21st Century: The Case for Restraint.* London: Routledge.

Thurow, Lester C. (1992). *Head to Head: The Coming Economic Battle Among Japan, Europe, and America.* New York: William Morrow & Co.

Tilly, Charles, ed. (1975). *The Formation of National States in Western Europe.* Princeton: Princeton University Press.

Tilly, Charles (1985). "War Making and State Making as Organized Crime." In *Bringing the State Back In,* edited by Dietrich Rueschemeyer, Peter B. Evans, and Theda Skocpol, 169–91. Cambridge: Cambridge University Press.

Tompkins, Andrew S. (2016). *Better Active than Radioactive!: Anti-nuclear Protest in 1970s France and West Germany.* Oxford: Oxford University Press.

Tooze, Adam (2018). "The Forgotten History of the Financial Crisis: What the World Should Have Learned in 2008." *Foreign Affairs* 97, no. 5: 199–210.

Tooze, Adam (2020). "Whose Century?" *London Review of Books* 42, no. 15. https://www.lrb.co.uk/the-paper/v42/n15/adam-tooze/whose-century.

Tooze, Adam (2021). *Shutdown: How Covid Shook the World's Economy.* New York: Allen Lane.

Trubowitz, Peter (1998). *Defining the National Interest: Conflict and Change in American Foreign Policy.* Chicago: University of Chicago Press.

Trubowitz, Peter (2011). *Politics and Strategy: Partisan Ambition and American Statecraft.* Princeton: Princeton University Press.

Trubowitz, Peter, and Brian Burgoon (2020). "The Retreat of the West." *Perspectives on Politics* 20, no. 1: 102–122.

Trubowitz, Peter, and Peter Harris (2019). "The End of the American Century? Slow Erosion of the Domestic Sources of Usable Power." *International Affairs* 95, no. 3: 619–639.

Trubowitz, Peter, and Jungkun Seo (2012). "The China Card: Playing Politics with Sino-American Relations." *Political Science Quarterly* 127, no. 2: 189–211.

Ulrich, Beck (2006). *Cosmopolitan Vision.* Cambridge: Polity Press.

Urata, Shujiro (2009). "Japan's Free Trade Agreement Strategy." *Japanese Economy* 36, no. 2: 46–77.

Van Der Brug, W., M. Fennema, and J.N. Tillie (2005). "Why Some Anti– Immigrant Parties Fail and Others Succeed: A Two-Step Model of Aggregate Electoral Support." *Comparative Political Studies* 38, no. 5: 537–573.

Vine, David (2021). "Lists of U.S. Military Bases Abroad, 1776–2021," American University Digital Research Archive.

Voce, Antonio and Seán Clarke (2021). "German election 2021: full results and analysis." *The Guardian*, September 6. https://www.theguardian.com/world/ng-interactive/2021/sep/26/german-election-results-exit-poll-and-possible-coalitions.

Voeten, Erik (2013). "Data and Analyses of Voting in the UN General Assembly." In *Routledge Handbook of International Organization*, edited by Bob Reinalda, 54–66. London: Routledge.

Voeten, Erik, Anton Strezhnev, and Michael Bailey (2009). "United Nations General Assembly Voting Data." https://doi.org/10.7910/DVN/LEJUQZ, Harvard Dataverse, V28, UNF:6:dki7hpeRB0FwTFJ00X/TCQ== [fileUNF].

Waal, Jeroen van der, and Willem de Koster (2018). "Populism and Support for Protectionism: The Relevance of Opposition to Trade Openness for Leftist and Rightist Populist Voting in the Netherlands." *Political Studies* 66, no. 3: 560–576.

Wagner, Wolfgang (2020). *The Democratic Politics of Military Interventions: Political Parties, Contestation, and Decisions to Use Force Abroad.* New York: Oxford University Press.

Wallerstein, Immanuel (1993). "The World-System after the Cold War." *Journal of Peace Research* 30, no. 1: 1–6.

Walt, Stephen M. (1987). *The Origins of Alliance.* Ithaca, NY: Cornell University Press.

Walt, Stephen M. (2018). *The Hell of Good Intentions.* New York: Farrar, Straus and Giroux.

Walt, Stephen M. (2019). "The End of Hubris." *Foreign Affairs* 98, no. 3: 26–35.

Walter, Stefanie (2010). "Globalization and the Welfare State: Testing the Microfoundations of the Compensation Hypothesis." *International Studies Quarterly* 54, no. 2: 403–426.

Waltz, Kenneth N. (1979). *Theory of International Politics.* Boston: McGraw-Hill.

Waltz, Kenneth N. (1993). "The Emerging Structure of International Politics." *International Security* 18, no. 2: 44–79.

Warwick, Paul, and Maria Zakharova (2013). "Measuring the Median: The Risks of Inferring Beliefs from Votes." *British Journal of Political Science* 43, no. 1: 157–175.

Westad, Odd Arne (2018a). "Has a New Cold War Really Begun? Why the Term Shouldn't Apply to Today's Great-Power Tensions." *Foreign Affairs*, March 27. https://www.for eignaffairs.com/articles/china/2018-03-27/has-new-cold-war-really-begun.

Westad, Odd Arne (2018b). *The Cold War: A World History*. New York: Penguin Books.

Westley, Christopher, William L. Anderson, and Scott A. Kjar (2011). "War and the Austrian School: Ludwig von Mises and Friedrich von Hayek." *Economics of Peace and Security Journal* 6, no. 1: 28–33.

Williams, Andrew (1998). *Failed Imagination: The Anglo-American New World Order from Wilson to Bush*. Manchester: Manchester University Press.

Wohlforth, William C. (2011). "Gilpinian Realism and International Relations." *International Relations* 25, no. 4: 499–511.

Wolfe, Robert (2012). "Protectionism and Multilateral Accountability During the Great Recession: Drawing Inferences from Dogs Not Barking." *Journal of World Trade* 46, no. 4: 777–814.

Wondreys, Jakub, and Cas Mudde (2022). "Victims of the Pandemic? European Far-Right Parties and COVID-19." *Nationalities Papers*, Cambridge Coronavirus Collection, 21: 1–18.

Wood, Adrian (2018). "The 1990s Trade and Wages Debate in Retrospect." *World Economy* 41, no. 4: 975–999.

Woods, Ngaire (2010). "Global Governance after the Financial Crisis: A New Multilateralism or the Last Gasp of the Great Powers?: Cooperation after the Crisis." *Global Policy* 1, no. 1: 51–63.

Woods, Ngaire, and Amrita Narlikar (2001). "Governance and the Limits of Accountability: The WTO, the IMF, and the World Bank." *International Social Science Journal* 53, no. 179: 569–583.

Wright, Robert (1997). "We're All One-Worlders Now." *Slate Magazine*. April 25. https:// slate.com/news-and-politics/1997/04/we-re-all-one-worlders-now.html.

Young, John W. (1996). *Cold War Europe, 1945–91: A Political History*. London: Arnold.

Zellner, Arnold (1962). "An Efficient Method of Estimating Seemingly Unrelated Regressions and Tests for Aggregation Bias." *Journal of the American Statistical Association* 57, no. 298: 348–368.

Zohlnhöfer, Reimut, Fabian Engler, and Kathrin Dümig (2018). "The Retreat of the Interventionist State in Advanced Democracies." *British Journal of Political Science* 48, no. 2: 535–562.

Zürn, Michael (2019). "Politicization Compared: At National, European, and Global Levels." *Journal of European Public Policy* 26, no. 7: 977–995.

Index

For the benefit of digital users, indexed terms that span two pages (e.g., 52–53) may, on occasion, appear on only one of those pages.

Tables and figures are indicated by *t* and *f* following the page number